ENGINEERING SIMULATION AND ITS APPLICATIONS

ENGINEERING SIMULATION AND ITS APPLICATIONS

Algorithms and Numerical Methods

XIN-SHE YANG
Middlesex University London
School of Science and Technology
London, United Kingdom

ELSEVIER

ACADEMIC PRESS
An imprint of Elsevier

Academic Press is an imprint of Elsevier
125 London Wall, London EC2Y 5AS, United Kingdom
525 B Street, Suite 1650, San Diego, CA 92101, United States
50 Hampshire Street, 5th Floor, Cambridge, MA 02139, United States

ISBN: 978-0-443-14084-6

For information on all Academic Press publications
visit our website at https://www.elsevier.com/books-and-journals

Publisher: Mara Conner
Acquisitions Editor: Craig Smith
Editorial Project Manager: Toni Louise Jackson
Production Project Manager: Punithavathy Govindaradjane
Cover Designer: Mark Rogers

Typeset by VTeX

Contents

About the author

Xin-She Yang obtained his PhD/DPhil in Applied Mathematics from the University of Oxford. He then worked at Cambridge University and the National Physical Laboratory (UK) as a Senior Research Scientist. Now he is Reader at Middlesex University London and an elected Fellow of the Institute of Mathematics and its Applications (FIMA). He was also the IEEE Computer Intelligence Society (CIS) Chair for the Task Force on Business Intelligence and Knowledge Management (2015–2020) and an Editor of Springer's Book Series *Springer Tracts in Nature-Inspired Computing* (STNIC).

With more than 20 years of research and teaching experience, he has authored 15 books and edited more than 25 books. He has published more than 300 research papers in international peer-reviewed journals and conference proceedings. With more than 84 500 citations, he has been on the prestigious lists of Web of Science Highly Cited Researchers for eight consecutive years (2016–2023).

Preface

Engineering simulation is an important part of essential skills for engineers, and thus engineering simulation will be a core course for almost all degrees in engineering disciplines. Simulation and optimization can be paramount in many applications such as engineering, business management, engineering design, and industrial applications. Quantitative models are necessary to study the behavior and characteristics of a system in engineering and to make reliable predictions possible. Such quantitative models are often written as mathematical models and/or numerical models. Their solutions require sophisticated numerical techniques and simulation tools.

Simulation of engineering systems requires a class of numerical techniques, such as numerical integration, numerical solutions of differential equations, statistical analysis, and others. This book covers all the essential quantitative methods for engineering simulation, including linear algebra, ordinary differential equations, partial differential equations, the finite difference method, the finite element method, the finite volume method, optimization, linear programming, probability and statistics, the Monte Carlo method, discrete event simulation, and queueing as well as applications.

Optimization techniques can be used to design better systems that can minimize costs and maximize efficiency. Linear programming can solve optimization problems related to supply chains, logistics, scheduling, and resource allocation in various engineering applications.

The emphasis of this book is on the essential algorithms and numerical methods as well as their main procedures. Dozens of worked examples are provided to show how such methods work. The diverse coverage of the different topics and contents means that this book includes all essential topics in a single textbook. Therefore this book can serve as a textbook for both undergraduates and graduates in engineering, computer science, and data science. It can also serve as a reference for lecturers and graduates for many courses in engineering, such as engineering simulation, design optimization, mathematical modeling, numerical methods, data analysis, engineering management, and other relevant courses. Industrial practitioners, engineering managers, and software developers may also find this book as a useful aide-memoire for algorithms and numerical methods.

Xin-She Yang
London
September 2023

Preface

Acknowledgments

I would like to thank many students who took the *Engineering Simulation* course and have provided some useful comments and feedback on the contents of the book. I would like to thank the staff at Elsevier for their help and professionalism, in particular Craig Smith, Toni Jackson and Jeromel Theodore Tenorio. Last but not least, I thank my family for their help and support.

Xin-She Yang
September 2023

CHAPTER ONE

Introduction to engineering simulation

Engineering simulation is a vast area with many different topics and applications. This chapter introduces the fundamentals of engineering simulation with the emphasis on mathematical models and numerical models. Relevant software tools will also be discussed.

1.1. Introduction

Simulation and optimization can be paramount in many applications such as engineering design, business management, manufacturing engineering, product design, and industrial applications. Obviously, quantitative models are required to analyze the behavior and characteristics of a system and to make any possible predictions. Such quantitative models are often written as mathematical models or numerical models.

The analysis of mathematical models requires a diverse range of mathematical methods, including calculus, ordinary differential equations (ODEs), partial differential equations (PDEs), Fourier transforms, Laplace transforms, statistical techniques, and many others. Numerical solutions of mathematical models require a class of numerical techniques, including numerical integration, finite difference methods, finite element methods, finite volume methods, Monte Carlo simulation, statistical sampling, and many others.

With a good mathematical model for modeling and simulating an engineering system, it may be necessary to carry out some optimization. The aims of optimization can be anything – to minimize the energy consumption, costs, or environmental impact, and to maximize the profit, output, performance, sustainability, or efficiency. It is no exaggeration to say that optimization is everywhere, from engineering design to business planning. Because resources, time, and money are always limited in real-world applications, we have to find solutions to optimally use these valuable resources under various constraints, ideally in a long-term, sustainable way. Mathematical optimization or mathematical programming is the study of such planning and design problems using mathematical tools and numerical algorithms. For example, linear programming is one of powerful tools for solving optimization problems related to supply chains, logistics, resource allocation, scheduling, manufacturing, and other applications. In addition, engineering optimization is a well-established area of research with many algorithms, techniques, and software tools.

Engineering Simulation and its Applications
https://doi.org/10.1016/B978-0-44-314084-6.00008-5

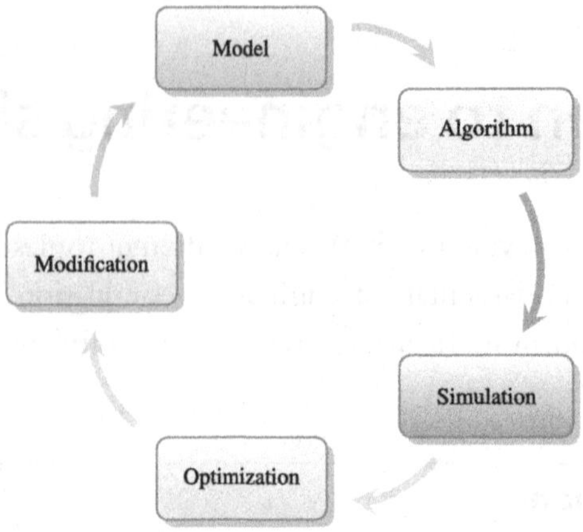

Figure 1.1 Components and procedure of modeling, simulation, and optimization.

1.2. What is a model?

A model is a representation or an approximation to a system or part of a system in a quantitative way. Such models are often called mathematical models or numerical models if they are represented on a computer. See Fig. 1.1.

- *Models* can be mathematical models, statistical models, numerical models, geometric models, and others.
- *Simulation* requires the use of a numerical simulator, or a solver, implemented in a programming language or as a software package.
- *Algorithms* are essential to both numerical simulation and optimization.

Modeling and simulation are two important components for engineering simulation tasks. However, it is rarely possible to get a mathematical model correctly in the first place, and modifications are usually needed. In addition, the parameters of the model under consideration usually need to be optimized.

- *Optimization* changes the design parameters or decision variables so as to make the design objective (also called the cost function) optimally (either maximum or minimum, depending on the actual design requirements).
- *Modification* of the model may be carried out iteratively. The results should be compared with experiments or real data, and further modifications of the model may be necessary, so as to explain the data more accurately.

Even with the most accurate models and most efficient algorithms, the interpretation of the analytical solution and/or numerical solutions requires care so as to extract and explain the results in a meaningful way.

"All models are wrong, but some models are useful."
— George Box (British statistician)

"Approximate solutions to correct models worth much more than exact solutions to wrong models."
— John Tukey (American mathematician)

There are different types of model. Loosely speaking, we can divide the models into four types: mathematical models, numerical model, geometry models, and others. Models can be static (not change with time), dynamic (vary with time), stochastic (models in terms of some expectation/average of model parameters), or mixed.

1. Mathematical models can take many forms, including continuous, discrete, and stochastic forms.
   - *Continuous models*: Continuous models usually use ordinary differential equations (ODEs), partial differential equations (PDEs), and even a set of both ODEs and PDEs.
   - *Discrete models*: Queueing models simulate discrete events, such as the arrivals of customers at a bank and the queueing process in a supermarket.
   - *Stochastic models*: Some models are probabilistic or statistical models, such as regression models and neural network models. Monte Carlo methods can also be used to simulate stochastic models and discrete models.
2. Numerical models: The representations of mathematical models as computer models often require discretization of continuous models. Numerical methods are often discrete, typically in terms of vectors, matrices, discrete systems such as a set of discrete ODEs or PDEs, computer files, and other forms.
3. Geometric models: Some models are represented as geometric models, such as the 3D objects or models in Solidworks and AutoCAD, mesh models in finite element simulation, surface/mesh models in animation, and others.
4. Other types of models: Some models cannot be explicitly written as one of the above models, but they can still simulate and represent the characteristics and behavior of systems under consideration. Such models can take various forms such as data, mixture of models and data, descriptive (both qualitative and quantitative), implicit models, and others.

This books mainly concerns mathematical models in both continuous and discrete forms. We will also introduce various numerical methods and algorithms for solving models based on differential equations.

1.3. Mathematical models

Most mathematical models can be expressed as algebraic equations, ODEs, PDEs, a set of ODEs or PDEs, or some probabilistic relationships. Let us briefly introduce them here, and we will provide more details in late chapters.

1.3.1 Algebraic equations

Many physical laws can be expressed as algebraic relationships. For example, Newton's second law $F = ma$ is a good example, though strictly speaking, we should express it in the vector form

$$\boldsymbol{F} = m\boldsymbol{a}, \tag{1.1}$$

because both force $\boldsymbol{F}$ and acceleration $\boldsymbol{a}$ are vectors. Another example is Ohm's law.

Example 1.1. Ohm's law relates the current I through a conductor with resistance R and voltage V applied across the conductor:

$$I = \frac{V}{R},$$

or

$$V = IR.$$

Here the main assumption is that the resistance does not vary with V or I. Obviously, in case of R depending on I, we can still write this as an equivalent approximate relationship. In fact, R usually depends on the temperature T, and the flow of current will generate heat (and thus vary the temperature).

Almost all the physical and chemical laws we learned in school are expressed as algebraic equations.

1.3.2 ODE models

A simple model for modeling the charging process of a smartphone battery with voltage $v(t)$ is

$$\tau \frac{dv}{dt} + v = v_0, \quad \tau = RC, \tag{1.2}$$

where v_0 is the charger voltage (typically, $v_0 = 5$ volts), and $\tau = RC$ is the time constant. Here R is the resistance of the battery, whereas the battery storage is loosely modeled as the capacitor C, as shown in Fig. 1.2.

This model comes from the fact that the total voltage in the circuit is

$$v_0 = iR + v, \tag{1.3}$$

where we have used the relationship between the current i and the voltage across the capacitor C as

$$i = C\frac{dv}{dt}. \tag{1.4}$$

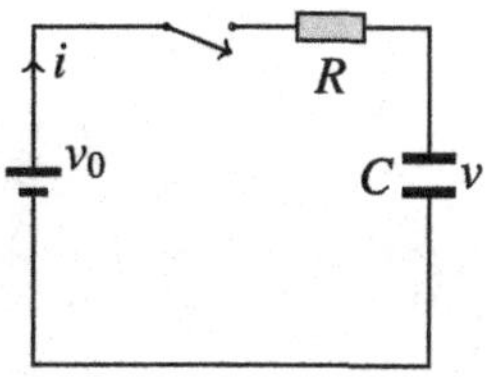

Figure 1.2 A simple RC model for a rechargeable battery.

If the battery is initially empty, then we have the initial value $v(0) = 0$ at $t = 0$ (a very crude approximation). It is straightforward to verify that the solution to Eq. (1.2) is

$$v(t) = v_0(1 - e^{-t/\tau}), \quad t \geq 0. \tag{1.5}$$

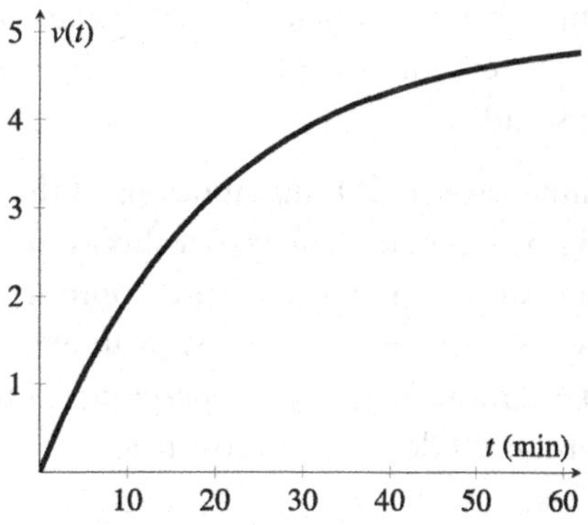

Figure 1.3 The charging curve obtained by the ODE model.

For $v_0 = 5$ volts and $\tau = 15$ minutes, the charging curve is shown in Fig. 1.3.

In practice, the voltage variation of a rechargeable battery is much more complicated, and the initial empty voltage is certainly not zero. Most modern chargers can initially deliver a nearly constant charging current. Thus the model here is very crude, omitting many realistic features. However, the curve can still provide some insight into the variation of electrical current at different stages of charging.

1.3.3 PDE models

To simulate the temperature variations (T) of a room with some heaters, we can use the heat conduction equation

$$\frac{\partial T}{\partial t} = K\nabla^2 T = K\left(\frac{\partial^2 T}{\partial x^2} + \frac{\partial^2 T}{\partial y^2} + \frac{\partial^2 T}{\partial z^2}\right), \tag{1.6}$$

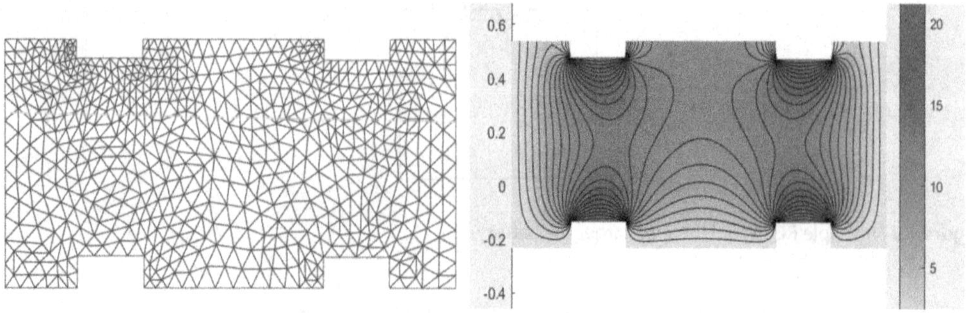

Figure 1.4 Mesh and contour maps for the temperature distribution in a room.

where K is the thermal diffusivity. Obviously, this requires both initial conditions $T(t=0, x, y, z)$ at different locations and boundary conditions at various boundaries.

For example, if we assume that all walls are insulated (i.e., $\nabla T = 0$) with no internal heat sources except for the heaters, the temperature distribution near four heaters with constant heat fluxes can be simulated.

Example 1.2. The two-dimensional (2D) distributions of the temperature on the floor (i.e., $z=0$) are shown in Fig. 1.4, where the left plot shows the mesh model of the room geometry, and the right plot shows the temperature contours. The initial temperature was assumed to be $T=0\,°\text{C}$ everywhere at $t=0$. We can expect that after a sufficiently long time (for example, a few hours or longer, depending on the size of the room), the temperature will become about 20 degrees in most places.

1.3.4 Functional and integral equations

Though most mathematical models are written as differential equations, however, sometimes it may be more convenient to write them in terms of integral equations. These integral forms can be discretized using various numerical methods, such as the finite volume method (FVM) widely used in computational fluid dynamics and aerospace engineering.

For example, the conservation of mass in modeling the sugar concentration of c in a glass of water can be written as

$$\frac{\partial}{\partial t}\left[\iiint_{\Omega} c dV\right] + \iint_{\Gamma} \boldsymbol{J} \cdot d\boldsymbol{S} = 0, \tag{1.7}$$

where Γ is the boundary of the domain Ω with surface element $d\boldsymbol{S}$, and $\boldsymbol{J}$ is the flux across the surface. This integral equation is equivalent to the partial difference equation

$$\frac{\partial c}{\partial t} + \nabla \cdot \boldsymbol{J} = 0, \tag{1.8}$$

written in a divergent form, where $\nabla \cdot \boldsymbol{J}$ is essentially the sugar source (e.g., adding a sugar cube).

In the calculus of variations, many quantities are expressed as functionals. The well-known Euler–Lagrange equation governs the variations of such functionals (e.g., Lagrangian or Hamiltonian) in theoretical physics and Lagrangian mechanics.

1.3.5 Discrete models

Both differential equations and integral equations are mathematical models for continuous systems. For other, discrete systems, such as queueing and iteration, discrete models are needed.

Example 1.3. For example, the well-known population growth of rabbits in terms of the Fibonacci sequence is the discrete recurrence model

$$F_n = F_n + F_{n-2}, \quad F_0 = F_1 = 1. \tag{1.9}$$

The models for discrete systems can take many different forms. For example, for a simple queueing system with a single queue and single server (a service desk/counter) at a bank or a coffee shop, the typical queue length (L) can be estimated by

$$L = \frac{\rho}{1-\rho} \tag{1.10}$$

with

$$\rho = \frac{\lambda}{\mu}, \tag{1.11}$$

where λ is the arrival rate (number of customers per unit time), and μ is the service time obeying an exponential distribution.

Clearly, it is required that $\rho < 1$ or $\lambda < \mu$. If the service is slower than the arrival, then the queue length will increase continuously. In fact, as $\rho \to 1$, L will become infinity ($L \to \infty$).

Little's law of a queuing system states that the average number L of items in the system is equal to the average arrival rate λ multiplied by the average time W that an item spends in the queuing system, that is,

$$L = \lambda W.$$

This simple law provides some good insight into queueing systems, and relevant quantities can be estimated without any detailed knowledge of a particular queueing system.

Example 1.4. For example, a coffee shop has an arrival rate of three people per minute, and the average queue length is 9. What the average waiting time for a customer?

We know that $\lambda = 3$ and $L = 9$, so

$$W = \frac{L}{\lambda} = \frac{9}{3} = 3,$$

which means that a customer usually waits 3 minutes before being served.

1.3.6 Statistical models

Many systems have intrinsic randomness, and thus the descriptions and proper modeling require statistical models. The numbers of telephone calls received in a call center can be described by a Poisson distribution. Statistical models are a very important class of models that are widely used in economics, finance, risk management, data mining, and machine learning.

Let use discuss an example about the Six Sigma (6σ) design methodology for manufacturing.

Six Sigma (6σ) is a quality control methodology, pioneered at Motorola in the 1980s, for eliminating defects in products. Assuming that the normal distribution applies to such scenarios, we have

$$p(x, \mu, \sigma) = \frac{1}{\sigma\sqrt{2\pi}} e^{-\frac{(x-\mu)^2}{2\sigma^2}},$$

where μ is the mean, and σ is the standard deviation. Clearly, this function is symmetric on both sides of $x = \mu$.

The exact area under the curve from $\mu - k\sigma$ to $\mu + k\sigma$ (where $k > 0$) can be calculated by

$$A_k = \frac{1}{2}\left[\mathrm{erf}(k/\sqrt{2}) - \mathrm{erf}(-k/\sqrt{2})\right] = \mathrm{erf}(k/\sqrt{2}), \tag{1.12}$$

where the error function is defined by

$$\mathrm{erf}(x) = \frac{2}{\sqrt{\pi}} \int_0^x e^{-u^2} du. \tag{1.13}$$

For different values of k or $\pm k\sigma$, we have

$$A_1 = 0.68269, \quad A_2 = 0.9545, \quad A_3 = 0.9973, \tag{1.14}$$

and

$$A_4 = 0.99993665, \quad A_{4.5} = 0.9999932. \tag{1.15}$$

Suppose the product is an electric motor with a no-load speed or the spin speed of $\omega = 3000.0 \pm 0.2$ round per minutes (rpm). If we try to use 3σ, then there would be 99.7% products without defects, and the defect rate is about 0.27%, still too high for a good product because there are about 2700 defective products out of 1 million.

Example 1.5. The beauty of the Six Sigma methodology is to use $\pm 4.5\sigma$ allowing the mean to shift $\pm 1.5\sigma$ (thus 6σ in essence). Since $k = 4.5$, we have

$$A_{4.5} = 0.999993204653751,$$

which gives 6.8 defective parts per million if the mean is not allowed to shift. Since the mean can shift $\pm 1.5\sigma$, the actual defective parts is half of the above value, that is, 3.4 parts per million, which is the essence of the Six Sigma Standards in manufacturing.

Coming back to the motor specification of $\omega = 3000.0 \pm 0.2$, or from $3000.0 - 0.2 = 2999.8$ to $3000.0 + 0.2 = 3000.2$, to ensure this standard specification with only about 3.4 defective motors per million, we have to ensure that manufacturing standard deviation σ to be even smaller. Since it requires that $6\sigma = 0.2$, we have

$$\sigma = \frac{0.2}{6} \approx 0.033,$$

which is the standard deviation to be achieved in the actual manufacturing process to ensure the desired quality target.

1.3.7 Data-driven models

As the data volumes have increased dramatically in the few last decades, various techniques are needed to deal with such big data, which have formed a new subject, called the big data science. As these data sets are usually unstructured with high complexity, no simple mathematical models can be constructed to explain the whole data. Even if it may be possible to construct some mathematical models, such models need to be modified as more data flow in. In addition, uncertainties and noise are often present in the data, which makes the already challenging data mining tasks even more difficult.

In such applications, models become data-driven, nondeterministic, and dynamic, and thus it may be impossible or meaningless to try to seek a deterministic and simple mathematical model. In this case, we have to live with models that are truly data-driven and noisy. This is a relatively new area, and the interested readers can refer to more advanced literature on data science.

In this book, we are mainly concerned with continuous and discrete models and their corresponding numerical implementations.

1.4. Numerical models

Though mathematical models can provide insights and more accurate representations of the system behavior in engineering applications, however, most governing equations used in engineering simulation are nonlinear, often in terms of partial differential equations. Such PDEs equations are very difficult to solve analytically, and in most cases, there are no closed-form analytical solutions. Therefore numerical representations or discretization of such models are necessary, and solutions are usually obtained numerically. There are different ways of discretizing ODEs and PDEs, and common used techniques are finite differences, finite elements, finite volumes, spectral methods, and others.

1.4.1 Finite differences

Finite difference approximations use Taylor expansions to approximate solutions and their derivatives. For example, a first-order ODE

$$y' = f(x, y), \quad x \in [a, b], \tag{1.16}$$

is typically discretized over N discrete intervals or $N+1$ discrete points at $x_n = a + nh$ for $n = 0, 1, 2, \ldots, N$. Here $h = \Delta x = x_n - x_{n-1}$ is given. The corresponding values of y at x_n are $y_n = y(x_n)$. The derivative is approximated by

$$y'_n \approx \frac{y_{n+1} - y_n}{\Delta x} = \frac{y_{n+1} - y_n}{h}. \tag{1.17}$$

Thus the ODE (1.16) becomes the finite difference equation

$$y_{n+1} \approx y_n + hf(x_n, y_n), \tag{1.18}$$

which is essentially an algebraic equation, also known as Euler's numerical scheme. We will introduce the finite difference methods later in this book.

1.4.2 Finite volumes

In engineering applications, conservation laws, such as the conservation of mass and energy, are usually written in integral forms. The integral volume can be decomposed into many small control volumes so as to approximate the integral to a desired accuracy. That is, a big volume domain Ω is decomposed into many nonoverlapping smaller control volumes Ω_i:

$$\Omega = \bigcup_{i=1}^{N} \Omega_i, \quad \Omega_i \cap \Omega_j = \emptyset. \tag{1.19}$$

Inside each smaller control volume domain Ω_i with the volume V_i, quantities such as $u(x)$ will not vary much, and an averaged or mean quantity

$$\bar{u}_i = \frac{1}{V_i} \int_{\Omega_i} u d\Omega_i \tag{1.20}$$

is used Then all relevant differential equations will be further discretized into a set of algebraic equations, typically written in a matrix form.

1.4.3 Finite elements

In finite element approximations, quantities at nodes or corners of small blocks or elements are calculated. The values at other places are then approximated using shape functions, and the differential equations under consideration are often written in the so-called weak form with integrals over the boundaries of an element and the integral inside the elements.

Elements are typically triangular and quadrilateral elements in the two-dimensional space or tetrahedrons and hexahedrons in the three-dimensional space. We will introduce finite element methods later in this book.

1.4.4 Meshless methods

Meshless (or meshfree) methods are a class of methods that approximate solutions to a problem on discrete nodes, rather than using elements or volumes. Such methods do not require connections between nodes and thus do not require elements or volumes. One such meshless method is the smoothed-particle hydrodynamics, and other methods include the partition of unity, element-free Galerkin method, boundary node method, discrete least squares meshfree method, and others.

1.4.5 Spectral methods

There are other types of numerical methods that use a combination of approximation techniques. For example, the spectral method uses the basis functions to first expand a solution $u(x, t)$ and then use the analytical methods to solve a reduced set of equations or use other numerical methods such as finite differences to do further approximations.

As an example, to solve the diffusion equation

$$\frac{\partial u}{\partial t} = D\frac{\partial^2 u}{\partial x^2}, \quad x \in [0, L], \tag{1.21}$$

where D is the diffusion coefficient, we can approximate a solution $u(x, t)$ by

$$u(x, t) \approx \sum_{k=0}^{N-1} a_k(t)\phi_k(x), \tag{1.22}$$

where ϕ_k $(k = 0, 1, \ldots, N-1)$ are the basis functions that vary with x only (not time t). The coefficients $a_k(t)$ are unknown functions of t to be determined.

Eq. (1.21) now becomes

$$\frac{\partial}{\partial t}\left[\sum_{k=0}^{N-1} a_k(t)\phi_k(x)\right] = D\frac{\partial}{\partial x}\left[\sum_{k=0}^{N-1} a_k(t)\phi_k(x)\right], \tag{1.23}$$

which leads to

$$\sum_{k=0}^{N-1} \frac{da_k(t)}{dt} \phi_k(x) = D \sum_{k=0}^{N-1} a_k(t) \frac{d^2 \phi_k(x)}{dx^2}. \tag{1.24}$$

For basis functions $\phi_k(x) = \exp[-i\omega_k x]$ with $\omega_k = 2\pi k/L$, we have a set of N ordinary differential equations

$$\frac{d^2 \phi_k}{dx^2} = -\omega_k^2 e^{-i\omega_k x}, \tag{1.25}$$

which can be further solved by standard ODE techniques. We can see that this spectral method converts a PDE problem into a set of ODE problems. If the basis functions are based on Fourier series, then we can usually use Fourier transforms to solve such problems.

Obviously, there are other numerical methods in the literature. We will introduce some of these methods in later chapters in this book.

1.5. Notes on software

There are many software packages that can do extensive engineering simulation, such as *Matlab®*, *Ansys*, and *Simulia*. For the contents of this book, you may find the following software packages useful:

- *Simulation Software*: There are many software packages that can do full-scale realistic simulation of real-world engineering systems. Powerful software packages such as *Ansys, Fluent, Simulia/Abaqus, Solidworks*, and many others are among the most widely used.
  Other software packages include *SimScale, SimSolid, Simu8, FlexSim, CATIA, Valispace*, and *COMSOL Multiphysics*. They are also widely used.
- *Programming and Toolboxes*: Matlab is a powerful programming language for scientific computing and many other tasks. For example, Matlab has its *Simulink®* toolbox, *Simscape* toolbox, and Optimization toolbox (e.g., linear programming `linprog`).
  Octave: Octave is a free, open-source software package, which can be considered as a main alternative for Matlab with very similar syntax. Most codes in Matlab can be run successfully in Octave without modifications. Another software is *Scilab*, which can run Matlab-style codes. In addition, Scilab has a toolbox `XCOS`, which has many similar functions to Simulink.
  Many *Python* add-on packages are also powerful for simulating various engineering systems.
  Other powerful symbolic computation and simulation software packages include *Mathematica, Maple, Maxima*, and *MapleSim*.
- *Discrete Event Simulation*: *WITNESS Horizon* software is for simulating discrete event simulation, such as queuing and manufacturing processes.

SimEvent: SimEvent is a discrete-event simulation Matlab toolbox, which has many functions, quite similar to those in Witness.

Vensim is a general-purpose software for system dynamics and discrete–continuous and agent simulation. *Simio* is a simulation and schedule software package.

There are many other software packages, either commercial or free, that can carry out various modeling and simulation tasks.

CHAPTER TWO

Ordinary differential equations

Most mathematical models in engineering, physics, chemistry, and applied sciences are formulated in terms of differential equations. If the variables or quantities (such as velocity, temperature, and pressure) change with other independent variables (such as spatial coordinates and time), then their relationship can in general be written as a differential equation or even a set of differential equations. In this chapter, we introduce the fundamentals of ordinary differential equations, and in the next chapter, we will focus on partial differential equations.

2.1. Ordinary differential equations

Newton's second law $F = ma$ is an algebraic equation. For a given force F and mass m, we can calculate the corresponding acceleration a. However, if this relationship is written in terms of the rate of change of linear momentum $p = mv$, where v is the velocity of this object, then we have

$$F = \frac{\mathrm{d}p}{\mathrm{d}t}, \tag{2.1}$$

which is a first-order differential equation. Alternatively, if we write Newton's second law in terms of displacement y, then $F = ma$ becomes

$$m\frac{\mathrm{d}^2 y}{\mathrm{d}t^2} = F, \tag{2.2}$$

which is a second-order differential equation.

In general, an ODE is a relationship between a function $y(x)$ (of an independent variable x) and its derivatives such as y' and y''. It can be written in a generic form as

$$\phi\left(x, y, y', y'', \ldots, y^{(n)}\right) = 0, \tag{2.3}$$

where we have used the following notation for derivatives:

$$y' = \frac{\mathrm{d}y}{\mathrm{d}x}, \quad y'' = \frac{\mathrm{d}^2 y}{\mathrm{d}x^2}, \quad y''' = \frac{\mathrm{d}^3 y}{\mathrm{d}x^3}, \quad y^{(n)} = \frac{\mathrm{d}^n y}{\mathrm{d}x^n}. \tag{2.4}$$

The solution of an ODE is a function $y = f(x)$ satisfying the ODE for all x in a given domain Ω. Here the domain Ω is the set formed by all feasible x values.

Engineering Simulation and its Applications
https://doi.org/10.1016/B978-0-44-314084-6.00009-7

The order of the differential equation is equal to the order n of the highest derivative in the equation. For example, the ODE $F = dp/dt$ is a first-order ODE, whereas the equation for damped harmonic motion

$$y''/\omega_n^2 + 2\zeta y'/\omega_n + y = f \tag{2.5}$$

is a second-order ODE. Here ω_n is the natural frequency, ζ is the damping coefficient, and f is the driving force.

An ordinary differential equation is called linear if it can be arranged into the following standard form:

$$a_n(x)y^{(n)} + \cdots + a_1(x)y' + a_0(x)y = f(x), \tag{2.6}$$

where all the coefficients depend on x only, not on y or any derivatives. If any of the coefficients is a function of y or its derivatives, then the equation is nonlinear. If the right-hand side is zero or $f(x) \equiv 0$, then the equation is homogeneous. It is called nonhomogeneous if $f(x) \neq 0$.

The following ODEs are nonlinear:

$$\frac{\mathrm{d}y}{\mathrm{d}x} + y^2 = \sin(x), \tag{2.7}$$

$$(y')^3 + y = x, \tag{2.8}$$

$$\frac{\mathrm{d}y}{\mathrm{d}x} + \frac{1}{y} = e^{-x}, \tag{2.9}$$

because y^2, $(y')^3$, and $1/y$ are nonlinear terms.

There are various techniques for solving linear ODEs; however, to find solutions of an ODE is not always straightforward. It is usually very complicated for nonlinear equations because there are no general solution techniques. Special techniques such as separation of variables may be only applicable to particular cases. Even for linear equations, the solutions are straightforward in only a very few simple cases, such as the ODEs with constant coefficients.

Mathematically speaking, solutions of differential equations generally fall into three types: closed forms, series forms, and integral forms. A closed-form solution is a solution that can be expressed in terms of elementary functions and some arbitrary constants. For example, $y = a\exp(-x) + x - 1$ with an undetermined coefficient a is a closed-form solution to $y' + y = x$. Series solutions are the ones that can be expressed in terms of a series when a closed-form is not possible for certain types of equations. The integral form of solutions or quadrature is sometimes the only possible form of solution. If all these forms are not possible, then the alternative is to use numerical solutions and some forms of approximations, such as asymptotic approximations.

2.1.1 First-order ODEs

The general form of a first-order linear ODE can be written as

$$y' + a(x)y = b(x), \tag{2.10}$$

where $a(x)$ and $b(x)$ are known functions.

By defining the integrating factor

$$w = \exp\left[\int a(x)dx\right] > 0 \tag{2.11}$$

we have

$$w' = \left\{\exp\left[\int a(x)dx\right]\right\}' = a(x)\exp\left[\int a(x)dx\right] = a(x)w. \tag{2.12}$$

Multiplying both sides of (2.10) by the integrating factor, we have

$$y'w + a(x)yw = b(x)w, \tag{2.13}$$

which can be written as

$$(yw)' = b(x)w. \tag{2.14}$$

By simple integration we have

$$yw = \int b(x)wdx + C \tag{2.15}$$

or

$$y = \frac{1}{w}\int b(x)wdx + \frac{C}{w}, \tag{2.16}$$

where C is an integration constant. Substituting w, this solution becomes

$$y = e^{-\int a(x)dx}\int b(x)e^{\int a(x)dx}dx + Ce^{-\int a(x)dx}. \tag{2.17}$$

However, the integrals may not lead to explicit expressions in many cases.

Example 2.1. Let us solve

$$y' + y = x. \tag{2.18}$$

Since $a(x) = 1$ and $b(x) = x$, the integrating factor becomes

$$w = \exp\left[\int a(x)dx\right] = e^x, \tag{2.19}$$

and

$$\exp\left[-\int a(x)dx\right] = \frac{1}{w} = e^{-x}. \tag{2.20}$$

Eq. (2.17) becomes

$$y = e^{-x}\int xe^{x}dx + Ce^{-x} = (x-1) + Ce^{-x}, \tag{2.21}$$

where we have used

$$\int xe^{x}dx = (x-1)e^{x}. \tag{2.22}$$

Nonlinear ODEs are much more complicated, though some nonlinear ODEs can be converted into first-order linear equations (2.10) by a transform or change of variables. Such transforms are rare, and in most cases nonlinear ODEs cannot be transformed into linear ODEs.

2.1.2 Higher-order ODEs

Higher-order ODEs are more complicated to solve even for linear equations. For the special case of higher-order ODEs where all the coefficients $a_n, \ldots, a_1$, and a_0 are real constants,

$$a_n y^{(n)} + \cdots + a_1 y' + a_0 y = f(x), \tag{2.23}$$

its general solution $y(x)$ consists of two parts, the complementary function $y_c(x)$ and the particular integral or particular solution $y_p^*(x)$. We have

$$y(x) = y_c(x) + y_p^*(x). \tag{2.24}$$

The complementary function is the solution of the linear homogeneous equation with constant coefficients, which can be written in a generic form as

$$a_n y_c^{(n)} + a_{n-1} y_c^{(n-1)} + \cdots + a_1 y_c' + a_0 = 0. \tag{2.25}$$

Assuming that $y = Ae^{\lambda x}$ with arbitrary constant $A \neq 0$ and using $y' = A\lambda e^{\lambda x}$, $y'' = A\lambda^2 e^{\lambda x}$, and $y^{(n)} = A\lambda^n e^{\lambda x}$, the ODE (2.25) becomes

$$\left[a_n\lambda^n + a_{n-1}\lambda^{n-1} + \cdots + a_1\lambda + a_0\right]Ae^{\lambda x} = 0. \tag{2.26}$$

Since $A \neq 0$ and $\exp[\lambda x] \neq 0$, we have the polynomial equation of characteristics or the auxiliary equation

$$a_n\lambda^n + a_{n-1}\lambda^{(n-1)} + \cdots + a_1\lambda + a_0 = 0, \tag{2.27}$$

which should in general have n roots. Then the solution can be expressed as a linear combination of all the basic solutions $\exp(\lambda_k x)$, that is,

$$y_c(x) = \sum_{k=1}^{n} c_k e^{\lambda_k x}, \tag{2.28}$$

where c_k $(k = 1, 2, \ldots, n)$ are the coefficients to be determined by initial conditions. Here we have assumed that the characteristic polynomial has n distinct zeros $\lambda_1, \ldots, \lambda_n$. In general, we can have complex roots, which always occur in pairs $\lambda = r \pm i\omega$, and the corresponding linearly independent terms can then be replaced by $e^{rx}[A\cos(\omega x) + B\sin(\omega x)]$.

Example 2.2. To solve the ODE

$$y'''(x) + 2y''(x) - y'(x) - 2y(x) = e^{2x}, \tag{2.29}$$

we have to find its complementary function y_c and its particular integral $y^*(x)$. The complementary function is given by

$$y'''(x) + 2y''(x) - y'(x) - 2y(x) = 0.$$

Assuming that $y_c = Ae^{\lambda x}$, we have the characteristic equation

$$\lambda^3 + 2\lambda^2 - \lambda - 2 = 0,$$

which is equivalent to

$$(\lambda + 1)(\lambda - 1)(\lambda + 2) = 0.$$

Its solutions are $\lambda = \pm 1, -2$, which lead to three basic solutions: $\exp(-x)$, $\exp(x)$, and $\exp(-2x)$. So the general complementary function becomes

$$y_c = ae^{-x} + be^{x} + ce^{-2x},$$

where a, b, and c are undetermined constants.

Since the function on the right-hand side is e^{2x}, we can assume that the particular function takes the form

$$y^*(x) = Ke^{2x}.$$

Substituting it into the original ODE (2.29), we have

$$(8K + 8K - 2K - 2K)e^{2x} = e^{2x}.$$

Dividing both sides by $e^{2x} \neq 0$, we have

$$12K = 1, \quad \text{that is,} \quad K = \frac{1}{12}.$$

So the particular function becomes

$$y^* = \frac{1}{12}e^{2x}.$$

Finally, the general solution becomes

$$y(x) = ae^{-x} + be^{x} + ce^{-2x} + \frac{1}{12}e^{2x}.$$

The constants a, b, and c will be determined by appropriate initial conditions.

The particular solution $y_p^*(x)$ is any $y(x)$ that satisfies the original inhomogeneous equation (2.23). Depending on the form of the function $f(x)$, the particular solutions can take various forms. For most combinations of basic functions such as $\sin x$, $\cos x$, e^{kx}, and x^n, the method of the undetermined coefficients is widely used.

For example, if $f(x) = \sin(\alpha x)$ or $\cos(\alpha x)$, then we can try $y_p^* = A\sin\alpha x + B\sin\alpha x$. We then substitute it into the original equation (2.23), so that the coefficients A and B can be determined. For a polynomial

$$f(x) = x^n \quad (n \geq 1), \tag{2.30}$$

the trial form is a polynomial

$$y_p^* = A + Bx + \cdots + Qx^n. \tag{2.31}$$

For $f(x) = e^{kx}x^n$, the trial form becomes

$$y_p^* = (A + Bx + \cdots + Qx^n)e^{kx}. \tag{2.32}$$

Similarly, for $f(x) = e^{kx}\sin\alpha x$ or $f(x) = e^{kx}\cos\alpha x$, the trial form is

$$y_p^* = e^{kx}(A\sin\alpha x + B\cos\alpha x). \tag{2.33}$$

In the case where $f(x)$ is a basic solution of the homogeneous ODE, it is not possible for $y_p = Af(x)$ to satisfy the original ODE. Therefore a different trial form of the particular integral should be used, which can be obtained by multiplying $f(x)$ by Ax, where A is the constant to be determined. For example, if $\exp(kx)$ is a basic solution of the homogeneous ODE, then the trial form should be

$$y_p^* = Axe^{kx}. \tag{2.34}$$

Determining the coefficients by using particular trial integrals is called the method of undetermined coefficients. More general cases and their particular solutions can be found in more specialized textbooks.

Example 2.3. To solve

$$y'' + 3y' + 2y = e^{-x}, \tag{2.35}$$

we can assume that $y_c = Ae^{\lambda x}$, and then its auxiliary or characteristic equation becomes

$$\lambda^2 + 3\lambda + 2 = (\lambda + 1)(\lambda + 2) = 0, \tag{2.36}$$

which gives

$$\lambda_1 = -1, \quad \lambda_2 = -2. \tag{2.37}$$

The two basic solutions are e^{-x} and e^{-2x}, and the complementary function is

$$y_c = Ae^{-x} + Be^{-2x}. \tag{2.38}$$

Since $f(x) = e^{-x}$ is the same as the basic solution e^{-x} with $\lambda_1 = -1$, we have to try the particular integral of the form

$$y_p = kxe^{-x}, \tag{2.39}$$

where k is the undetermined coefficient.

From $y_p' = k(1-x)e^{-x}$ and $y_p'' = k(x-2)e^{-x}$, after substituting into the original ODE, we obtain

$$k(x-2)e^{-x} + 3k(1-x)e^{-x} + 2kxe^{-x} = e^{-x}, \tag{2.40}$$

which can be simplified as

$$ke^{-x} = e^{-x}, \tag{2.41}$$

which gives $k = 1$. This means that the particular integral now becomes

$$y_p = xe^{-x}. \tag{2.42}$$

Finally, the general solution can be written as

$$y(x) = Ae^{-x} + Be^{-2x} + xe^{-x}. \tag{2.43}$$

2.1.3 Differential operator and particular integrals

To find the particular integrals of linear ODEs, a very useful technique is to use differential operators. A differential operator D is defined as

$$D \equiv \frac{\mathrm{d}}{\mathrm{d}x}, \quad D^2 = \frac{\mathrm{d}^2}{\mathrm{d}x^2}. \tag{2.44}$$

Since we know that $De^{\lambda x} = \lambda e^{\lambda x}$ and $D^n e^{\lambda x} = \lambda^n e^{\lambda x}$, they are equivalent to the mappings $D \mapsto \lambda$ and $D^n \mapsto \lambda^n$ when applied to $\exp(\lambda x)$. Thus any polynomial $P(D)$ will be mapped to its corresponding $P(\lambda)$, that is,

$$P(D)e^{\lambda x} = e^{\lambda x}P(\lambda). \tag{2.45}$$

This means that the particular integral for $f(\boldsymbol{x}) = \exp(\lambda x)$ is

$$y_p = \frac{1}{P(D)}e^{\lambda x} = \frac{1}{P(\lambda)}e^{\lambda x}, \quad P(\lambda) \neq 0. \tag{2.46}$$

The beauty of the differential operator method is that the expression of differential operators can be factorized in the same way as for polynomials, and then each factor can be solved separately. In fact, if $P(D) = Q(D)R(D)$, then we have

$$P(D)y = Q(D)R(D)y = f(x), \tag{2.47}$$

which gives

$$y = \frac{1}{P(D)}f(x) = \frac{1}{Q(D)}\left[\frac{1}{R(D)}f(x)\right] = \frac{1}{R(D)}\left[\frac{1}{Q(D)}f(x)\right], \tag{2.48}$$

that is, the application of $P(D)$ can be sequentially carried out in two stages. The differential operator method is very useful in finding particular integrals.

On the other hand, the integral operator

$$D^{-1}f(x) = \frac{1}{D}f(x) = \int f(x)dx, \tag{2.49}$$

is just the inverse of differentiation. The rigorous derivations of differential operator rules are beyond the scope of this book. However, many operations are linked to differential equations. For example, the differential operator with a constant k

$$y(x) = \frac{1}{(D+k)}f(x) \tag{2.50}$$

is essentially equivalent to

$$(D+k)y(x) = f(x) \tag{2.51}$$

or the ODE

$$y'(x) + ky(x) = f(x). \tag{2.52}$$

Using the solution from (2.17) with $a(x) = k$ and setting $C = 0$, we have

$$y(x) = \frac{1}{(D+k)}f(x) = e^{-kx}\int e^{+kx}f(x)dx. \tag{2.53}$$

The reason we can set $C = 0$ is that our aim is finding a particular integral, not a general solution in this step.

Example 2.4. For example, the particular integral of the differential equation in the previous example

$$y'''(x) + 2y''(x) - y'(x) - 2y(x) = e^{2x}$$

can be found by

$$P(D)y_p^* = e^{2x}, \quad P(D) = D^3 + 2D^2 - D - 2, \tag{2.54}$$

or

$$y_p^* = \frac{e^{2x}}{P(D)} = \frac{1}{(D^3 + 2D^2 - D - 2)} e^{2x}.$$

Since $D^n \mapsto \lambda^n = 2^n$ for $\exp(2x)$, where $n = 1, 2, 3$, we have

$$y_p^* = \frac{e^{2x}}{(2^3 + 2 \times 2^2 - 2 - 2)} = \frac{e^{2x}}{12},$$

which is exactly what we got earlier.

It is worth pointing out that the differential operator technique cannot be used directly to find the particular integral if $f(x)$ on the right-hand side is part of the complementary function (i.e., $P(\lambda) = 0$). Some modifications are needed. In addition, we may have to use the so-called exponential-shift property and other properties in the calculations.

It is straightforward to show that

$$D[e^{\lambda x}y(x)] = e^{\lambda x}(D + \lambda)y(x), \quad D^2[e^{\lambda x}y(x)] = e^{\lambda x}(D + \lambda)^2 y(x), \tag{2.55}$$

and

$$D^n[e^{\lambda x}y(x)] = e^{\lambda x}(D + \lambda)^n y(x), \tag{2.56}$$

where $n \geq 1$ is an integer.

For the case of $P(\lambda) = 0$, the particular integral can be calculated by

$$y_p = \frac{xe^{\lambda x}}{P'(\lambda)}, \tag{2.57}$$

where P' is the derivative polynomial. The proof of this result requires rigorous mathematics, which is not the focus here.

Let us use an example to show how this method works. From the linear differential operator

$$P(D) = D^2 + 3D + 2 \tag{2.58}$$

we have

$$P'(D) = 2D + 3. \tag{2.59}$$

To obtain a particular integral in (2.42), we use

$$y_p = \frac{xe^{\lambda x}}{P'(\lambda)} = \frac{xe^{-x}}{P'(-1)} = \frac{xe^{-1}}{2(-1)+3} = xe^{-x}, \tag{2.60}$$

which is the same as that we obtained earlier. As we can see, the algebra may not be simple in this case. In principle, we can also find the particular integral by direct factorization and inversion.

Example 2.5. For example, to find the particular integral of

$$y'' + 3y' + 2y = e^{-x}, \tag{2.61}$$

we have

$$(D^2 + 3D + 2)y_* = (D+1)(D+2)y_* = e^{-x}, \tag{2.62}$$

which becomes

$$y_* = \frac{1}{(D+1)(D+2)} e^{-x}. \tag{2.63}$$

Using (2.53), the preceding equation becomes

$$\begin{aligned} y_* &= \frac{1}{(D+1)}\left[\frac{1}{(D+2)}e^{-x}\right] = \frac{1}{(D+1)}\left[e^{-2x}\int e^{2x}e^{-x}dx\right] \\ &= \frac{1}{(D+1)}\left[e^{-2x}e^{x}\right] = \frac{1}{(D+1)}e^{-x} \\ &= e^{-x}\left[\int e^{x}e^{-x}dx\right] = e^{-x}\int dx = e^{-x}x = xe^{-x}, \end{aligned} \tag{2.64}$$

which is the same as we obtained before.

It is worth pointing out that a slightly different calculation

$$\frac{1}{(D+2)}\left[\frac{1}{(D+1)}e^{-x}\right] = xe^{-x} - e^{-x} \tag{2.65}$$

gives a seemingly different result. Since e^{-x} is part of the complementary function $y_c = A\exp(-x) + B\exp(-2x)$, the term $-e^{-x}$ can be absorbed into y_c, and then $y_* = x\exp(-x)$ is still the same particular integral.

As we have seen, the calculations are quite complicated here. The differential operator method can be suitable for systematic derivations using symbolic mathematic software tools. For our purpose of figuring out the particular integrals here, the standard method of undetermined coefficients may be preferable.

Higher-order differential equations can be conveniently written as a system of ODEs. In fact, an nth-order linear ODE can always be written as a linear system of n first-order ODEs. A linear system of ODEs is more suitable for mathematical analysis and numerical integration.

2.2. System of linear ODEs

For a linear ODE of order n (see (2.23)), we can write as a system of linear ODEs by using additional variables

$$y_1 = \frac{dy}{dx}, \quad y_2 = \frac{dy_1}{dx} = \frac{d^2y}{dx^2}, \tag{2.66}$$

and others. With these notations, we can rewrite

$$a_n y^{(n)} + \cdots + a_2 y'' + a_1 y' + a_0 y = f(x) \tag{2.67}$$

as a linear system of n ODEs

$$\frac{dy}{dx} = y_1, \tag{2.68}$$

$$\frac{dy_1}{dx} = y_2, \tag{2.69}$$

$$\cdots, \tag{2.70}$$

$$\frac{dy_{(n-2)}}{dx} = y_{n-1}, \tag{2.71}$$

$$a_n y'_{n-1} = -a_{n-1} y_{n-1} - \cdots - a_1 y_1 - a_0 y + f(x), \tag{2.72}$$

which is a dynamical system for

$$u = [y \ y_1 \ y_2 \ \ldots \ y_{n-1}]^T. \tag{2.73}$$

In essence, this converts the nth-order ODE for $y(x)$ with independent variable x into a system in a higher-dimensional phase space for u where all equations are first-order linear ODEs.

Example 2.6. For the second-order ODE

$$y'' + 3y' + 2y = e^{-x},$$

we set $z = dy/dx$, and we have

$$y' = z, \tag{2.74}$$

$$z' = -3z - 2y + e^{-x}. \tag{2.75}$$

For a second-order linear ODE, we can always write it in the following form:

$$\frac{du}{dx} = a_1 u + b_1 v + c_1 + f(x), \tag{2.76}$$

$$\frac{dv}{dx} = a_2 u + b_2 v + c_2 + g(x), \tag{2.77}$$

where $f(x)$ and $g(x)$ are known functions. If the independent variable x does not appear explicitly on the right-hand sides (e.g., $f = 0$ and $g = 0$), then the system is said to be autonomous. Such a system has important properties. For simplicity and in keeping with the convention, we use $t = x$ and $\dot{u} = du/dt$ in the following discussion. In general, a homogeneous linear system of nth order with constant coefficients can be written as

$$\begin{pmatrix} \dot{u}_1 \\ \dot{u}_2 \\ \vdots \\ \dot{u}_n \end{pmatrix} = \begin{pmatrix} a_{11} & a_{12} & \ldots & a_{1n} \\ a_{21} & a_{22} & \ldots & a_{2n} \\ \vdots & & & \vdots \\ a_{n1} & a_{n2} & \ldots & a_{nn} \end{pmatrix} \begin{pmatrix} u_1 \\ u_2 \\ \vdots \\ u_n \end{pmatrix} \tag{2.78}$$

or, in the matrix form,

$$\dot{\boldsymbol{u}} = \boldsymbol{A}\boldsymbol{u}, \tag{2.79}$$

where

$$\boldsymbol{u} = \begin{pmatrix} u_1 \\ u_2 \\ \vdots \\ u_n \end{pmatrix}, \quad \boldsymbol{A} = \begin{pmatrix} a_{11} & a_{12} & \cdots & a_{1n} \\ a_{21} & a_{22} & \cdots & a_{2n} \\ \vdots & \vdots & \ddots & \vdots \\ a_{n1} & a_{n2} & \cdots & a_{nn} \end{pmatrix}. \tag{2.80}$$

By using $\boldsymbol{u} = \boldsymbol{v}\exp(\lambda t)$ where $\boldsymbol{v}$ is a vector to be determined this becomes an eigenvalue problem for matrix $\boldsymbol{A}$,

$$(\boldsymbol{A} - \lambda \boldsymbol{I})\boldsymbol{v} = 0, \tag{2.81}$$

which will have nonzero solutions only if the determinant is zero, that is,

$$\det(\boldsymbol{A} - \lambda \boldsymbol{I}) = 0. \tag{2.82}$$

Here $\boldsymbol{v}$ is the eigenvector for a given eigenvalue λ. We will introduce the eigenvalue problems later in this book.

Example 2.7. The system

$$\begin{cases} \dot{u} = u - v, \\ \dot{v} = 2u + 3v \end{cases} \tag{2.83}$$

can be written as

$$\begin{pmatrix} \dot{u} \\ \dot{v} \end{pmatrix} = \begin{pmatrix} 1 & -1 \\ 2 & 3 \end{pmatrix} \begin{pmatrix} u \\ v \end{pmatrix}. \tag{2.84}$$

Obviously, such systems can be analyzed by using dynamical system theories and numerical methods. We will discuss this in more detail later when appropriate.

2.3. Notes on software

Many software packages can solve ODEs symbolically, such as *Mathematica*, *Maple*, *Maxima*, symbolic mathematics toolbox of *Matlab*®, and *Python*'s Sympy.

Other popular software packages include *Geogebra*, *Desmos*, *Sagemath*, *R*, and many others.

CHAPTER THREE

Partial differential equations

Many processes in engineering can be modeled by using partial differential equations (PDEs). For example, the heat transfer problems in the three-dimensional (3D) space can be modeled by the heat conduction equation

$$\frac{\partial T}{\partial t} = \kappa \nabla^2 T, \quad \nabla^2 T = \frac{\partial^2 T}{\partial x^2} + \frac{\partial^2 T}{\partial y^2} + \frac{\partial^2 T}{\partial z^2}, \tag{3.1}$$

where $T(x, y, z, t)$ is the temperature that varies with x, y, z and time t, and κ is a constant that depends on the thermal properties of the media.

PDEs are much more complicated compared with ODEs. Solution techniques for PDEs tend to be problem-type specific, and there are no universal solution techniques for nonlinear equations. Even their numerical solutions are usually not straightforward to obtain. Thus we will mainly focus on some linear PDEs that are of special interest to engineering simulation.

In general, a PDE is a relationship containing one or more partial derivatives. Similar to the concept of ODEs, the highest nth partial derivative is referred to as the order n of the PDE. The general form of a PDE can be written as

$$\phi\left(u, x, y, \ldots, \frac{\partial u}{\partial x}, \frac{\partial u}{\partial y}, \frac{\partial^2 u}{\partial x^2}, \frac{\partial^2 u}{\partial y^2}, \frac{\partial^2 u}{\partial x \partial y}, \ldots\right) = 0, \tag{3.2}$$

where u is the dependent variable, and $x, y, \ldots$ are the independent variables.

Example 3.1. A simple example of PDEs is the linear first-order PDE, which can be written as

$$a(x, y)\frac{\partial u}{\partial x} + b(x, y)\frac{\partial u}{\partial y} = f(x, y) \tag{3.3}$$

for two independent variables and one dependent variable u. If the right-hand side is zero or simply $f(x, y) = 0$, then this PDE is said to be homogeneous. The PDE is said to be linear if a, b, and f are functions of x, y only, not u itself.

In many textbooks, especially in pure mathematics, subscript notations are used to simplify the form of PDEs. For simplicity, we also use such notations:

$$u_x \equiv \frac{\partial u}{\partial x}, \quad u_y \equiv \frac{\partial u}{\partial y}, \quad u_{xx} \equiv \frac{\partial^2 u}{\partial x^2}, \tag{3.4}$$

$$u_{yy} \equiv \frac{\partial^2 u}{\partial y^2}, \quad u_{xy} \equiv \frac{\partial^2 u}{\partial x \partial y}. \tag{3.5}$$

Engineering Simulation and its Applications
https://doi.org/10.1016/B978-0-44-314084-6.00010-3

Thus we can write the previous PDE (3.3) compactly as

$$au_x + bu_y = f. \tag{3.6}$$

In the rest of the chapters in this book, we will use such notations whenever no confusion occurs.

3.1. First-order PDEs

A first-order PDE of linear type can be written as

$$a(x, y)u_x + b(x, y)u_y = f(x, y), \tag{3.7}$$

which can be solved using the method of characteristics. This method uses a new parameter s to convert the PDE into a set of ODEs

$$\frac{dx}{ds} = a, \quad \frac{dy}{ds} = b, \quad \frac{du}{ds} = f, \tag{3.8}$$

which essentially forms a system of first-order ODEs evolving along the characteristics of the PDE.

Example 3.2. A simple example of first-order PDEs is the first-order hyperbolic equation

$$u_t + cu_x = 0, \tag{3.9}$$

where c is a constant. This can be written as a set of three ODEs

$$\frac{dt}{ds} = 1, \quad \frac{dx}{ds} = c, \quad \frac{du}{ds} = 0. \tag{3.10}$$

Since $du/ds = 0$, u is constant (independent of s). From $dt/ds = 1$ we have $t = s$, where we assumed that $s = 0$ when $t = 0$. From $dx/ds = c$ we have $x = cs + x_0$, where x_0 is the initial value. Combining the two results, we have

$$x_0 = x - ct. \tag{3.11}$$

For a given initial profile $u = \psi(x_0)$, the solution becomes

$$u(x, t) = \psi(x_0) = \psi(x - ct), \tag{3.12}$$

which essentially means that the initial profile or shape travels along the x-axis with constant speed c. In this case the shape of the wave does not change, though its position is constantly changing.

3.2. Classification of second-order PDEs

Though second-order PDEs can in general be very complicated, second-order linear PDEs can have compact forms, and most PDEs in engineering applications can be formulated as second-order PDEs.

In general, a linear second-order PDE (with two independent variables x and y) can be written in the generic form

$$au_{xx} + bu_{xy} + cu_{yy} + gu_x + hu_y + ku = f, \tag{3.13}$$

where a, b, c, g, h, k, and f are functions of x and y only. If $f(x, y, u)$ is also a function of u, then we say that this equation is quasilinear.

For the classification purpose of PDEs, we can define the quantity

$$\Delta = b^2 - 4ac = b(x, y)^2 - 4a(x, y)c(x, y), \tag{3.14}$$

which is a function of x and y in general.

- *Elliptic PDEs*: If $\Delta = b^2 - 4ac < 0$, then the PDE is said to be elliptic. One famous example is the Laplace equation

$$u_{xx} + u_{yy} = 0, \tag{3.15}$$

where $\Delta = -4 < 0$ because $a = 1$, $b = 0$, and $c = 1$.

- *Hyperbolic PDEs*: If $\Delta > 0$, then it is hyperbolic. One example is the wave equation

$$u_{tt} = v^2 u_{xx}, \tag{3.16}$$

where v is the wave speed. Here $\Delta = 4v^2 > 0$ because $a = 1$, $b = 0$, and $c = -v^2$.

- *Parabolic PDEs*: If $\Delta = 0$, then it is parabolic. The 1D heat conduction equation

$$u_t = \kappa u_{xx} \tag{3.17}$$

is parabolic because $\Delta = 0$ with $a = 0$, $b = 0$, and $c = -\kappa$.

These three types of classic PDEs are widely used, and they occur in a vast range of applications. In fact, almost all textbooks on PDEs deal with these three basic types of PDEs.

3.3. Common PDEs in engineering

In engineering simulation, there are quite a few types of PDEs, and we will briefly introduce some of these commonly used PDEs.

3.3.1 Heat conduction equation

Time-dependent problems, such as diffusion and heat conduction, are governed by the heat conduction equation

$$\frac{\partial u}{\partial t} = \kappa \nabla^2 u, \quad \nabla^2 u = \frac{\partial^2 u}{\partial x^2} + \frac{\partial^2 u}{\partial y^2} + \frac{\partial^2 u}{\partial z^2}, \tag{3.18}$$

which is a parabolic PDE. Here κ is a constant.

Written in the n-dimensional case with notations $x_1 = x$, $x_2 = y$, $x_3 = z$, etc., the above PDE can be extended to the general reaction–diffusion equation

$$u_t = \kappa \nabla^2 u + f(u, x_1, ..., x_n, t), \tag{3.19}$$

where f is a known function for modeling the source.

3.3.2 Poisson's equation

For heat transfer problems, the temperature distribution can reach a steady state if time is sufficiently long. The distribution of the final temperature profile will no longer change with time, though it is still a function of spatial coordinates. For example, in the two-dimensional space (x, y), the steady state of heat conduction with a source $f(x, y)$ is governed by the Poisson equation

$$\kappa \nabla^2 u = f(x, y), \quad (x, y) \in \Omega, \tag{3.20}$$

or

$$u_{xx} + u_{yy} = q(x, y) \tag{3.21}$$

for two independent variables x and y. Here κ is thermal diffusivity, and $q = f(x, y)/\kappa$.

If there is no heat source ($q = 0$), then this becomes the Laplace equation

$$\frac{\partial^2 u}{\partial x^2} + \frac{\partial^2 u}{\partial y^2} = 0. \tag{3.22}$$

Its solutions are often referred to as harmonic functions.

To determine the temperature distribution u completely and uniquely, appropriate initial and boundary conditions are needed. For initial conditions, an initial temperature profile $u(x, y, t = 0)$ is should be given. For example, we can set all the initial temperature as zero.

For boundary conditions, we can specify different types, depending on the physics and insulation conditions. A simple boundary condition is to specify the temperature $u = u_0$ on the boundary $\partial\Omega$ of the domain Ω. This type of problem is the Dirichlet problem. On the other hand, if the temperature is not known, but the gradient $\partial u/\partial \boldsymbol{n}$

is known on the boundary where $\boldsymbol{n}$ is the outward-pointing unit normal, then this forms the Neumann problem. Furthermore, some problems may have a mixed type of boundary condition in the combination of

$$au + b\frac{\partial u}{\partial \boldsymbol{n}} = \gamma, \tag{3.23}$$

which may naturally occur as a radiation or cooling boundary condition. Here a and b are known constants.

3.3.3 Wave equation

The vibrations of a string and traveling sound waves are governed by the hyperbolic wave equation. The 1D wave equation in its simplest form is

$$\frac{\partial^2 u}{\partial t^2} = a^2 \frac{\partial^2 u}{\partial x^2}, \tag{3.24}$$

where a is the velocity of the wave. Using a transformation of the pair of independent variables

$$\xi = x + at, \quad \eta = x - at \tag{3.25}$$

for $t > 0$ and $-\infty < x < \infty$, the wave equation becomes

$$\frac{\partial^2 u}{\partial \xi \partial \eta} = 0. \tag{3.26}$$

Integrating it with respect to η and then integrating with respect to ξ, we have

$$u = f(\xi) + g(\eta). \tag{3.27}$$

Substituting back in terms of x and t, we have

$$u(x, t) = f(x + at) + g(x - at), \tag{3.28}$$

where f and g are arbitrary functions of $x + at$ and $x - at$, respectively. We can see that there are two directions in which the wave can travel. One wave moves to the right along the x-axis, and one travels to the left at a constant speed a.

3.4. Sound wave: a worked example

As an example, let us look at the acoustics of a flute. The air pressure change $u(x, t)$ with time t and location x inside the pipe of a flute, which is governed by the wave equation

$$\frac{\partial^2 u}{\partial t^2} = a^2 \frac{\partial^2 u}{\partial x^2}, \tag{3.29}$$

where a is the speed of sound. The vibrations of the air form a series of standing waves with different frequencies, depending on the length of the flute and its boundary conditions.

The boundary conditions can be either open or closed. If the ends of the flute are open, then we have $u(0, t) = 0$ or $u(L, t) = 0$, where L is the length of the flute. Here we have implicitly assumed that the pressure outside the pipe is constant, and thus its change is zero. If the end is closed at $x = L$, then we have $\partial u(L, t)/\partial x = 0$, which corresponds to the boundary condition when we blow across the opening end of an empty bottle. For simplicity, we will only discuss the case where both ends are open, that is,

$$u(0, t) = 0, \quad u(L, t) = 0. \tag{3.30}$$

This problem is exactly the same as the vibration of a string with both ends fixed.

We now use the separation of variables (see the next section for details) by letting

$$u(x, t) = \phi(x)T(t),$$

where $\phi(x)$ is a function of x only, whereas $T(t)$ is a function of time t. Substituting it into the wave equation, we have

$$\phi T'' = a^2 \phi'' T,$$

which can be written as

$$\frac{1}{a^2}\frac{T''}{T} = \frac{\phi''}{\phi}.$$

Since the left-hand side only depends on t, whereas the right-hand side only depends on x, both sides should be equal to the same constant, say, $-\lambda$ (here the negative sign is purely for convenience), that is,

$$\frac{1}{a^2}\frac{T''}{T} = \frac{\phi''}{\phi} = -\lambda, \tag{3.31}$$

which is equivalent to two ODEs

$$T'' = -a^2 \lambda T, \quad \phi'' = -\lambda \phi. \tag{3.32}$$

The general solution for ϕ is

$$\phi(x) = A \sin(\sqrt{\lambda} x) + B \cos(\sqrt{\lambda} x), \tag{3.33}$$

where A and B are constants. As the boundary conditions on $u=0$ lead to

$$\phi(0)=0, \quad \phi(L)=0, \tag{3.34}$$

we now have

$$\phi(x)=\sin\left(\sqrt{\lambda_n}x\right)=\sin\left(\frac{n\pi x}{L}\right), \quad \lambda_n=\frac{n^2\pi^2}{L^2}, \tag{3.35}$$

where λ_n $(n=1,2,\ldots)$ are often referred to as the eigenvalues of this problem. Similarly, the equation for T becomes

$$T''+\omega_n^2 T=0, \quad w_n=\frac{n\pi a}{L}, \tag{3.36}$$

whose solution is

$$T(t)=C_n\cos(\omega_n t)+D_n\sin(\omega_n t), \tag{3.37}$$

where C_n and D_n are coefficients. Therefore the basic frequencies of the harmonics are

$$f_n=\frac{\omega_n}{2\pi}=\frac{na}{2L} \quad (n=1,2,\ldots). \tag{3.38}$$

Here $n=1$ corresponds to the fundamental frequency, $n=2$ corresponds to the second harmonics, and so on. So changing the effective length L by cutting holes in the pipe can create differences in pitch. The distance between holes will affect the notes of the flute. By changing the force of the air flow we effectively change n, also resulting in differences in pitch.

Finally, the general solution for u is given by superposing all the basic solutions, and we have

$$u(x,t)=\sum_{n=1}^{\infty}\sin\frac{n\pi a}{L}\left[C_n\cos\frac{n\pi at}{L}+D_n\sin\frac{n\pi at}{L}\right]. \tag{3.39}$$

It is worth pointing out that for a pipe with one end open and the other end closed, the frequencies are given by

$$f_n=\frac{na}{4L} \quad (n=1,3,5,\ldots). \tag{3.40}$$

So the pitch can also be changed by closing one end.

3.5. PDE solution techniques

Though there are different techniques for solving PDEs, different techniques may require different conditions and thus may only apply to certain types of PDEs. Therefore each type of PDEs usually requires a different solution technique in practice. In addition, for nonlinear PDEs, there may not be any good solution techniques at all, especially for second- or higher-order PDEs.

For linear PDEs on regular domains with appropriate boundary and initial conditions, there are a few methods that can work well. These methods include separation of variables, the method of series expansion, and transform methods such as the Laplace and Fourier transforms.

3.5.1 Separation of variables

The main idea of separation of variables is to assume that the solution can be written as a product of functions, where each function depends on only one of its independent variables, and thus such functions can be separated into different terms.

For example, for a solution $u(x, y, t)$ that is a function of x, y, t, the separation of variables attempts to express the solution as a product of three functions $X(x)$, $Y(y)$, and $T(t)$ in the form

$$u = X(x)Y(y)T(t), \tag{3.41}$$

where $X(x)$, $Y(y)$, $T(t)$ are functions of x, y, t, respectively. Then the solution is obtained by determining these functions so that u satisfies the PDE and the required boundary conditions (often in terms of eigenvalue problems). The assumption of writing a solution as factors of separate functions is a very strong assumption, which may not work in many cases. However, for linear PDEs in a regular domain with sufficiently nice conditions, this method can work very well.

To demonstrate how the separation of variables works, let us use a classic example of heat conduction in the one-dimensional (1D) space. Now we try to solve the 1D heat conduction equation

$$u_t = ku_{xx}, \tag{3.42}$$

in the domain $x \in [0, L]$ and $t > 0$ with the initial value and boundary conditions

$$u(0, t) = 0, \quad \frac{\partial u}{\partial x}\Big|_{x=L} = 0, \quad u(x, 0) = \psi. \tag{3.43}$$

Assuming that $u(x, t) = X(x)T(t)$, we have

$$u_t = \frac{\partial u}{\partial t} = X(x)T'(t) \tag{3.44}$$

and

$$u_x = \frac{\partial u}{\partial x} = X'(x)T(t), \quad u_{xx} = \frac{\partial^2 u}{\partial x^2} = X''(x)T(t). \tag{3.45}$$

Substituting these into the original PDE (3.42), we have

$$X(x)T'(t) = kX''(x)T(t). \tag{3.46}$$

Since we should assume that $u(x, t) \neq 0$ (otherwise, we have a trivial solution that is zero everywhere), we can divide both sides of the preceding equation by $u(x, t) = X(x)T(t)$ and get

$$\frac{X''(x)}{X(x)} = \frac{T'(t)}{kT(t)}. \tag{3.47}$$

As the left-hand side depends only on x and the right-hand side depends only on t, therefore both sides must be equal to the same constant, and the constant can be taken as $-\lambda^2$, that is,

$$\frac{X''(x)}{X(x)} = \frac{T'(t)}{kT(t)} = -\lambda^2. \tag{3.48}$$

The negative sign is just for convenience because we will see below that the finiteness of the solution $T(t)$ requires that eigenvalues $\lambda^2 > 0$ or λ are real. Hence we now get two ODEs

$$X''(x) + \lambda^2 X(x) = 0 \tag{3.49}$$

and

$$T'(t) + k\lambda^2 T(t) = 0. \tag{3.50}$$

Up to this step, the method of separation of variables has essentially converted a PDE into two linear ODEs, which has significantly simplified the solution task. As we will see later, λ can be considered as the eigenvalue to this problem.

The basic solution of $T(t)$ to the linear ODE $T' + k\lambda^2 T = 0$ is

$$T = A_n e^{-\lambda^2 kt}, \tag{3.51}$$

where A_n is a constant to be determined. The basic solution of $X(x)$ to $X'' + \lambda^2 X = 0$ is simply

$$X(t) = \alpha \cos \lambda x + \beta \sin \lambda x. \tag{3.52}$$

So the basic or fundamental solution for u becomes

$$u(x, t) = X(x)T(t) = (\alpha \cos \lambda x + \beta \sin \lambda x)e^{-\lambda^2 kt}, \tag{3.53}$$

where we have absorbed the coefficient A_n into α and β because they are the undetermined coefficients anyway. The value of λ varies with the boundary conditions, which forms an eigenvalue problem.

The general solution for u should be derived by superposing solutions of (3.53), and we have

$$u = \sum_{n=1}^{\infty} X_n T_n = \sum_{n=1}^{\infty} (\alpha_n \cos \lambda_n x + \beta_n \sin \lambda_n x)e^{-\lambda_n^2 kt}. \tag{3.54}$$

If we try to determine these coefficients α_n and β_n, then we need to use appropriate boundary and initial conditions. From the boundary condition $u(0, t) = 0$ at $x = 0$ we have

$$0 = \sum_{n=1}^{\infty} \alpha_n e^{-\lambda_n^2 kt}, \tag{3.55}$$

which leads to $\alpha_n = 0$ since $\exp(-\lambda^2 kt) > 0$. Thus the general solution becomes

$$u = \sum_{n=1}^{\infty} \beta_n \sin(\lambda_n x) e^{-\lambda_n^2 kt}. \tag{3.56}$$

From the other boundary condition $\frac{\partial u}{\partial x}\Big|_{x=L} = 0$ at $x = L$ we have

$$\sum_{n=1}^{\infty} \beta_n \lambda_n \cos(\lambda_n L) e^{-\lambda_n^2 kt} = 0. \tag{3.57}$$

Since this condition is true at $t = 0$ (thus $\exp(-\lambda_n^2 kt) = 0$ at $t = 0$) and not all β_n are zero (otherwise, we have a trivial zero solution), the above condition implies that

$$\lambda_n \cos \lambda_n L = 0, \tag{3.58}$$

which leads to $\cos(\lambda_n L) = 0$ or

$$\lambda_n L = \frac{(2n+1)\pi}{2} \quad (n = 0, 1, 2, \ldots). \tag{3.59}$$

Therefore λ cannot be continuous, and it only takes an infinite number of discrete values, called eigenvalues.

For each eigenvalue

$$\lambda = \lambda_n = \frac{(2n+1)\pi}{2L} \quad (n = 0, 1, 2, \ldots), \tag{3.60}$$

it has a corresponding eigenfunction $X_n = \sin(\lambda_n x)$. Substituting into the solution for $T(t)$, we have

$$T_n(t) = A_n e^{-\frac{[(2n+1)\pi]^2}{4L^2} kt}. \tag{3.61}$$

Expanding the initial condition into a Fourier series so as to determine the coefficients, we have

$$u(x, t) = \sum_{n=0}^{\infty} \beta_n \sin\left(\frac{(2n+1)\pi x}{2L}\right) e^{-\left[\frac{(2n+1)\pi}{2L}\right]^2 kt}, \tag{3.62}$$

where

$$\beta_n = \frac{2}{L}\int_0^L \psi(x)\sin\left[\frac{(2n+1)\pi\xi}{2L}\right]d\xi. \tag{3.63}$$

In the particular case where the initial condition $u(x, t=0) = \psi = u_0$ is constant, the requirement for $u = u_0$ at $t = 0$ becomes

$$u_0 = \sum_{n=0}^{\infty} \beta_n \sin\frac{(2n+1)\pi x}{2L}. \tag{3.64}$$

Using the orthogonal relationships

$$\int_0^L \sin\frac{m\pi x}{L}\sin\frac{n\pi x}{L}dx = 0, \quad m \neq n, \tag{3.65}$$

and

$$\int_0^L \left(\sin\frac{n\pi x}{L}\right)^2 dx = \frac{L}{2} \quad (n = 1, 2, \ldots) \tag{3.66}$$

and multiplying both sides of Eq. (3.64) by $\sin\frac{(2n+1)\pi x}{2L}$, we have the integral

$$\beta_n \frac{L}{2} = \int_0^L \sin\frac{(2n+1)\pi x}{2L} u_0 dx = \frac{2L}{(2n+1)\pi} \quad (n = 0, 1, 2, \ldots), \tag{3.67}$$

which leads to

$$\beta_n = \frac{4u_0}{(2n+1)\pi} \quad (n = 0, 1, 2, \ldots). \tag{3.68}$$

Therefore the solution becomes

$$u = \frac{4u_0}{\pi}\sum_{n=0}^{\infty}\frac{1}{(2n+1)}e^{-\frac{(2n+1)^2\pi^2 kt}{4L^2}}\sin\frac{(2n+1)\pi x}{2L}. \tag{3.69}$$

This solution is essentially the same as the classic heat conduction problem discussed by Carslaw and Jaeger in 1959. The same solution can also be obtained using the Fourier series of u_0 in $0 < x < L$.

3.5.2 Laplace transform

Integral transform methods, such as the Laplace transforms, can reduce the number of independent variables. In most cases, a PDE is converted into an ODE after such transforms.

For example, the PDE for the 1D heat conduction can be transformed into an ODE. By solving the transformed ODE and then inverting back we can obtain the solution for the original PDE. Let us look at an example to show how this works.

Example 3.3. We now solve the heat conduction in a semiinfinite interval $[0, \infty)$,

$$u_t = k u_{xx} \tag{3.70}$$

with the initial and boundary conditions

$$u(x, 0) = 0, \quad u(0, t) = T_0. \tag{3.71}$$

Using the notation

$$\bar{u}(x, s) = \int_0^\infty u(x, t) e^{-st} dt \tag{3.72}$$

for the Laplace transform of $u(x, t)$, the above PDE then becomes

$$s\bar{u} = k \frac{d^2 \bar{u}}{dx^2}, \quad \bar{u}_{x=0} = \frac{T_0}{s}, \tag{3.73}$$

which is an ODE whose general solution can be written as

$$\bar{u} = A \exp\left[-\sqrt{\frac{s}{k}} x\right] + B \exp\left[\sqrt{\frac{s}{k}} x\right]. \tag{3.74}$$

The finiteness of the solution as $x \to \infty$ requires that $B = 0$, and the boundary conditions lead to

$$\bar{u} = \frac{T_0}{s} \exp\left[-\sqrt{\frac{s}{k}} x\right]. \tag{3.75}$$

By the inversion of the Laplace transform we have

$$u = T_0 \text{erfc}\left(\frac{x}{2\sqrt{kt}}\right), \tag{3.76}$$

where $\text{erfc}(x)$ is the complementary error function given by

$$\text{erfc}(x) = 1 - \text{erf}(x) = \frac{2}{\sqrt{\pi}} \int_x^\infty e^{-\eta^2} d\eta. \tag{3.77}$$

Here the error function $\text{erf}(x)$ is defined by

$$\text{erf}(x) = \frac{2}{\sqrt{\pi}} \int_0^x e^{-\eta^2} d\eta. \tag{3.78}$$

There are other important methods for PDEs. These include series expansion methods, asymptotic methods, approximate methods, Green's function, conformal mapping, Fourier transform, Z-transform, hybrid methods, perturbation methods, and naturally numerical methods.

3.6. Notes on software

For solving ODEs and PDEs, there are some software packages that can handle symbolic computations. Here we briefly outline a few commonly used packages.

- *Mathematica* is very powerful and can handle almost all symbolic computations. It can solve ODEs and PDEs using analytical methods and numerical methods. An online version *Wolframalpha* is very useful to do some quick calculations.
- *Maple* is also very powerful and can deal with ODEs and PDEs with many other functionalities.
- *Matlab*® is mainly for scientific computation using matrix representations. Matlab's symbolic toolbox can handle ODEs and some PDEs well.
- *Python* has a symbolic package, called *SymPy*, which can solve both ODEs and PDEs.
- Other packages can also handle ODEs well and sometimes PDEs to a different degree, including *Geogebra*, *Desmos*, *Maxima*, *R*, *SageMath*, and others.

There are other programming languages or packages that can be extended to do symbolic computation as well. For example, the popular *Gnu Octave* can do calculus and solve some ODEs if the relevant symbolic mathematics package is installed.

CHAPTER FOUR

Computational linear algebra

Linear algebra is an essential foundation for engineering simulation because many numerical methods, such as finite difference methods and finite element methods, use vectors and matrices as well as the solutions of large, sparse matrix systems. This chapter introduces the fundamentals of vectors, matrices, eigenvalues, eigenvectors, and iteration methods.

4.1. Vectors

A vector is a quantity with both direction and magnitude. Typical examples in engineering are forces, velocities, and displacements.

In the three-dimensional (3D) space (x, y, z), shown in Fig. 4.1, the position of a point P is uniquely determined by its position vector

$$\boldsymbol{r} = x\boldsymbol{i} + y\boldsymbol{j} + z\boldsymbol{k} = \begin{pmatrix} x \\ y \\ z \end{pmatrix}, \tag{4.1}$$

where $\boldsymbol{i}$, $\boldsymbol{j}$, and $\boldsymbol{k}$ are the unit vectors along the x-axis, y-axis, and z-axis directions, respectively. In addition, x, y, and z are often called the coordinates of the point P or the components of the position vector $\boldsymbol{r}$. It is worth pointing out that $\boldsymbol{r}$ is a column vector.

The norm or modulus of $\boldsymbol{r}$ is its length

$$r = |\boldsymbol{r}| = \sqrt{x^2 + y^2 + z^2}. \tag{4.2}$$

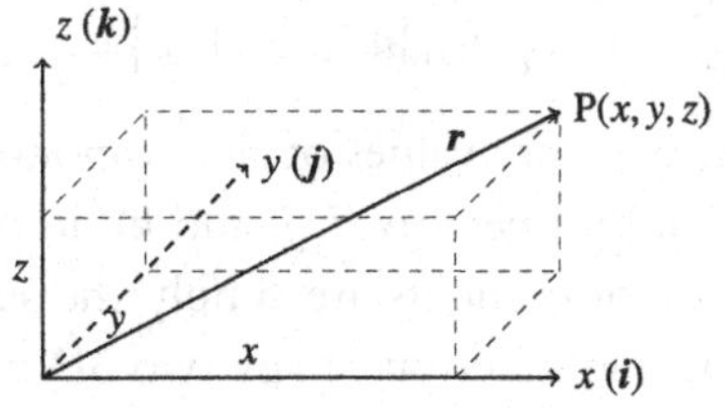

Figure 4.1 The coordinates in the three-dimensional space.

Engineering Simulation and its Applications
https://doi.org/10.1016/B978-0-44-314084-6.00011-5

The length of a unit vector is 1, and we can write the three unit vectors as

$$\boldsymbol{i} = \begin{pmatrix} 1 \\ 0 \\ 0 \end{pmatrix}, \quad \boldsymbol{j} = \begin{pmatrix} 0 \\ 1 \\ 0 \end{pmatrix}, \quad \boldsymbol{k} = \begin{pmatrix} 0 \\ 0 \\ 1 \end{pmatrix}. \tag{4.3}$$

In general, a vector $\boldsymbol{u}$ in an n-dimensional space can be written as

$$\boldsymbol{u} = \begin{pmatrix} u_1 & u_2 & \cdots & u_n \end{pmatrix}^T = \begin{pmatrix} u_1 \\ u_2 \\ \vdots \\ u_n \end{pmatrix}, \tag{4.4}$$

where $u_i\,(i = 1, 2, \ldots, n)$ are its components. Here the notation T means transpose, which converts a row vector to a column vector or vice versa.

The length or modulus of $\boldsymbol{u}$ is $|\boldsymbol{u}|$ or, more formally,

$$||\boldsymbol{u}|| = \sqrt{u_1^2 + u_2^2 + \cdots + u_n^2}. \tag{4.5}$$

More generally, we define the p-norm, or L_p-norm, of an n-dimensional vector as

$$\|\boldsymbol{u}\|_p = (|u_1|^p + |u_2|^p \cdots + |u_n|^p)^{1/p} = \left(\sum_{i=1}^{n} |u_i|^p\right)^{1/p}, \quad p > 0. \tag{4.6}$$

The three commonly used norms are with $p = 1, 2$, and ∞. Clearly, the modulus $|\boldsymbol{r}|$ we have just mentioned is the L_2-norm or Cartesian norm when $p = 2$.

The L_1-norm can be calculated by

$$\|\boldsymbol{u}\|_1 = |u_1| + |u_2| + \cdots + |u_n|, \tag{4.7}$$

which is the sum of the absolute values of all its components. The L_∞-norm is the max norm, that is,

$$\|\boldsymbol{u}\|_\infty = \max\{|u_1|, |u_2|, \ldots, |u_n|\} = u_{\max}, \tag{4.8}$$

which is the maximum of the absolute values of all components.

Since the basic directions of unit vectors ($\boldsymbol{i}$, $\boldsymbol{j}$, and $\boldsymbol{k}$) do not change, the addition of two vectors is a vector whose components are simply the sum of their corresponding components. We can define the subtraction of any two 3D vectors $\boldsymbol{u}$ and $\boldsymbol{v}$ as

$$\boldsymbol{u} - \boldsymbol{v} = \boldsymbol{u} + (-\boldsymbol{v}), \tag{4.9}$$

where $-\boldsymbol{v}$ is obtained by reversing the direction of $\boldsymbol{v}$. In general, we have

$$\boldsymbol{u}_1 \pm \boldsymbol{u}_2 = \begin{pmatrix} x_1 \\ y_1 \\ z_1 \end{pmatrix} \pm \begin{pmatrix} x_2 \\ y_2 \\ z_2 \end{pmatrix} = \begin{pmatrix} x_1 \pm x_2 \\ y_1 \pm y_2 \\ z_1 \pm z_2 \end{pmatrix}. \tag{4.10}$$

The addition of any two vectors $\boldsymbol{u}$ and $\boldsymbol{v}$ is commutative, that is,

$$\boldsymbol{u} + \boldsymbol{v} = \boldsymbol{v} + \boldsymbol{u}. \tag{4.11}$$

All the above mathematical operations can be extended to the n-dimensional cases.

For two n-dimensional vectors

$$\boldsymbol{u} = \begin{pmatrix} u_1 & u_2 & \dots & u_n \end{pmatrix}^T \quad \text{and} \quad \boldsymbol{v} = \begin{pmatrix} v_1 & v_2 & \dots & v_n \end{pmatrix}^T, \tag{4.12}$$

their dot product, also called the inner product or scalar product, is defined by

$$\boldsymbol{u}^T \boldsymbol{v} = \boldsymbol{u} \cdot \boldsymbol{v} = \sum_{i=1}^{n} u_i v_i = u_1 v_1 + u_2 v_2 + \dots + u_n v_n. \tag{4.13}$$

Here the transpose notation $\boldsymbol{u}^T \boldsymbol{u}$ is commonly used in many textbooks. The dot product can be used for testing the orthogonality of two vectors. Two vectors are orthogonal or perpendicular to each other if their dot product is zero (i.e., $\boldsymbol{u} \cdot \boldsymbol{v} = 0$). For example, the vectors

$$\boldsymbol{u} = \begin{pmatrix} 1 & 1 & 1 & 0 & 1 \end{pmatrix}^T \quad \text{and} \quad \boldsymbol{v} = \begin{pmatrix} 1 & -2 & 1 & 5 & 0 \end{pmatrix}^T \tag{4.14}$$

are orthogonal because

$$\boldsymbol{u} \cdot \boldsymbol{v} = 1 \times 1 + 1 \times (-2) + 1 \times 1 + 0 \times 5 + 1 \times 0 = 0. \tag{4.15}$$

In a particular case when calculating the dot product of a vector with itself, we have

$$\boldsymbol{u}^T \boldsymbol{u} \equiv \boldsymbol{u} \cdot \boldsymbol{u} \equiv ||\boldsymbol{u}||^2 = u_1^2 + u_2^2 + \dots + u_n^2, \tag{4.16}$$

which is the modulus squared of the vector.

4.2. Matrix algebra

Matrices can be considered as an extension of vectors, and they are widely used in engineering simulation and scientific computing.

A matrix is a rectangular array of numbers. For example, the arrays

$$A = \begin{pmatrix} 1 & 2 & 3 \\ 4 & 5 & 6 \end{pmatrix}, \quad B = \begin{pmatrix} 1 & 2 \\ 2.3 & 4.5 \end{pmatrix}, \quad C = \begin{pmatrix} 1 & 0 & 2.5 & 3.7 \\ 1.7 & -1.5 & 7 & 8.9 \end{pmatrix} \tag{4.17}$$

are all matrices. In most mathematics textbooks, a matrix is denoted by an uppercase letter in bold font. The size of a matrix is determined by its numbers of rows and columns. Since the matrix $\boldsymbol{A}$ has 2 rows and 3 columns, the size of $\boldsymbol{A}$ is thus 2×3 (or 2 by 3). Similarly, the size of $\boldsymbol{B}$ is 2×2 (or 2 by 2), and the size of $\boldsymbol{C}$ is 2×4.

Each number in a matrix is called an entry or element, and the location of the entry is given by its row and column numbers. We usually use a lower case letter with subscripts to denote such entries. For the above matrix $\boldsymbol{A}$, we can write

$$\boldsymbol{A} = \begin{pmatrix} 1 & 2 & 3 \\ 4 & 5 & 6 \end{pmatrix} = \begin{pmatrix} a_{11} & a_{12} & a_{13} \\ a_{21} & a_{22} & a_{23} \end{pmatrix}, \tag{4.18}$$

and we have $a_{11} = 1$, $a_{12} = 2$, $a_{13} = 3$, $a_{21} = 4$, $a_{22} = 5$, and $a_{23} = 6$. Use the same convention of notations, we can say that b_{21} of the 2nd row and 1st column of $\boldsymbol{B}$ is $b_{21} = 2.3$, and $c_{23} = 7$ of $\boldsymbol{C}$.

In general, if a matrix with m rows and n columns is arranged in a rectangular array, then we can write it as

$$\boldsymbol{A} = \begin{pmatrix} a_{11} & a_{12} & \cdots & a_{1n} \\ a_{21} & a_{22} & \cdots & a_{2n} \\ \vdots & \vdots & \ddots & \vdots \\ a_{m1} & a_{m2} & \cdots & a_{mn} \end{pmatrix}, \tag{4.19}$$

where a_{ij} $(i = 1, 2, \ldots, m; j = 1, 2, \ldots, n)$ are numbers, m is the number of rows, and n is the number of columns. In this case the matrix $\boldsymbol{A}$ is said to have a size of $m \times n$. Sometimes, to show its elements, we can write

$$\boldsymbol{A} = [a_{ij}], \quad (i = 1, 2, \ldots, m; \; j = 1, 2, \ldots, n), \tag{4.20}$$

where we use $[a_{ij}]$ to explicitly show the elements of $\boldsymbol{A}$.

If the number of rows m is equal to the number of columns n (i.e., $m = n$), then we say that the matrix is a square matrix.

The transpose of a matrix can be formally defined as

$$\boldsymbol{A}^T = [a_{ij}]^T = [a_{ji}] \quad \text{for all } (i, j). \tag{4.21}$$

Sometimes, it makes a statement simpler if we write $\forall(i, j)$ to mean for all values of $(i = 1, 2, \ldots, m; \; j = 1, 2, \ldots, n)$.

If a matrix is a square matrix satisfying

$$A^T = A \text{ or } a_{ij} = a_{ji} \quad \forall(i,j), \tag{4.22}$$

then it is called a symmetric matrix. The expression $A^T = A$ emphasizes the overall form, whereas $a_{ij} = a_{ji}$ focuses on the properties of elements, though both forms are essentially identical and thus used interchangeably.

Example 4.1. The sizes of the matrices

$$A = \begin{pmatrix} 2 & -2 & 0 \\ 7 & 8 & -9 \end{pmatrix} \quad \text{and} \quad B = \begin{pmatrix} 2 & -1 \\ -1 & 3 \end{pmatrix}$$

are 2 by 3 and 2 by 2, respectively. Their transposes are

$$A^T = \begin{pmatrix} 2 & 7 \\ -2 & 8 \\ 0 & -9 \end{pmatrix} \quad \text{and} \quad B^T = \begin{pmatrix} 2 & -1 \\ -1 & 3 \end{pmatrix}.$$

Since $B^T = B$, the matrix B is a square and symmetric matrix.

In principle, each element a_{ij} of a matrix A can be a real or complex number. If all elements are real numbers, then the matrix is called a real matrix. If at least one element contains a complex number, then the matrix is called a complex matrix. For the moment, we will focus mainly on real matrices.

Matrix addition and subtraction are possible only if both matrices are of the same size. If $A = [a_{ij}]$ and $G = [g_{ij}]$ are of the same size $m \times n$, then their sum $S = [s_{ij}]$ can be obtained by adding their corresponding entries, that is,

$$s_{ij} = a_{ij} + g_{ij} \quad \forall(i,j), \tag{4.23}$$

where S has the same size $m \times n$. Their differences also form the matrix $M = [m_{ij}]$ with

$$m_{ij} = a_{ij} - g_{ij}, \tag{4.24}$$

which also has the same size. If a matrix is multiplied by a scalar $k \neq 0$, then we have

$$kA = [ka_{ij}] \quad \forall(i,j). \tag{4.25}$$

Matrix multiplication requires that the number of columns of the first matrix is equal to the number of rows of the second matrix. If $A = [a_{ij}]$ is an $m \times n$ matrix, and $B = [b_{jk}]$

is an $n \times p$ matrix, then $\boldsymbol{C} = \boldsymbol{AB}$ is an $m \times p$ matrix. We have

$$\boldsymbol{C} = [c_{ik}] = \begin{pmatrix} \boxed{c_{11}} & c_{12} & \cdots & c_{1p} \\ c_{21} & c_{22} & \cdots & c_{2p} \\ \vdots & \vdots & \ddots & \vdots \\ c_{m1} & c_{m2} & \cdots & c_{mp} \end{pmatrix} = \boldsymbol{AB} = [a_{ij}][b_{jk}]$$

$$= \begin{pmatrix} \boxed{a_{11}} & \boxed{a_{12}} & \cdots & \boxed{a_{1n}} \\ a_{21} & a_{22} & \cdots & a_{2n} \\ \vdots & \vdots & \ddots & \vdots \\ a_{m1} & a_{m2} & \cdots & a_{mn} \end{pmatrix} \begin{pmatrix} \boxed{b_{11}} & b_{12} & \cdots & b_{1p} \\ \boxed{b_{21}} & b_{22} & \cdots & b_{2p} \\ \vdots & \vdots & \ddots & \vdots \\ \boxed{b_{n1}} & b_{n2} & \cdots & b_{np} \end{pmatrix}, \tag{4.26}$$

where

$$c_{ik} = a_{i1}b_{1k} + a_{i2}b_{2k} + a_{i3}b_{3k} + \cdots + a_{in}b_{nk} = \sum_{j=1}^{n} a_{ij}b_{jk}. \tag{4.27}$$

Here the entry c_{ik} is the dot product of the ith row of $\boldsymbol{A}$ and the kth column of $\boldsymbol{B}$, which is the sum of multiplying the ith row of $\boldsymbol{A}$ by the corresponding entry in the kth column of $\boldsymbol{B}$. For example, we have

$$c_{11} = \sum_{j=1}^{n} a_{1j}b_{j1} = a_{11}b_{11} + a_{12}b_{21} + \cdots + a_{1n}b_{n1}, \tag{4.28}$$

and these entries are highlighted in boxes in Eq. (4.26). Similarly, we have

$$c_{23} = \sum_{j=1}^{n} a_{2j}b_{j3} = a_{21}b_{13} + a_{22}b_{23} + \cdots + a_{2n}b_{n3}, \tag{4.29}$$

and so on.

In general, if the product of two matrices $\boldsymbol{A}$ and $\boldsymbol{B}$ exists, then their transposes have the following property:

$$(\boldsymbol{AB})^T = \boldsymbol{B}^T\boldsymbol{A}^T. \tag{4.30}$$

There are two special matrices: the zero matrix and the identity matrix. The zero matrix is the matrix with all zero elements. For example, we have the 1×4 zero matrix as $\boldsymbol{O} = (0\ 0\ 0\ 0)$.

If the diagonal elements are 1s and all the other elements are zeros, it is called the unit matrix or the identity matrix. For example, the 3×3 unit matrix can be written as

$$I = \begin{pmatrix} 1 & 0 & 0 \\ 0 & 1 & 0 \\ 0 & 0 & 1 \end{pmatrix}. \tag{4.31}$$

For an $n \times n$ identity matrix, we can write it as

$$I = \begin{pmatrix} 1 & 0 & 0 & \cdots & 0 \\ 0 & 1 & 0 & \cdots & 0 \\ 0 & 0 & 1 & \cdots & 0 \\ \vdots & \vdots & \vdots & \ddots & 0 \\ 0 & 0 & 0 & \cdots & 1 \end{pmatrix}. \tag{4.32}$$

If a matrix A is of the same size as the unit matrix, then it is commutative with I, that is,

$$IA = AI = A. \tag{4.33}$$

Example 4.2. For $A = \begin{pmatrix} 11 & -2 \\ -3 & 5 \end{pmatrix}$, we can check that

$$AI = \begin{pmatrix} 11 & -2 \\ -3 & 5 \end{pmatrix} \begin{pmatrix} 1 & 0 \\ 0 & 1 \end{pmatrix} = \begin{pmatrix} 11 & -2 \\ -3 & 5 \end{pmatrix}.$$

Similarly, we have

$$IA = \begin{pmatrix} 1 & 0 \\ 0 & 1 \end{pmatrix} \begin{pmatrix} 11 & -2 \\ -3 & 5 \end{pmatrix} = \begin{pmatrix} 11 & -2 \\ -3 & 5 \end{pmatrix},$$

which indeed means that

$$AI = IA.$$

In general, the inverse A^{-1} of a square matrix A, if it exists, is defined by

$$A^{-1}A = AA^{-1} = I, \tag{4.34}$$

where I is the unit or identity matrix of the same size as A.

It is worth pointing out that a matrix is not invertible, that is, A^{-1} does not exist, if its determinant $\det(A)$ is zero. We will formally define the determinant shortly. Let us first look at a simple example.

Example 4.3. For example, a 2×2 matrix $\boldsymbol{A}$ and its inverse $\boldsymbol{A}^{-1}$,

$$\boldsymbol{A} = \begin{pmatrix} a & b \\ c & d \end{pmatrix} \quad \text{and} \quad \boldsymbol{A}^{-1} = \begin{pmatrix} \alpha & \beta \\ \gamma & \kappa \end{pmatrix},$$

are related by

$$\boldsymbol{A}\boldsymbol{A}^{-1} = \begin{pmatrix} a & b \\ c & d \end{pmatrix}\begin{pmatrix} \alpha & \beta \\ \gamma & \kappa \end{pmatrix} = \begin{pmatrix} a\alpha + b\gamma & a\beta + b\kappa \\ c\alpha + d\gamma & c\beta + d\kappa \end{pmatrix} = \begin{pmatrix} 1 & 0 \\ 0 & 1 \end{pmatrix} = \boldsymbol{I}.$$

This requires that

$$a\alpha + b\gamma = 1, \; a\beta + b\kappa = 0, \; c\alpha + d\gamma = 0, \; c\gamma + d\kappa = 1.$$

These four equations determine the four unknowns α, β, γ, and κ. After some algebraic calculations, we have

$$\alpha = \frac{d}{\Delta}, \quad \beta = \frac{-b}{\Delta}, \quad \gamma = \frac{-c}{\Delta}, \quad \kappa = \frac{a}{\Delta},$$

where $\Delta = ad - bc \neq 0$ is the determinant of $\boldsymbol{A}$. Therefore the inverse is

$$\boldsymbol{A}^{-1} = \frac{1}{ad - bc}\begin{pmatrix} d & -b \\ -c & a \end{pmatrix}.$$

It is straightforward to verify that $\boldsymbol{A}^{-1}\boldsymbol{A} = \begin{pmatrix} 1 & 0 \\ 0 & 1 \end{pmatrix}$.

In the case of the rotation matrix

$$\boldsymbol{R}_\theta = \begin{pmatrix} \cos\theta & -\sin\theta \\ \sin\theta & \cos\theta \end{pmatrix}, \tag{4.35}$$

we have

$$\begin{aligned} \boldsymbol{R}^{-1} &= \frac{1}{\cos\theta\cos\theta - (-\sin\theta)\sin\theta}\begin{pmatrix} \cos\theta & \sin\theta \\ -\sin\theta & \cos\theta \end{pmatrix} \\ &= \frac{1}{\cos^2\theta + \sin^2\theta}\begin{pmatrix} \cos\theta & \sin\theta \\ -\sin\theta & \cos\theta \end{pmatrix} = \begin{pmatrix} \cos\theta & \sin\theta \\ -\sin\theta & \cos\theta \end{pmatrix}, \end{aligned} \tag{4.36}$$

where we have used $\cos^2\theta + \sin^2\theta = 1$.

We have seen that the determinant $\Delta = ad - bc$ is very important. We now define it more generally.

The determinant of an $n \times n$ square matrix $\boldsymbol{A} = [a_{ij}]$ is the number obtained by the cofactor expansion either by row or by column

$$\det(\boldsymbol{A}) \equiv |A| = \sum_{j=1}^{n} (-1)^{i+j} a_{ij} |\boldsymbol{M}_{ij}|, \tag{4.37}$$

where $|\boldsymbol{M}_{ij}|$ is the cofactor or the determinant of a minor matrix $\boldsymbol{M}$ of $\boldsymbol{A}$ obtained by deleting row i and column j. This is a recursive relationship. For example, $\boldsymbol{M}_{12}$ of a 3×3 matrix is obtained by deleting the first row and the second column

$$\begin{vmatrix} -a_{11}- & -a_{12}- & -a_{13}- \\ a_{21} & a_{22} & a_{23} \\ a_{31} & a_{32} & a_{33} \end{vmatrix} \Longrightarrow |\boldsymbol{M}|_{12} = \begin{vmatrix} a_{21} & a_{23} \\ a_{31} & a_{33} \end{vmatrix}. \tag{4.38}$$

Obviously, the determinant of a 1×1 matrix $|a_{11}| = a_{11}$ is the number itself. The determinant of a 2×2 matrix is

$$\det(\boldsymbol{A}) = \begin{vmatrix} a_{11} & a_{12} \\ a_{21} & a_{22} \end{vmatrix} = a_{11}a_{22} - a_{12}a_{21}. \tag{4.39}$$

The determinant of a 3×3 matrix is given by

$$\begin{vmatrix} a_{11} & a_{12} & a_{23} \\ a_{21} & a_{22} & a_{23} \\ a_{31} & a_{32} & a_{33} \end{vmatrix} = (-1)^{1+1} a_{11} \begin{vmatrix} a_{22} & a_{23} \\ a_{32} & a_{33} \end{vmatrix} + (-1)^{1+2} a_{12} \begin{vmatrix} a_{21} & a_{23} \\ a_{31} & a_{33} \end{vmatrix}$$
$$+(-1)^{1+3} a_{13} \begin{vmatrix} a_{21} & a_{22} \\ a_{31} & a_{32} \end{vmatrix} = a_{11}(a_{22}a_{33} - a_{32}a_{23})$$
$$-a_{12}(a_{21}a_{33} - a_{31}a_{23}) + a_{13}(a_{21}a_{32} - a_{31}a_{22}). \tag{4.40}$$

Here we have used the expansion along the first row $i = 1$. We can also expand it along any other rows or columns, and the results will be the same.

As the determinant of a matrix is a scalar or a simple number, it is not difficult to understand the following properties:

$$\det(\boldsymbol{AB}) = \det(\boldsymbol{A}) \det(\boldsymbol{B}), \quad \det(\boldsymbol{A}^T) = \det(\boldsymbol{A}). \tag{4.41}$$

If $\det(\boldsymbol{A}) = 0$, then the square matrix is called singular, and its inverse does not exist. For example, the determinant of

$$\boldsymbol{B} = \begin{pmatrix} 1 & 2 \\ 2 & 4 \end{pmatrix} \tag{4.42}$$

is $\det(\boldsymbol{B}) = 1 \times 4 - 2 \times 2 = 0$, so its inverse does not exist, and the matrix is not invertible. In fact, the second row is twice of the first row, and the second column is twice the first column. In this case, we say that the rows or columns of this singular matrix are not linearly independent.

There are many applications of determinants. The inverse of a matrix exists only if $\det(\boldsymbol{A}) \neq 0$. Here we use it to calculate the inverse $\boldsymbol{A}^{-1}$ using

$$\boldsymbol{A}^{-1} = \frac{\mathrm{adj}(\boldsymbol{A})}{\det(\boldsymbol{A})} = \frac{\boldsymbol{B}^T}{\det(\boldsymbol{A})}, \quad \boldsymbol{B} = \left[(-1)^{i+j}|M_{ij}|\right], \tag{4.43}$$

where the matrix $\boldsymbol{B}^T$ is called the adjoint of matrix $\boldsymbol{A}$ of the same size as $\boldsymbol{A}$, and $i, j = 1, \ldots, n$. Each part of the element $\boldsymbol{B}$ is expressed in terms of a cofactor so that

$$b_{ij} = (-1)^{i+j}|M_{ij}|. \tag{4.44}$$

The matrix $\boldsymbol{B}$ itself is called the cofactor matrix, whereas $\mathrm{adj}(\boldsymbol{A}) = \boldsymbol{B}^T$ is sometimes used to denote the adjoint matrix. This seems too complicated, so let us compute the inverse of a 3×3 matrix as an example. To compute the inverse of

$$\boldsymbol{A} = \begin{pmatrix} 1 & 1 & -2 \\ 1 & 0 & 2 \\ 2 & 1 & 1 \end{pmatrix},$$

we first construct its adjoint matrix $\boldsymbol{B}^T$ with

$$\boldsymbol{B} = [b_{ij}] = \left[(-1)^{i+j}|M_{ij}|\right].$$

The first element b_{11} can be obtained by

$$b_{11} = (-1)^{1+1}\begin{vmatrix} 0 & 2 \\ 1 & 1 \end{vmatrix} = (-1)^2 \times (0 \times 1 - 2 \times 1) = -2.$$

The element b_{12} is

$$b_{12} = (-1)^{1+2}\begin{vmatrix} 1 & 2 \\ 2 & 1 \end{vmatrix} = -1 \times (1 \times 1 - 2 \times 2) = 3,$$

whereas the element b_{21} is

$$b_{21} = (-1)^{2+1}\begin{vmatrix} 1 & -2 \\ 1 & 1 \end{vmatrix} = (-1)^3 \times (1 \times 1 - 1 \times (-2)) = -3.$$

Following a similar procedure, we have $\boldsymbol{B}$ and its transpose $\boldsymbol{B}^T$:

$$\boldsymbol{B}=\begin{pmatrix} -2 & 3 & 1 \\ -3 & 5 & 1 \\ 2 & -4 & -1 \end{pmatrix}, \quad \boldsymbol{B}^T=\begin{pmatrix} -2 & -3 & 2 \\ 3 & 5 & -4 \\ 1 & 1 & -1 \end{pmatrix}.$$

Then the determinant of $\boldsymbol{A}$ is

$$\det(\boldsymbol{A})=\begin{vmatrix} 1 & 1 & -2 \\ 1 & 0 & 2 \\ 2 & 1 & 1 \end{vmatrix}=1\times\begin{vmatrix} 0 & 2 \\ 1 & 1 \end{vmatrix}-1\times\begin{vmatrix} 1 & 2 \\ 2 & 1 \end{vmatrix}+(-2)\times\begin{vmatrix} 1 & 0 \\ 2 & 1 \end{vmatrix}$$
$$=1\times(0\times1-2\times1)-1\times(1\times1-2\times2)-2\times(1\times1-2\times0)$$
$$=1\times(-2)-1\times(-3)-2\times1=-1.$$

Finally, the inverse becomes

$$\boldsymbol{A}^{-1}=\frac{\boldsymbol{B}^T}{\det(\boldsymbol{A})}=\frac{1}{-1}\begin{pmatrix} -2 & -3 & 2 \\ 3 & 5 & -4 \\ 1 & 1 & -1 \end{pmatrix}=\begin{pmatrix} 2 & 3 & -2 \\ -3 & -5 & 4 \\ -1 & -1 & 1 \end{pmatrix}.$$

This inverse result will be used in the next example to solve a linear system.

4.3. System of linear equations

A system of linear equations can be written compactly as a matrix equation, and the solution of such a linear system will become straightforward if the inverse of a square matrix is used. Let us demonstrate this by an example. For a linear system consisting of three simultaneous equations, we have

$$a_{11}x+a_{12}y+a_{13}z=b_1, \tag{4.45}$$

$$a_{21}x+a_{22}y+a_{23}z=b_2, \tag{4.46}$$

$$a_{31}x+a_{32}y+a_{33}z=b_3, \tag{4.47}$$

which can be written as

$$\begin{pmatrix} a_{11} & a_{12} & a_{13} \\ a_{21} & a_{22} & a_{23} \\ a_{31} & a_{32} & a_{33} \end{pmatrix}\begin{pmatrix} x \\ y \\ z \end{pmatrix}=\begin{pmatrix} b_1 \\ b_2 \\ b_3 \end{pmatrix} \tag{4.48}$$

or more compactly as

$$\boldsymbol{A}\boldsymbol{u}=\boldsymbol{b}, \tag{4.49}$$

where

$$A = \begin{pmatrix} a_{11} & a_{12} & a_{13} \\ a_{21} & a_{22} & a_{23} \\ a_{31} & a_{32} & a_{33} \end{pmatrix}, \quad u = \begin{pmatrix} x \\ y \\ z \end{pmatrix}, \quad b = \begin{pmatrix} b_1 \\ b_2 \\ b_3 \end{pmatrix}. \tag{4.50}$$

Multiplying both sides by A^{-1}, we have

$$A^{-1}Au = A^{-1}b, \quad \text{or} \quad Iu = A^{-1}b. \tag{4.51}$$

Therefore its solution can be written as

$$u = A^{-1}b.$$

Now let us look at an example of the solution of a simple linear system.

Example 4.4. To solve the system of three equations

$$x + y - 2z = -3, \quad x + 2z = 7, \quad 2x + y + z = 7,$$

we first write these equations as $Au = b$:

$$\begin{pmatrix} 1 & 1 & -2 \\ 1 & 0 & 2 \\ 2 & 1 & 1 \end{pmatrix} \begin{pmatrix} x \\ y \\ z \end{pmatrix} = \begin{pmatrix} -3 \\ 7 \\ 7 \end{pmatrix}.$$

We know from the preceding example that the inverse of A is

$$A^{-1} = \begin{pmatrix} 2 & 3 & -2 \\ -3 & -5 & 4 \\ -1 & -1 & 1 \end{pmatrix}.$$

We now have $u = A^{-1}b$ or

$$\begin{pmatrix} x \\ y \\ z \end{pmatrix} = \begin{pmatrix} 2 & 3 & -2 \\ -3 & -5 & 4 \\ -1 & -1 & 1 \end{pmatrix} \begin{pmatrix} -3 \\ 7 \\ 7 \end{pmatrix} = \begin{pmatrix} 2 \times (-3) + 3 \times 7 + (-2) \times 7 \\ -3 \times (-3) + (-5) \times 7 + 4 \times 7 \\ -1 \times (-3) + (-1) \times 7 + 1 \times 7 \end{pmatrix} = \begin{pmatrix} 1 \\ 2 \\ 3 \end{pmatrix},$$

which gives a unique set of solutions $x = 1$, $y = 2$, and $z = 3$.

In general, a linear system of n equations for n unknowns can be written in a compact form as

$$\begin{pmatrix} a_{11} & a_{12} & \cdots & a_{1n} \\ a_{21} & a_{22} & \cdots & a_{2n} \\ \vdots & \vdots & & \\ a_{n1} & a_{n2} & \cdots & a_{nn} \end{pmatrix} \begin{pmatrix} u_1 \\ u_2 \\ \vdots \\ u_n \end{pmatrix} = \begin{pmatrix} b_1 \\ b_2 \\ \vdots \\ b_n \end{pmatrix} \tag{4.52}$$

or simply

$$Au = b. \tag{4.53}$$

Its solution can be obtained by inverse:

$$u = A^{-1}b. \tag{4.54}$$

However, this is not always possible. If the determinant $\det(A) = 0$, then the system becomes degenerate or ill-posed, and there may be no solution or an infinite number of solutions. For example, the system of $x + 2y = 5$ and $2x + 4y = 10$ can have an infinite number of solutions, because

$$A = \begin{pmatrix} 1 & 2 \\ 2 & 4 \end{pmatrix} \tag{4.55}$$

has no inverse and the two equations are not linearly independent. Multiplying the first equation by 2 gives the second equation. These two equations overlap as a single line on the Cartesian plane. On the other hand, the system of $x + 2y = 5$ and $2x + 4y = 11$ does not have any solution and corresponds to two parallel lines that do not cross each other.

For large systems, direct inverse is not a good option. There are many other more efficient methods to obtain the solutions, including the powerful Gauss–Jordan elimination, matrix decomposition, and iteration methods. We will introduce some of these methods later in this chapter.

4.4. Eigenvalues and eigenvectors

For the linear system $Au = b$, it becomes an eigenvalue problem if $b = \lambda u$. Formally, an eigenvalue λ and its corresponding eigenvector u of a square matrix A satisfy

$$Au = \lambda u. \tag{4.56}$$

Multiplying both sides by the identity matrix I of the same size as that of A, we have

$$IAu = I\lambda u, \quad \text{or} \quad Au = \lambda Iu, \tag{4.57}$$

where we have used $IA = A$ and $I\lambda = \lambda I$. The above equation can also be written as

$$(A - \lambda I)u = 0. \tag{4.58}$$

To satisfy this equation, we can either have $u = 0$ (a trivial solution) or

$$A - \lambda I = 0.$$

Therefore any nontrivial solution requires

$$\det|\boldsymbol{A} - \lambda \boldsymbol{I}| = 0. \tag{4.59}$$

In engineering simulation, especially in structural analysis, eigenvalue problems are related to the natural frequencies of basic vibration modes of structures. In this context the eigenvector corresponding to an eigenvalue provides information about the mode shapes of vibrations in structures. Therefore eigenvalue problems are very useful for analyzing responses of bridges and buildings, subject to time-varying loads such as winds, earthquake, and probabilistic loads. In addition, eigenvalues and eigenvectors can be used to detect any flaws such as cracks that may develop in structures under dynamic loading. Nondestructive testings often use the change in eigenvalues to figure out subtle changes in critical components such as turbine blades and high-precision structures.

Example 4.5. Let us first look at a simple example. For a 2×2 matrix

$$\boldsymbol{A} = \begin{pmatrix} 2 & 3 \\ 3 & 2 \end{pmatrix},$$

its eigenvalues can be obtained by solving

$$\det|\boldsymbol{A} - \lambda \boldsymbol{I}| = \begin{vmatrix} 2-\lambda & 3 \\ 3 & 2-\lambda \end{vmatrix}$$
$$= (2-\lambda)(2-\lambda) - 3 \times 3 = (2-\lambda)^2 - 9 = 0,$$

which can be written as

$$(2-\lambda)^2 = 3^2 \quad \text{or} \quad 2-\lambda = \pm 3.$$

Thus two eigenvalues are

$$\lambda_1 = -1, \quad \lambda_2 = 5.$$

Here we have seen that a 2×2 matrix can have two eigenvalues. In general, for a real matrix $\boldsymbol{A}$ of size $n \times n$, we have

$$\boldsymbol{A} = \begin{pmatrix} a_{11} & a_{12} & \cdots & a_{1n} \\ a_{21} & a_{22} & \cdots & a_{2n} \\ \vdots & \vdots & \ddots & \vdots \\ a_{n1} & a_{n2} & \cdots & a_{nn} \end{pmatrix}, \tag{4.60}$$

and its eigenvalues can be determined by

$$\det \begin{vmatrix} a_{11}-\lambda & a_{12} & \cdots & a_{1n} \\ a_{21} & a_{22}-\lambda & \cdots & a_{2n} \\ \vdots & \vdots & \ddots & \vdots \\ a_{n1} & a_{n2} & \cdots & a_{nn}-\lambda \end{vmatrix} = 0, \tag{4.61}$$

which is equivalent to a polynomial of order n. In general, the characteristic equation has n solutions ($\lambda_i, i = 1, 2, \ldots, n$), though it is usually not easy to find them if n is large.

In many applications, eigenvalues are estimated using numerical methods or by certain approximation techniques. In practice, analytical methods are rarely used to calculate them accurately for large-scale problems.

For an eigenvalue λ, there is a corresponding eigenvector $\boldsymbol{u} = [u_1, u_2, \ldots, u_n]^T$ that satisfies

$$\boldsymbol{A}\boldsymbol{u} = \lambda \boldsymbol{u}. \tag{4.62}$$

If we multiply it by a nonzero scalar or number $\beta \neq 0$, we get

$$\boldsymbol{A}\boldsymbol{u}\beta = \lambda \boldsymbol{u}\beta, \tag{4.63}$$

which can be written as

$$\boldsymbol{A}(\beta \boldsymbol{u}) = \lambda(\beta \boldsymbol{u}). \tag{4.64}$$

Thus $\beta \boldsymbol{u}$ is also an eigenvector that corresponds to the same eigenvalue λ. In other words, there are infinitely many eigenvectors for different values of β. This means that we can only determine the direction of the eigenvector $\boldsymbol{u}$ but not its length.

In practice, the length of the eigenvector is usually set to unity, which allows us to determine the eigenvector uniquely. Even with the unity requirement, there are still two vectors $\boldsymbol{u}$ and $-\boldsymbol{u}$ (opposite unit vectors) that correspond to the same eigenvalue, and some care should be taken. In some software packages, the first component may be set as $u_1 = 1$, and the other components ($u_2, \ldots, u_n$) are found. Then the vector is rescaled by dividing by the norm or length of the vector to form a unity eigenvector.

Example 4.6. To obtain the eigenvector for each eigenvalue in the previous example, we assume that

$$\boldsymbol{v} = \begin{pmatrix} a \\ b \end{pmatrix}.$$

For the eigenvalue $\lambda_1 = -1$, we can substitute this into

$$(\boldsymbol{A} - \lambda \boldsymbol{I})\boldsymbol{v} = 0,$$

and we have

$$\begin{pmatrix} 2-(-1) & 3 \\ 3 & 2-(-1) \end{pmatrix}\begin{pmatrix} a \\ b \end{pmatrix}=0, \quad \begin{pmatrix} 3 & 3 \\ 3 & 3 \end{pmatrix}\begin{pmatrix} a \\ b \end{pmatrix}=0.$$

This is equivalent to

$$3a+3b=0, \qquad \text{or} \qquad a=-b.$$

This equation has an infinite number of solutions; each corresponds to the vector parallel to the unit eigenvector. If we set $a=1$, then we have $b=-1$. To normalize its length, we can divide both components by $\sqrt{2}$, and we have the first set of eigenvalue and eigenvector

$$\lambda_1=-1, \quad \boldsymbol{v}_1=\frac{1}{\sqrt{2}}\begin{pmatrix} 1 \\ -1 \end{pmatrix}.$$

Similarly, the second eigenvalue $\lambda_2=5$ gives

$$\boldsymbol{v}_2=\frac{1}{\sqrt{2}}\begin{pmatrix} 1 \\ 1 \end{pmatrix}.$$

When a real square matrix is symmetric (i.e., $\boldsymbol{A}^T=\boldsymbol{A}$), its eigenvalues are all real. If two eigenvalues λ_1 and λ_2 are distinct (i.e., $\lambda_1 \neq \lambda_2$ and $\lambda_1, \lambda_2 \in \mathbb{R}$), their corresponding nonzero eigenvectors $\boldsymbol{u}_1$ and $\boldsymbol{u}_2$ are orthogonal to each other. From the basic definitions we have

$$\boldsymbol{A}\boldsymbol{u}_1=\lambda_1\boldsymbol{u}_1, \quad \boldsymbol{A}\boldsymbol{u}_2=\lambda_2\boldsymbol{u}_2. \tag{4.65}$$

Multiplying both sides of the first equation by $\boldsymbol{u}_2^T$, we have

$$\boldsymbol{u}_2^T\boldsymbol{A}\boldsymbol{u}_1=\boldsymbol{u}_2^T\lambda_1\boldsymbol{u}_1=\lambda_1\boldsymbol{u}_2^T\boldsymbol{u}_1. \tag{4.66}$$

Here it is in fact a premultiplication because $\boldsymbol{u}_2^T$ is applied as the first factor on both sides. Since $\boldsymbol{A}$ is real and symmetric (i.e., $\boldsymbol{A}^T=\boldsymbol{A}$) and $\boldsymbol{u}^T\boldsymbol{A}=(\boldsymbol{A}^T\boldsymbol{u})^T$, we have

$$\boldsymbol{u}_2^T\boldsymbol{A}\boldsymbol{u}_1=(\boldsymbol{A}^T\boldsymbol{u}_2)^T\boldsymbol{u}_1=(\boldsymbol{A}\boldsymbol{u}_2)^T\boldsymbol{u}_1=(\lambda_2\boldsymbol{u}_2)^T\boldsymbol{u}_1=\lambda_2\boldsymbol{u}_2^T\boldsymbol{u}_1, \tag{4.67}$$

where we have used $\boldsymbol{A}\boldsymbol{u}_2=\lambda_2\boldsymbol{u}_2$. Therefore the above two equations give

$$\lambda_1\boldsymbol{u}_2^T\boldsymbol{u}_1=\lambda_2\boldsymbol{u}_2^T\boldsymbol{u}_1, \qquad \text{or} \quad (\lambda_1-\lambda_2)\boldsymbol{u}_2^T\boldsymbol{u}_1=0, \tag{4.68}$$

which implies

$$\boldsymbol{u}_2^T\boldsymbol{u}_1=0 \quad \text{if } \lambda_1 \neq \lambda_2, \tag{4.69}$$

that is, two eigenvectors with two distinct eigenvalues are orthogonal to each other.

Example 4.7. In the preceding example the two eigenvalues are different, $\lambda_1 \neq \lambda_2$, and their corresponding eigenvectors are

$$v_1 = \frac{1}{\sqrt{2}}\begin{pmatrix} 1 \\ -1 \end{pmatrix}, \quad v_2 = \frac{1}{\sqrt{2}}\begin{pmatrix} 1 \\ 1 \end{pmatrix}. \tag{4.70}$$

Their dot product becomes

$$v_1^T v_2 = \frac{1}{\sqrt{2}}\begin{pmatrix} 1 & -1 \end{pmatrix}\frac{1}{\sqrt{2}}\begin{pmatrix} 1 \\ 1 \end{pmatrix} = \frac{1}{2}[1 \times 1 + (-1) \times 1] = 0. \tag{4.71}$$

Indeed, v_1 and v_2 are orthogonal to each other.

The orthogonal property is useful for structural analysis and signal processing. In real-world applications, eigenvalues or natural frequencies of complex structures are real and distinct. Therefore the vibration modes as eigenvectors are orthogonal, which means that any vibrations can be decomposed or represented as a linear combination of the basic mode shapes (eigenvectors).

Care should be taken when a matrix has some repeated eigenvalues. For example, the 2×2 identity matrix

$$I = \begin{pmatrix} 1 & 0 \\ 0 & 1 \end{pmatrix}, \tag{4.72}$$

has a repeated eigenvalue of 1. In this case, any two-dimensional vector is an eigenvector of this identity matrix. If an eigenvalue has multiplicity (or repeated eigenvalues), some orthonormalization is needed.

4.5. Definite matrices

The eigenvalues of a real symmetric matrix are also linked to its definiteness. A real symmetric matrix A is called positive definite if all its eigenvalues are strictly positive, that is, $\lambda_i > 0$. If all the eigenvalues are nonnegative ($\lambda_i \geq 0$), the matrix is said to be positive semidefinite. Similarly, if all the eigenvalues are strictly negative ($\lambda_i < 0$), then the matrix is said to be negative definite, but the matrix becomes negative semidefinite if $\lambda_i \leq 0$.

Multiplying the eigenvalue equation

$$Au = \lambda u \tag{4.73}$$

by u^T, we have

$$u^T A u = u^T \lambda u = \lambda u^T u, \tag{4.74}$$

which gives

$$\lambda = \frac{\boldsymbol{u}^T \boldsymbol{A}\boldsymbol{u}}{\boldsymbol{u}^T \boldsymbol{u}}. \tag{4.75}$$

The eigenvalues of a positive definite matrix $\boldsymbol{A}$ are positive ($\lambda_i > 0$), which means that

$$\boldsymbol{u}^T \boldsymbol{A}\boldsymbol{u} > 0 \tag{4.76}$$

for all $\boldsymbol{u}$ and $\boldsymbol{u}^T \boldsymbol{u} > 0$.

Example 4.8. The eigenvalues of

$$\boldsymbol{B} = \begin{pmatrix} 5 & -1 \\ -1 & 5 \end{pmatrix} \tag{4.77}$$

are 4 and 6, and thus $\boldsymbol{B}$ is positive definite.

The eigenvalues of

$$\boldsymbol{C} = \begin{pmatrix} -1 & 2 \\ 2 & -9 \end{pmatrix} \tag{4.78}$$

are $-5 + 2\sqrt{5}$ and $-5 - 2\sqrt{5}$, which are both negative, which means that $\boldsymbol{C}$ is negative definite.

However, the matrix

$$\boldsymbol{A} = \begin{pmatrix} 2 & 3 \\ 3 & 2 \end{pmatrix} \tag{4.79}$$

is neither positive definite nor negative definite because its eigenvalues are -1 and 5.

The definiteness of a matrix is useful to determine the local optimality in optimization problems. We will explore this point later in this book.

There are many other techniques concerning matrix operations, including diagonalization, eigendecomposition, singular value decomposition (SVD), lower and upper triangular matrix decomposition (called LU decomposition), Jordan normal form, matrix exponential, and others.

4.6. Iteration methods

For a linear system $\boldsymbol{A}\boldsymbol{u} = \boldsymbol{b}$, its solution $\boldsymbol{u} = \boldsymbol{A}^{-1}\boldsymbol{b}$ generally involves the inversion of a large matrix. Direct inversion becomes impractical if the matrix is very large (e.g., $n > 100,000$). Many efficient algorithms have been developed for solving such systems. Jacobi and Gauss–Seidel iteration methods are just two examples.

4.6.1 Jacobi iteration method

The basic idea of the Jacobi-type iteration method is to decompose an $n \times n$ square matrix $\boldsymbol{A}$ into three simpler matrices

$$\boldsymbol{A} = \boldsymbol{D} + \boldsymbol{L} + \boldsymbol{U}, \tag{4.80}$$

where $\boldsymbol{D}$ is a diagonal matrix, and $\boldsymbol{L}$ and $\boldsymbol{U}$ are strictly lower and upper triangular matrices, respectively. Here "strict" means that the lower (or upper) triangular matrices do not include the diagonal elements, that is to say, all the diagonal elements of the triangular matrices are zeros.

Example 4.9. For the matrix

$$\boldsymbol{A} = \begin{pmatrix} 5 & 1 & -2 \\ 3 & 7 & 1 \\ 2 & 2 & -7 \end{pmatrix}, \tag{4.81}$$

we can decompose it as

$$\boldsymbol{A} = \begin{pmatrix} 5 & 1 & -2 \\ 3 & 7 & 1 \\ 2 & 2 & -7 \end{pmatrix} = \boldsymbol{D} + (\boldsymbol{L} + \boldsymbol{U})$$

$$= \begin{pmatrix} 5 & 0 & 0 \\ 0 & 7 & 0 \\ 0 & 0 & -7 \end{pmatrix} + \begin{pmatrix} 0 & 0 & 0 \\ 3 & 0 & 0 \\ 2 & 2 & 0 \end{pmatrix} + \begin{pmatrix} 0 & 1 & -2 \\ 0 & 0 & 1 \\ 0 & 0 & 0 \end{pmatrix}. \tag{4.82}$$

The inverse of $\boldsymbol{D}$ is

$$\boldsymbol{D}^{-1} = \begin{pmatrix} 1/5 & 0 & 0 \\ 0 & 1/7 & 0 \\ 0 & 0 & -1/7 \end{pmatrix}. \tag{4.83}$$

Using such a decomposition, the linear system $\boldsymbol{Au} = \boldsymbol{b}$ becomes

$$\boldsymbol{Au} = (\boldsymbol{D} + \boldsymbol{L} + \boldsymbol{U})\boldsymbol{u} = \boldsymbol{b}, \tag{4.84}$$

which can be written as an iteration procedure

$$\boldsymbol{Du}^{(n+1)} = \boldsymbol{b} - (\boldsymbol{L} + \boldsymbol{U})\boldsymbol{u}^{(n)}, \tag{4.85}$$

where n is the iteration counter ($n = 1, 2, \ldots$), and by $\boldsymbol{u}^{(n)}$ we denote the value of the vector $\boldsymbol{u}$ at iteration n. Without confusing with the exponent notation, some books use $\boldsymbol{u}^n$ or $\boldsymbol{u}_n$ to mean $\boldsymbol{u}^{(n)}$.

The preceding equation can be used to calculate the next approximate solution $\boldsymbol{u}^{(n+1)}$ from the current estimate $\boldsymbol{u}^{(n)}$. As the inverse of any diagonal matrix $\boldsymbol{D} = \text{diag}[d_{ii}]$ is easy, we have

$$\boldsymbol{u}^{(n+1)} = \boldsymbol{D}^{-1}[\boldsymbol{b} - (\boldsymbol{L} + \boldsymbol{U})\boldsymbol{u}^{(n)}], \tag{4.86}$$

which is the main Jacobi-type iteration formula.

Writing in terms of the elements, we have

$$u_i^{(n+1)} = \frac{1}{d_{ii}}[b_i - \sum_{j \neq i} a_{ij} u_j^{(n)}], \tag{4.87}$$

where $d_{ii} = a_{ii}$ are the diagonal elements only.

This iteration usually starts from an initial guess $\boldsymbol{u}^{(0)}$ (say, $\boldsymbol{u}^{(0)} = \boldsymbol{0}$). However, this iteration scheme is only stable under the condition that the square matrix is strictly diagonally dominant, that is,

$$|a_{ii}| > \sum_{j=1, j \neq i}^{n} |a_{ij}| \tag{4.88}$$

for all $i = 1, 2, \ldots, n$. Thus some care should be taken in implementation to check if this condition is met.

4.6.2 Gauss–Seidel iteration

In Jacobi iterations, both $\boldsymbol{u}^{(n+1)}$ and $\boldsymbol{u}^{(n)}$ should be stored, and thus a running update of elements is not possible. The Gauss–Seidel iteration method is a procedure that improves this by providing an efficient way of solving $\boldsymbol{A}\boldsymbol{u} = \boldsymbol{b}$. The Gauss–Seidel iteration uses the same decomposition as the Jacobi iteration by splitting $\boldsymbol{A}$ into

$$\boldsymbol{A} = \boldsymbol{L} + \boldsymbol{D} + \boldsymbol{U}, \tag{4.89}$$

but the difference from the Jacobi method is that $\boldsymbol{L} + \boldsymbol{D}$ is used instead of $\boldsymbol{D}$ for the inverse. Thus the running update is possible. The nth step iteration is updated by

$$(\boldsymbol{L} + \boldsymbol{D})\boldsymbol{u}^{(n+1)} = \boldsymbol{b} - \boldsymbol{U}\boldsymbol{u}^{(n)}, \tag{4.90}$$

that is,

$$\boldsymbol{u}^{(n+1)} = (\boldsymbol{L} + \boldsymbol{D})^{-1}[\boldsymbol{b} - \boldsymbol{U}\boldsymbol{u}^{(n)}]. \tag{4.91}$$

Starting with an initial vector $\boldsymbol{u}^{(0)}$, this procedure stops if a prescribed criterion is reached. For numerical stability, Gauss–Seidel iteration requires similar criteria of convergence as for the Jacobi-type iteration method.

Let us use an example to show how this method works. It is straightforward to verify that the equation system

$$2x+y=4, \tag{4.92}$$
$$4y+z+w=9, \tag{4.93}$$
$$x+2y+5z+w=2, \tag{4.94}$$
$$4z+5w=6, \tag{4.95}$$

has a unique solution set

$$x=1, \quad y=2, \quad z=-1, \quad w=2. \tag{4.96}$$

This system of four linear equations can be written as

$$\boldsymbol{A}\boldsymbol{u}=\boldsymbol{b} \tag{4.97}$$

with

$$\boldsymbol{A}=\begin{pmatrix} 2 & 1 & 0 & 0 \\ 0 & 4 & 1 & 1 \\ 1 & 2 & 5 & 1 \\ 0 & 0 & 4 & 5 \end{pmatrix}, \quad \boldsymbol{u}=\begin{pmatrix} x \\ y \\ z \\ w \end{pmatrix}, \quad \boldsymbol{b}=\begin{pmatrix} 4 \\ 9 \\ 2 \\ 6 \end{pmatrix}. \tag{4.98}$$

It is easy to verify that $\boldsymbol{A}$ is strictly diagonally dominant. Therefore the condition for Gauss–Seidel iterations is met. The relevant matrices are

$$\boldsymbol{L}+\boldsymbol{D}=\begin{pmatrix} 2 & 0 & 0 & 0 \\ 0 & 4 & 0 & 0 \\ 1 & 2 & 5 & 0 \\ 0 & 0 & 4 & 5 \end{pmatrix}, \quad \boldsymbol{U}=\begin{pmatrix} 0 & 1 & 0 & 0 \\ 0 & 0 & 1 & 1 \\ 0 & 0 & 0 & 1 \\ 0 & 0 & 0 & 0 \end{pmatrix}. \tag{4.99}$$

We leave it as an exercise for the readers to show that

$$(\boldsymbol{L}+\boldsymbol{D})^{-1}=\begin{pmatrix} 0.5 & 0 & 0 & 0 \\ 0 & 0.25 & 0 & 0 \\ -0.1 & -0.1 & 0.2 & 0 \\ 0.08 & 0.08 & -0.16 & 0.2 \end{pmatrix}. \tag{4.100}$$

Example 4.10. The Gauss–Seidel iteration for solving this linear system becomes

$$\boldsymbol{u}^{(n+1)}=\begin{pmatrix} 0.5 & 0 & 0 & 0 \\ 0 & 0.25 & 0 & 0 \\ -0.1 & -0.1 & 0.2 & 0 \\ 0.08 & 0.08 & -0.16 & 0.2 \end{pmatrix}\left[\begin{pmatrix} 4 \\ 9 \\ 2 \\ 6 \end{pmatrix}-\begin{pmatrix} 0 & 1 & 0 & 0 \\ 0 & 0 & 1 & 1 \\ 0 & 0 & 0 & 1 \\ 0 & 0 & 0 & 0 \end{pmatrix}\boldsymbol{u}^{(n)}\right]. \tag{4.101}$$

Starting with

$$u^{(0)} = \begin{pmatrix} 0 \\ 0 \\ 0 \\ 0 \end{pmatrix},$$

the above iteration formula gives

$$u^{(1)} = \begin{pmatrix} 2.0000 \\ 2.2500 \\ -0.9000 \\ 1.9200 \end{pmatrix}, \quad u^{(2)} = \begin{pmatrix} 0.8750 \\ 1.9950 \\ -0.9570 \\ 1.9656 \end{pmatrix}, \quad u^{(3)} = \begin{pmatrix} 1.0025 \\ 1.9979 \\ -0.9928 \\ 1.9942 \end{pmatrix}, \tag{4.102}$$

$$u^{(4)} = \begin{pmatrix} 1.0011 \\ 1.9996 \\ -0.9989 \\ 1.9991 \end{pmatrix}, \quad u^{(5)} = \begin{pmatrix} 1.0002 \\ 1.9999 \\ -0.9998 \\ 1.9999 \end{pmatrix}, \quad u^{(6)} = \begin{pmatrix} 1.0000 \\ 2.0000 \\ -1.0000 \\ 2.0000 \end{pmatrix}. \tag{4.103}$$

As we can see, the solution is very close to the exact solution after five iterations. After six iterations, the difference is less than 10^{-5} (or accurate up to five decimal places).

4.6.3 Relaxation method

The convergence of the Gauss–Seidel iteration method is slow in practice. The relaxation method can be more efficient, and a popular method is the successive overrelaxation method with two steps

$$v^{(n)} = (L + D + U)u^{(n)} - b \tag{4.104}$$

and

$$u^{(n+1)} = u^{(n)} - \omega(L + D)^{-1}v^{(n)}, \tag{4.105}$$

where $0 < \omega < 2$ is the overrelaxation parameter. Combining the above equations and rearranging them, we have

$$u^{(n+1)} = (1 - \omega)u^{(n)} + \omega\tilde{u}^{(n)}, \tag{4.106}$$

where

$$\tilde{u}^{(n)} = (L + D)^{-1}(b - Uu^{(n)}) \tag{4.107}$$

is the standard Gauss–Seidel procedure. Therefore this method is essentially the weighted average between the previous iteration and the successive Gauss–Seidel iteration. Clearly, if $\omega = 1$, then it reduces to the standard Gauss–Seidel iteration method.

Broadly speaking, a small value of $0 < \omega < 1$ corresponds to underrelaxation with slower convergence, whereas $1 < \omega < 2$ leads to overrelaxation and faster convergence. It has been proved theoretically that the scheme will not converge if $\omega < 0$ or $\omega > 2$.

4.7. Notes on software

Vectors and matrices are essential elements of any programming language. All programming languages have vectors (1D arrays) and matrices (2D arrays). Thus there is no need to provide more details on software packages. Obviously, *Matlab*®, *Scilab*, *Python*, *Octave*, and many others are all efficient in handling vectors and matrices.

CHAPTER FIVE

Finite difference methods for ODEs

There are many different types of numerical methods for solving ODEs and PDEs. This chapter introduces the fundamentals of numerical methods for solving ODEs. Finite difference methods are among the most popular methods for computer simulation. It has the advantage of simplicity and clarity, especially in 1D configuration and other cases with regular geometry.

The foundation for the finite difference method is the Taylor expansion, which essentially transforms an ODE into a coupled set of algebraic equations by replacing the continuous derivatives with finite difference approximations on a grid of mesh or nodal points that span the domain of interest. However, the nodes at the boundary often require certain special treatment or approximations.

5.1. Integration of ODEs

As we have seen in earlier chapters, any second-order ODE can be written as a system of two first-order ODEs. In fact, any nth-order ODE can be reformulated as a system of n first-order ODEs. Therefore we can focus on the numerical methods for solving first-order ODEs. The techniques for solving a system is almost the same as that for solving a single ODE with some modifications.

For a first-order ODE, which is in general nonlinear, we can write it as

$$\frac{dy}{dx} = f(x, y). \tag{5.1}$$

For example, we can rewrite

$$\frac{dy}{dx} + xy^2 = \sin(x) - 1 \tag{5.2}$$

as

$$\frac{dy}{dx} = f(x, y), \quad f(x, y) = \sin(x) - 1 - xy^2. \tag{5.3}$$

To find the actual solution, it requires an initial condition $y(x_0) = y_0$ at $x = x_0$, that is,

$$y_0 = y(x_0) \quad \text{at} \quad x = x_0. \tag{5.4}$$

Naively, we can try to find the solution by direct integration

$$y(x) = y_0 + \int_{x_0}^{x} f(x, y(x))dx, \tag{5.5}$$

Engineering Simulation and its Applications
https://doi.org/10.1016/B978-0-44-314084-6.00012-7

but this is not possible because the unknown solution $y(x)$ appears in the integrand. However, it may be possible if some approximations can be carried out. For example, we can split the integration interval into many smaller intervals and assume that $y(x)$ is approximately constant within each smaller interval.

Numerical methods are the most common techniques for obtaining approximate solutions. There are various schemes with different orders of accuracy and convergent rates. These schemes include the simple Euler scheme, Runge–Kutta method, relaxation method, and many others.

5.2. Finite differences

Finite difference methods are a class of methods for solving differential equations. Let us start with the simplest Euler method for solving first-order ODEs.

5.2.1 Euler scheme

For the integration in the interval $[a, b]$, the main idea is to divide the interval into N smaller uniform intervals of the same width h, starting at $x_0 = a$. Using the notations $h = \Delta x = x_{n+1} - x_n = x_n - x_{n-1}$ and $y_n = y(x_n)$, we have

$$x_n = x_0 + n\Delta x = a + nh \quad (n = 0, 1, 2, \ldots, N). \tag{5.6}$$

We can now assume that $y(x)$ is approximately constant within each small interval $[x_n, x_{n+1}]$, but its values can change in different intervals. Thus we can use $y(x) \approx y_n = y(x_n)$, which is the calculated value y_n at x_n.

Now the explicit Euler scheme can simply be written as

$$y_{n+1} = y_n + \int_{x_n}^{x_{n+1}} f(x, y)dx \approx y_n + f(x_n, y_n)(x_{n+1} - x_n), \tag{5.7}$$

which becomes

$$y_{n+1} \approx y_n + hf(x_n, y_n). \tag{5.8}$$

This is a forward difference method as it is equivalent to the approximation of the first derivative

$$y'_n \approx \frac{y_{n+1} - y_n}{\Delta x} = \frac{y_{n+1} - y_n}{h}. \tag{5.9}$$

The order of accuracy can be estimated using the Taylor expansion

$$\begin{aligned} y_{n+1} &= y_n + hy'|_n + \frac{h^2}{2}y''|_n + \cdots \\ &= y_n + hf(x_n, y_n) + O(h^2), \end{aligned} \tag{5.10}$$

where $O(h^2)$ is the order notation, which basically means that the error in each interval is h^2 multiplied by a constant. For example, terms such as $10h^2$, $0.1h^2$, and $37h^2$ are all $O(h^2)$. It is worth mentioning that h is often called the step size in the literature, and the Euler scheme is essentially doing the time-stepping from $x = a$ to $x = b$ if we imagine the independent variable x is time or a pseudotime variable.

The error in each smaller interval is $O(h^2)$, but since there are $N = (b - a)/h$ intervals, the overall error E over all N intervals for the Euler scheme is

$$E = NO(h^2) = \frac{(b-a)}{h} O(h^2) \approx O(h). \tag{5.11}$$

Therefore the Euler method is first-order accurate, that is, its error is $O(h)$.

5.2.2 Numerical stability

For any numerical algorithms, the algorithm must be stable to reach convergent solutions. Thus stability is an important issue in numerical analysis.

Let us define E_n as the discrepancy between the approximate numerical solution y_n and the true solution $\tilde{y}(x)$ at x_n, that is,

$$E_n = \tilde{y}(x_n) - y_n, \quad E_{n+1} = \tilde{y}(x_n + h) - y_{n+1}. \tag{5.12}$$

We can also approximate the true solution by using Taylor expansion

$$\tilde{y}(x_n + h) \approx \tilde{y}_n + f(x_n, \tilde{y}_n)h + O(h^2). \tag{5.13}$$

Now subtracting Eq. (5.8) from Eq. (5.13), we have

$$E_{n+1} = E_n + [f(x_n, \tilde{y}) - f(x_n, y_n)]h, \tag{5.14}$$

which can be written as

$$E_{n+1} = E_n + [1 + f'_y(x_n, y_n)]h, \tag{5.15}$$

where we have used the approximations

$$f(x_n, \tilde{y}_n) \approx f(x_n, y_n) + f'_y(x_n, y_n)E_n, \quad f'_y = \frac{df}{dy}, \tag{5.16}$$

which is essentially a Taylor series of f at y_n.

Putting all the above together, we have

$$E_{n+1} = [1 + hf'_n]E_n, \quad f'_n = f'_y(x_n, y_n). \tag{5.17}$$

To ensure that the errors are not increasing, we require the following stability condition:

$$-1 \leq 1 + f'_n h \leq +1, \quad \text{or} \quad |1 + hf'_n| \leq 1, \tag{5.18}$$

that is,

$$-2 \le hf'_n \le 0, \tag{5.19}$$

or in practice

$$h \le \frac{2}{|f'_n|}. \tag{5.20}$$

The stability essentially restricts the interval size h, which is usually small. Otherwise, this scheme will be unstable.

Example 5.1. To solve the equation

$$\frac{dy}{dx} = f(y) = e^{-y} - y,$$

we use the explicit Euler scheme:

$$y_{n+1} \approx y_n + hf(y_n) = y_n + h(e^{-y_n} - y_n).$$

The step size for numerical stability requires

$$0 < h \le \frac{2}{|f'_y|} = \frac{2}{1 + e^{-y_n}}. \tag{5.21}$$

For a higher-order ODE, we can first write it into a system of first-order ODEs and then solve the system using any suitable numerical scheme. Let us look at the nonlinear pendulum equation

$$\ddot{\theta} + \zeta\dot{\theta} + a\sin\theta = 0, \tag{5.22}$$

where ζ is the damping coefficient, and $a = g/L$ is a constant with L being the length of the pendulum and g being the acceleration due to gravity. This equation is a nonlinear ODE, which does not have a closed-form analytical solution, so we have to solve it numerically.

Example 5.2. By introducing an additional variable $v = \dot{\theta}$ we can rewrite the pendulum equation as a system of two ODEs

$$\dot{\theta} = v, \tag{5.23}$$

$$\dot{v} = -\zeta v - a\sin\theta. \tag{5.24}$$

Using a time step $h = \Delta t$, the Euler scheme can be written as

$$\theta_{n+1} = \theta_n + hv_n, \tag{5.25}$$

$$v_{n+1} = v_n - h[\zeta v_n + a\sin\theta_n], \tag{5.26}$$

which can be implemented in any programming language.

5.2.3 Implicit Euler scheme

If we want to use a larger h so as to reduce the overall computational costs, then we can use the implicit Euler scheme by approximating the derivative with a backward difference

$$y'_n = \frac{y_n - y_{n-1}}{h}, \tag{5.27}$$

and the right-hand side of Eq. (5.5) is evaluated at the new y_{n+1} location at the end of the interval.

Now the implicit Euler scheme becomes

$$y_{n+1} = y_n + hf(x_{n+1}, y_{n+1}). \tag{5.28}$$

However, the right-hand side also contains the unknown y_{n+1}. Thus we have to rearrange this equation to solve y_{n+1}. If $f(x, y)$ is highly nonlinear, a further approximation to $f(x, y)$ is needed, which leads to a nonlinear algebraic equation for each step or interval.

Using the same notation E_n for errors and $\tilde{y}_n$ for true solutions, we can expand backward for $\tilde{y}$ at the point $x = x_{n+1}$:

$$\begin{aligned}\tilde{y}(x_n) &= \tilde{y}_{n+1} + f(x_{n+1}, \tilde{y}_{n+1})(x_n - x_{n+1}) + O(h^2)\\ &\approx \tilde{y}_{n+1} - hf(x_{n+1}, \tilde{y}_{n+1}) + O(h^2),\end{aligned} \tag{5.29}$$

which gives

$$\tilde{y}_{n+1} = \tilde{y}_n + hf(x_{n+1}, \tilde{y}_{n+1}) + O(h^2). \tag{5.30}$$

Now subtracting (5.28) from Eq. (5.30), we have

$$E_{n+1} = E_n + h[f(x_{n+1}, \tilde{y}_{n+1}) - f(x_{n+1}, y_{n+1})] = E_n + hf'_{n+1}E_{n+1}, \tag{5.31}$$

where we have used

$$f'_{n+1} = f'_y(x_{n+1}, y_{n+1}), \quad f'_y = \frac{df}{dy}, \tag{5.32}$$

and

$$f(x_{n+1}, \tilde{y}_{n+1}) = f(x_{n+1}, y_{n+1}) + f'_{n+1}E_{n+1}, \quad E_{n+1} = \tilde{y}_{n+1} - y_{n+1}. \tag{5.33}$$

Thus the stability condition for the implicit scheme, also called the backward Euler scheme, becomes

$$E_{n+1} \approx \frac{1}{(1 - hf'_{n+1})} E_n, \tag{5.34}$$

which is always stable if $f'(y) = df/dy \leq 0$. This means that any step size is acceptable. However, the step size cannot be too large because the accuracy reduces as the step size increases and the errors grow by a factor $1/(1 - hf')$.

Another practical issue is that for most problems such as nonlinear ODEs, the evaluation of y' and $f'(x, y)$ requires the value of y_{n+1}, which is unknown. Thus an iteration procedure is needed to pass to a new value y_{n+1}, and the iteration starts with a guess value, which is usually taken to be zero for most cases. The implicit scheme generally gives better stability.

Example 5.3. Let us revisit the previous example. To solve the equation

$$\frac{dy}{dx} = f(y) = e^{-y} - y, \tag{5.35}$$

we can now use an implicit scheme:

$$y_{n+1} \approx y_n + hf(y_{n+1}) = y_n + h(e^{-y_{n+1}} - y_{n+1}).$$

Since $f_y' = -1 - e^{-y_{n+1}} < 0$, this implicit Euler scheme is always stable. However, at each step, we have a nonlinear algebraic equation.

To find y_{n+1} for a given y_n, we have

$$(1 + h)y_{n+1} - he^{-y_{n+1}} = y_n, \tag{5.36}$$

which requires an iterative root-finding algorithm.

5.3. Leap-frog method

The Euler schemes, either explicit forward or implicit backward, essentially have first-order accuracy with errors $O(h)$. To make numerical methods more accurate, we have to do more elaborate approximations. One simple and yet interesting approach is the leap-frog scheme, which uses a central difference scheme by approximating the derivatives at two consecutive steps:

$$y_n' \approx \frac{y_{n+1} - y_{n-1}}{2\Delta x} = \frac{y_{n+1} - y_{n-1}}{2h}, \tag{5.37}$$

which leads to the leap-frog scheme for solving $y' = f(x, y)$

$$y_{n+1} = y_{n-1} + 2hf(x_n, y_n). \tag{5.38}$$

The central difference method is second-order accurate with $O(h^2)$. As an exercise, you can show that the accuracy is $O(h^2)$ using Taylor expansions for $y(x_n + h)$ and $y(x_n - h)$

at $x = x_n$, following the similar error estimation procedure that we did earlier for the Euler schemes.

In addition, similarly to Eq. (5.17), the errors for the leap-frog method become

$$E_{n+1} = E_{n-1} + 2hf'_y E_n, \tag{5.39}$$

or

$$E_{n+1} = (1 + 2hf'_y \xi)E_{n-1}, \quad \xi = \frac{E_n}{E_{n-1}}. \tag{5.40}$$

This scheme is stable only if $|\xi| \leq 1$ and $|1 + 2hf'_y \xi| \leq 1$. Therefore the central scheme is not necessarily always a better scheme than the forward scheme in terms of stability.

5.4. Runge–Kutta method

We have so far seen that both step sizes and stability of the Euler method and the central difference method are limited. The good news is that there are a class of numerical methods that can allow large step sizes and still have good numerical stability. The Runge–Kutta method is among the most widely used numerical integrators.

The two-step Runge–Kutta method uses a trial step to the midpoint of the interval by a central difference and combines with the forward difference at two steps:

$$\hat{y}_{n+1/2} = y_n + \frac{h}{2} f(x_n, y_n), \tag{5.41}$$

$$y_{n+1} = y_n + hf(x_n + h/2, \hat{y}_{n+1/2}). \tag{5.42}$$

The first equation is essentially a forward Euler scheme to predict or estimate the value at $x_n + h/2$, whereas the second equation attempts to correct and improve the estimates for y_{n+1}. This scheme is second-order accurate with higher stability, compared with previous simple schemes. In the standard Euler schemes, we only calculate or estimate the gradient or derivative $y' = f(x, y)$ once, but here we calculate the derivative $f(x, y)$ twice at x_n and $x_n + h/2$. It seems that the use of more derivative calculations can improve the accuracy. Obviously, we can view this scheme as a predictor–corrector method. In fact, we can use multisteps to devise higher-order methods if the right combinations are used to eliminate the error terms order by order.

The popular classical Runge–Kutta method can be written as

$$a = f(x_n, y_n), \quad b = f(x_n + h/2, y_n + ah/2), \tag{5.43}$$

$$c = f(x_n + h/2, y_n + bh/2), \quad d = f(x_n + h, y_n + ch), \tag{5.44}$$

$$y_{n+1} = y_n + \frac{h}{6}\left[a + 2(b + c) + d\right], \tag{5.45}$$

where four gradients or derivative estimates are used because a, b, c, and d are all derivative estimates. As a result, the Runge–Kutta method is fourth-order accurate with the overall errors of $O(h^4)$. Thus this method is often referred to as the RK4 method.

Example 5.4. Let us solve the following nonlinear ODE numerically:

$$\frac{dy}{dx} + y^2 = -1, \quad x \in [0, 2],$$

with the initial condition

$$y(0) = 1.$$

It is straightforward to verify by direct differentiation that its true solution is

$$y(x) = -\tan\left(x - \frac{\pi}{4}\right). \tag{5.46}$$

On the interval $[0, 2]$, let us first solve the equation using the Euler scheme for $h = 0.5$. There are five points $x_i = ih$ $(i = 0, 1, 2, 3, 4)$. As $dy/dx = f(y) = -1 - y^2$, we have the Euler scheme

$$y_{n+1} = y_n + hf(y) = y_n - h - hy_n^2.$$

From the initial condition $y_0 = 1$ we now have

$$y_1 = y_0 - h - hy_0^2 = 1 - 0.5 - 0.5 \times 1^2 = 0,$$
$$y_2 \approx -0.5, \quad y_3 \approx -1.125, \quad y_4 \approx -2.2578.$$

These are significantly different (about 30%) from the exact solutions

$$y_0^* = 1, \quad y_1^* \approx 0.2934079, \quad y_2^* = -0.21795809,$$
$$y_3^* = -0.86756212, \quad y_4^* = -2.68770693.$$

Now let us use the Runge–Kutta method to solve the same equation to see if it is better. Since $f(x_n, y_n) = -1 - y_n^2$, we have

$$a = f(x_n, y_n) = -(1 + y_n^2), \quad b = -\left[1 + \left(y_n + \frac{ah}{2}\right)^2\right],$$
$$c = -\left[1 + \left(y_n + \frac{bh}{2}\right)^2\right], \quad d = -[1 + (y_n + ch)^2],$$

and

$$y_{n+1} = y_n + \frac{h}{6}[a + 2(b + c) + d].$$

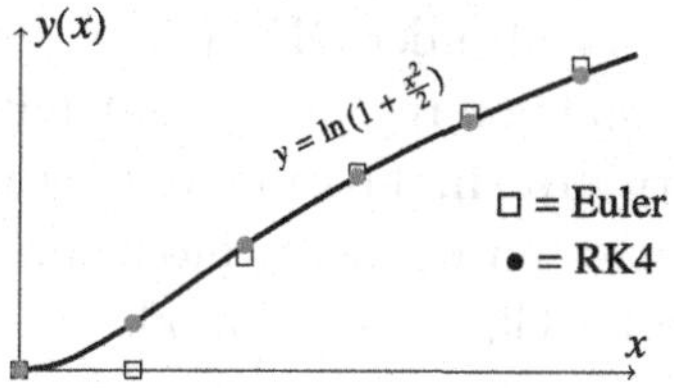

Figure 5.1 Numerical solutions by the Euler method (□) and the RK4 method (•).

From $y_0 = 1$ and $h = 0.5$ we have

$$a = -(1 + y_0^2) = -2.00, \quad b = -[1 + (y_0 + ah/2)^2] = -1.25,$$
$$c = -[1 + (y_0 + bh/2)^2] = -1.47266, \quad d = -[1 + (y_0 + ch)^2] = -1.06953,$$

and

$$y_1 = y_0 + \frac{0.5}{6}[a + 2(b + c) + d] \approx 0.29043.$$

Similarly, we have

$$y_2 \approx -0.22062, \quad y_3 \approx -0.87185, \quad y_4 \approx -2.67667.$$

These values are within about 1% of the analytical solutions y_n^*, as shown in Fig. 5.1.

We can see that even with the same step size, the Runge–Kutta method is much more efficient and accurate than the Euler scheme.

It is worth pointing out that this example concerns a nonlinear ODE, which can lead to some numerical difficulties at $x = \pi/2 + \pi/4$ because $\tan(x - \pi/4) \to \infty$. Generally speaking, higher-order schemes are better than lower-order schemes, but not always, because we often have to balance the computational efforts, stability, and the desired solution quality.

5.5. Shooting methods

Whatever the numerical methods we use to solve ODEs, we have to apply the initial conditions and boundary conditions. For a first-order ODE for $y(t)$, one initial condition $y(a) = y_0$ is needed at $t = a$ or, more commonly, at $t = 0$. For a second-order ODE for $y(t)$, it requires two initial conditions $y(0) = y_0$ and $y'(0) = k$ (i.e., initial gradient). In general, for an nth-order ODE, n initial conditions should be given. This type of ODE problem is called the initial value problem (IVP).

The numerical methods for solving ODEs that we have introduced so far work mainly for IVPs. However, there is another type of ODE boundary condition, which is not an IVP. For example, for a second-order ODE of $y(t)$, one initial condition $y(0) = \alpha$ is given at $t = 0$, but the other condition is given at a different time $t = \tau$. This condition is not at $t = 0$ and is not the derivative. In this case, we have an ODE with two boundary conditions. For this type of two-point boundary problem, the numerical methods that we discussed earlier cannot work well, and some modifications are needed.

Example 5.5. Now let us try to solve the following two-point boundary problem in the interval $[0, \tau]$, where $\tau > 0$ is a given constant:

$$\frac{d^2y(t)}{dt^2} = f(t, y, y'), \quad t \in [0, \tau], \tag{5.47}$$

with boundary conditions

$$y(0) = \alpha, \quad y(\tau) = \beta, \tag{5.48}$$

where $y' \equiv dy/dt$, and both α and β are constant. It is worth pointing out that the boundary condition $y(0) = \alpha$ at $t = 0$ is also an initial condition.

If we start the integration from $t = 0$, then the condition $y(0) = \alpha$ is not sufficient to determine a unique solution. The same is true if we start the integration from $t = \tau$. It seems that the direct numerical integration does not work. In fact, this problem is a two-point boundary problem because its boundary conditions are provided at two points or different times.

Shooting methods are a class of methods for solving such two-point boundary conditions. In general, the boundary conditions can be provided at more than two points, and the boundary conditions are often written in terms of functions, either a linear function $ay + by' = c$ or a nonlinear function $\psi(y, y') = 0$. The shooting method to be outlined here will work in both cases; however, for simplicity, we will use the simplest conditions given in Eq. (5.48).

Because a single initial condition $y(0) = \alpha$ is not sufficient to ensure a unique solution if we start the integration from $t = 0$; we have to introduce an additional condition $y'(0) = s$, where s is a parameter to be considered as constant during the integration. In this case the discrepancy in general between the value $y(\tau, s)$ (for a given s) and the actual prescribed boundary value $y(\tau) = \beta$ will be a function of s, that is,

$$\Delta(s) = y(\tau, s) - \beta. \tag{5.49}$$

The aim is now to minimize $\Delta(s)$, and the true solution will be obtained when $s = s_*$ which is the root of

$$\Delta(s_*) = 0. \tag{5.50}$$

For higher-order ODEs or a system of first-order ODEs, the discrepancy Δ should become a discrepancy vector. In principle, the root(s) s_* can be found using the standard

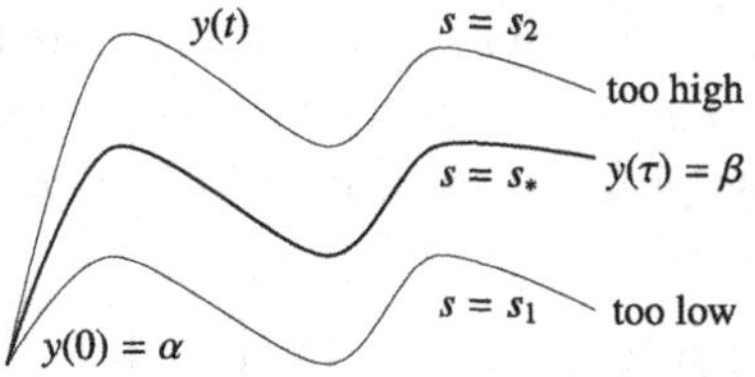

Figure 5.2 The shooting method with various values of the parameter s.

root-finding algorithms such as the Newton–Raphson method. This method can deal with boundary conditions in any form, even nonlinear or inexplicit functions. In addition, the numerical integration can be carried out using any of the efficient schemes such as the Runge–Kutta method.

In practice, the basic step of a shooting method is to start from a guess value $s = s_0$ and integrate the equation to get a trial solution. Then this trial solution is tested to see if it satisfies the other condition $y(\tau) = \beta$ at $t = \tau$. If the condition at the other end is not satisfied (usually not), we adjust the parameter s and carry out the integration again. This iterative procedure continues by varying the values of the parameter s until the solution satisfies both boundary conditions or within a prescribed accuracy.

Here the parameter $y'(0) = s$ acts as a velocity if the solution $y(t)$ is considered as a trajectory (see Fig. 5.2). This process is similar to shooting and aiming so as to hit the target at $y(\tau) = \beta$ (hence the name of the shooting method).

Example 5.6. We now try to solve the following two-point boundary problem:

$$y''(t) - 2y'(t) + y(t) = t \tag{5.51}$$

with boundary conditions

$$y(0) = 0, \quad y(1) = 1. \tag{5.52}$$

The analytical solution can be obtained using the standard technique of ODEs with constant coefficients. We have

$$y(t) = t + 2(1 - e^t) + 2(1 - e^{-1})te^t. \tag{5.53}$$

In general, we may not know the exact solution, and we have to use numerical methods. To solve this problem using the standard shooting method, we first rewrite the above second-order ODE as a linear system by letting $u_1 = y(t)$ and $u_2 = du_1/dt = y'(t)$:

$$\frac{\mathrm{d}\boldsymbol{u}}{\mathrm{d}t} = \frac{\mathrm{d}}{\mathrm{d}t}\begin{pmatrix} u_1 \\ u_2 \end{pmatrix} = \begin{pmatrix} u_2 \\ t + 2u_2 - u_1 \end{pmatrix}. \tag{5.54}$$

This is a system of first-order ODEs, which can be integrated directly if we use a guess value for $u_2(0) = y'(0) = s$ at $t = 0$. That is to say, the boundary value problem is now converted into an initial value problem with the initial values as

$$\boldsymbol{u}(0) = \begin{pmatrix} u_1(0) \\ u_2(0) \end{pmatrix} = \begin{pmatrix} 0 \\ s \end{pmatrix}. \tag{5.55}$$

For simplicity, let us use the bisection method to find the appropriate value s by starting from the initial guess $s = 0$. For $s = 0$, we can integrate the system using the Runge–Kutta method with $h = 0.25$ in a manner similar to the previous example. After some numerical calculations, we have $u_1(1) = y(1) \approx 0.2817$, which is too low for the given boundary condition $y(1) = 1$.

We then try this again using $s = 1$, and we have $u_1(1) = 3$, which is too high. Now we try their midpoint $s = (0 + 1)/2$, and we get $u_1(1) \approx 1.6409$, which is still too high.

Again, we then try $s = (0 + 0.5)/2 = 0.25$, and we get $u_1(1) \approx 0.961$, which is lower than $y(1) = 1$. So we now try $s = (0.25 + 0.5)/2$, and we get $u_1(1) \approx 1.301$ (too high). We continue in this way until we reach $s = 0.2656$ after seven iterations. We can then continue the iterations until a prescribed accuracy.

If we use the guess $y'(0) = s$ to solve the equation analytically, then we have

$$y(t) = 2 + t - 2e^t + (1 + s)te^t. \tag{5.56}$$

To satisfy $y(1) = 1$ at $t = 1$, we have the solution $s_* = 1 - 2e^{-1}$. The solution after seven iterations corresponds to $s = 0.2656$, which is quite close (within about 0.5%) to the true value of $y'(0) = 1 - 2e^{-1} \approx 0.264241117657$.

This is a relatively simple example, but it does demonstrate how the shooting method works. In fact, nonlinear equations with more complex boundary conditions can be solved using shooting methods. In the standard shooting method we discussed here, we start the integration (or shooting) from one boundary and try to match the target at the other boundary. Sometimes, it may be difficult to do so. In this case, it is possible or even more efficient to shoot from both sides (boundaries) and try to match a common target at a convenient midlocation. This forms the shooting-to-a-fitting-point method. There are other variations of shooting methods as well, and the interested readers can refer to more advanced literature.

5.6. Notes on software

ODE solvers using the Runge–Kutta method have been implemented in almost every programming language and major software packages. For example, in Matlab®, the ODE solver *ode45* is mainly based on the RK4 method and its variants. More specifically, it is based on the Dormand–Prince formulas.

In Python's package *scipy*, the scipy.integrate.RK45() is also based on the Dormand–Prince formulae. The package *deSolve* for R also implemented the RK4 method.

Since the RK4 steps are easy to implement, we can use any programming language to do the implementation, and in most cases, they are already implemented and tested.

CHAPTER SIX

Finite difference methods for PDEs

For differential equations with two or more independent variables, we have to use partial differential equations (PDEs). To solve PDEs numerically, simple integration is not possible because PDE-based problems can have complicated domains with initial and boundary conditions. In practice, boundary conditions are more complex, and the solution domain can be irregular. In addition, nonlinear problems are very common in real-world applications. Here we start with the simplest first-order PDEs and then extend discussion to more complicated cases.

6.1. First-order PDEs

One of the simplest first-order PDEs is the one-dimensional scalar equation

$$\frac{\partial u}{\partial t} + c\frac{\partial u}{\partial x} = 0, \tag{6.1}$$

where c is a constant or the velocity of advection.

Since there are two independent variables t and x, we have to approximate two derivatives in two dimensions. There is no reason to use the same type of approximations for time and space. In fact, it is advantageous to use different schemes to approximate different derivatives. By using the forward Euler scheme for time t and the central scheme for space x we have

$$\frac{u_j^{n+1} - u_j^n}{\Delta t} + c\left[\frac{u_{j+1}^n - u_{j-1}^n}{2h}\right] = 0, \tag{6.2}$$

where $t = n\Delta t$ for $(n = 0, 1, 2, \ldots)$, $x = x_0 + jh$ for $(j = 0, 1, 2, \ldots)$, and $h = \Delta x$. By u_j^n we denote the value of u at $t = n\Delta t$ and at location $x = jh$.

Stability analysis is useful to see how the method behaves numerically. We now use the von Neumann stability analysis with two indices, j for spatial coordinate x and n for time. The main idea of stability analysis is first to assume the independent solutions or eigenmodes, also called Fourier modes, in spatial coordinate x in the form

$$u_j^n = \xi^n e^{ikhj}, \tag{6.3}$$

where $i = \sqrt{-1}$ is the imaginary unit. The number k is also called the equivalent wavenumber. It is worth pointing out that u_j^n is a standard notation, not a power function, to denote the value of u at time step n at node j. Such notations are commonly used in numerical analysis. However, n in ξ^n is an exponent.

Engineering Simulation and its Applications
https://doi.org/10.1016/B978-0-44-314084-6.00013-9

Substituting (6.3) into Eq. (6.2), we have

$$\frac{\xi^{n+1}e^{ikhj} - \xi^n e^{ikhj}}{\Delta t} + c\left[\frac{\xi^n e^{ikh(j+1)} - \xi^n e^{ikh(j-1)}}{2h}\right] = 0. \tag{6.4}$$

After dividing it by $\xi^n e^{ikhj} \neq 0$, we have

$$\xi - 1 + \frac{c\Delta t}{h}\left[\frac{e^{ikh} - e^{-ikh}}{2}\right] = 0, \tag{6.5}$$

which becomes

$$\xi = 1 - i\frac{c\Delta t}{h}\sin(kh), \tag{6.6}$$

where we have used the identity

$$\sin\theta = \frac{e^{i\theta} - e^{-i\theta}}{2}, \quad \theta = kh. \tag{6.7}$$

The stability criterion $|\xi| \leq 1$ requires

$$\sqrt{1 + \beta^2 \sin^2(kh)} \leq 1, \quad \beta = \frac{c\Delta t}{h}, \tag{6.8}$$

or

$$\beta^2 \sin^2(kh) \leq 0. \tag{6.9}$$

However, this inequality is impossible to satisfy, and this scheme is thus unconditionally unstable.

To avoid the difficulty of instability, we can use other schemes such as the upwind scheme. For the upwind scheme, we use the one-step forward difference instead of the central difference:

$$\frac{u_j^{n+1} - u_j^n}{\Delta t} + c\left[\frac{u_j^n - u_{j-1}^n}{h}\right] = 0. \tag{6.10}$$

Following similar steps for stability analysis, we now have

$$|\xi| = \left|1 - \beta[1 - \cos(kh) + i\sin(kh)]\right| \leq 1, \tag{6.11}$$

which is equivalent to $0 < \beta \leq 1$, that is,

$$0 < \frac{c\Delta t}{h} \leq 1. \tag{6.12}$$

This is the well-known Courant–Friedrichs–Lewy stability condition, often referred to as the Courant stability condition. Thus the upwind scheme is conditionally stable.

6.2. Second-order PDEs: wave equation

For higher-order PDEs, such as the second-order wave equation, we can in principle rewrite a second-order PDE as a system of first-order PDEs and then solve it using standard techniques for solving first-order PDEs. However, it is may be more effective to solve such PDEs by direct discretization using finite difference schemes.

The wave equation

$$\frac{\partial^2 u}{\partial t^2} = c^2 \frac{\partial^2 u}{\partial x^2} \tag{6.13}$$

consists of two second derivatives. The first derivatives are approximated at each time step n as

$$u_i' = \frac{u_{i+1}^n - u_i^n}{\Delta x}, \quad u_{i-1}' = \frac{u_i^n - u_{i-1}^n}{\Delta x}, \tag{6.14}$$

where i denotes the node or location at $x_i = i\Delta x$. Then the second derivative can be approximated by

$$u_i'' = \frac{u_i' - u_{i-1}'}{\Delta x} = \frac{u_{i+1}^n - 2u_i^n + u_{i-1}^n}{(\Delta x)^2}, \tag{6.15}$$

which forms a central difference scheme with second-order accuracy.

Similarly to this central difference scheme for spatial coordinate x, we can also use a similar central difference scheme for time or time-stepping. In this case, we can use the central difference schemes in both time and space. Therefore the finite difference scheme for the wave equation becomes

$$\frac{u_i^{n+1} - 2u_i^n + u_i^{n-1}}{(\Delta t)^2} = c^2 \frac{u_{i+1}^n - 2u_i^n + u_{i-1}^n}{(\Delta x)^2}. \tag{6.16}$$

Essentially, this scheme is a two-level scheme with second-order accuracy. To find the solution u^{n+1} at $t = n + 1$, this difference equation can be expressed in terms of the known values or data u_i^n and u_i^{n-1} at two previous time steps $t = n$ and $t = n - 1$.

We leave it as an exercise for the reader to implement the above method using any programming language for the case of $i = 1, 2, \ldots, 100$, $n = 1, 2, \ldots, 500$, $c = 1$, $\Delta t = 0.01$, and $\Delta x = 0.02$. The initial condition for the wave equation (6.13) is

$$u(x, 0) = e^{-x^2} \tag{6.17}$$

together with the wave reflection boundary conditions at both ends

$$u(-L, t) = 0, \quad u(L, t) = 0, \quad L = 1. \tag{6.18}$$

If implemented properly, you will see two traveling waves (one travels to the left, and one travels to the right), as shown in Fig. 6.1.

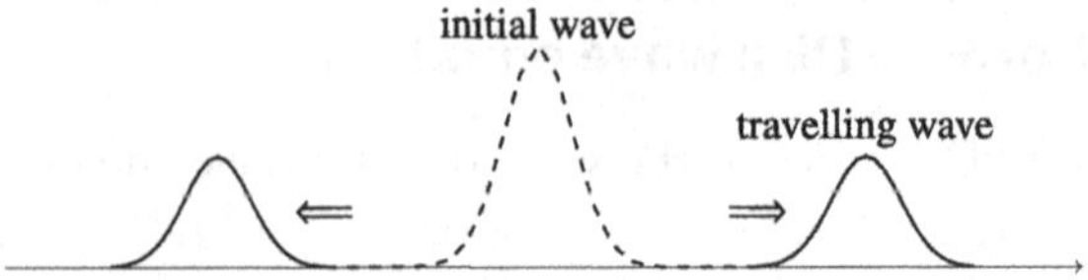

Figure 6.1 Travelling wave solution of the wave equation: $u_{tt} - c^2 u_{xx} = 0$.

6.3. Second-order PDEs: parabolic equation

Both the heat conduction and the diffusion equation are second-order parabolic PDEs. For the 1D diffusion equation with a constant diffusion coefficient D

$$\frac{\partial u}{\partial t} = \frac{\partial}{\partial x}(D\frac{\partial u}{\partial x}), \tag{6.19}$$

we can use the forward Euler scheme for the time derivative and the centered second-order approximations for space derivatives. We have

$$\frac{u_j^{n+1} - u_j^n}{\Delta t} = D\frac{(u_{j+1}^n - 2u_j^n + u_{j-1}^n)}{h^2}, \quad h = \Delta x, \tag{6.20}$$

which can be written as

$$u_j^{n+1} = u_j^n + \frac{D\Delta t}{h^2}(u_{j+1}^n - 2u_j^n + u_{j-1}^n). \tag{6.21}$$

Here u_j^n means the value of $u(x, t)$ at time $t = n\Delta t$ and node $x_j = jh$.

Similarly to the earlier von Neumann stability analysis, assuming that

$$u_j^n = \xi^n e^{ikhj}, \tag{6.22}$$

we have

$$\xi^{n+1} e^{ikhj} = \xi^n e^{ikhj} + \frac{D\Delta t}{h^2}\left[\xi^n e^{ikh(j+1)} - 2\xi^n e^{ikhj} + \xi^n e^{ikh(j-1)}\right]. \tag{6.23}$$

Dividing this expression by $\xi^n \exp(ikhj)$ and using

$$\sin^2(kh/2) = -\frac{(e^{ikh} - 2 + e^{-ikh})}{4}, \tag{6.24}$$

we have

$$\xi = 1 - \frac{4D\Delta t}{h^2}\sin^2\left(\frac{kh}{2}\right). \tag{6.25}$$

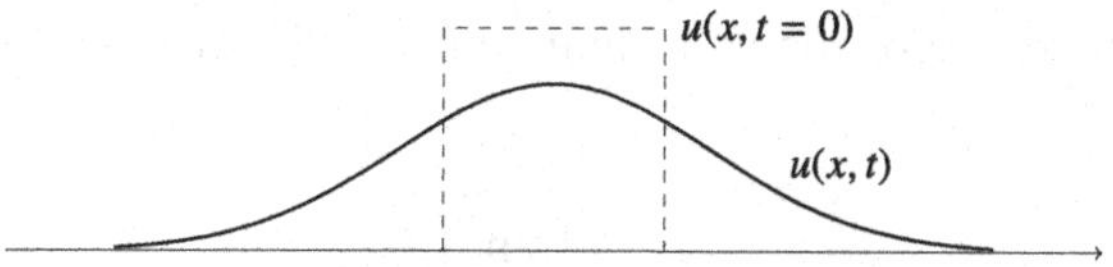

Figure 6.2 The 1-D time-dependent diffusion equation: $u_t - \kappa u_{xx} = 0$.

The stability requirement $|\xi| \le 1$ or

$$\left|1 - \frac{4D\Delta t}{h^2}\sin^2(kh/2)\right| \le 1 \tag{6.26}$$

requires

$$\frac{4D\Delta t}{h^2} \le 2, \tag{6.27}$$

where we have used $|\sin(kh/2)| \le 1$. Thus the constraint on the time step becomes

$$\Delta t \le \frac{h^2}{2D}. \tag{6.28}$$

This scheme is thus conditionally stable.

As an example, we leave it as an exercise to simulate the 1D heat conduction equation $u_t = u_{xx}$ with an initial condition in the interval [0, 1]

$$u(x, 0) = [H(x - 1/5) - H(x)], \tag{6.29}$$

where $H(x)$ is the Heaviside function, that is,

$$H(x) = 1, \quad x \ge 0, \quad H(x) = 0, \quad x < 0. \tag{6.30}$$

The temperature varies with both time and space. The evolution of the temperature profile at $t = 15$ is shown in Fig. 6.2, where the initial profile is plotted as a dashed curve.

For the explicit time-stepping scheme we used here, the step size needs to be sufficiently small; otherwise, the numerical scheme can become unstable. There are many ways to improve this, and one of most widely used schemes is the implicit scheme.

To avoid the limitation due to very small time steps, we now use an implicit scheme for time derivative via the backward Euler scheme. For the second-order spatial derivative, we still use the central difference scheme. Now we have

$$u_j^{n+1} - u_j^n = \frac{D\Delta t}{h^2}\left(u_{j+1}^{n+1} + 2u_j^{n+1} + u_{j-1}^{n+1}\right). \tag{6.31}$$

By using a similar procedure of the von Neumann stability analysis we can obtain

$$\xi = \frac{1}{1 + \frac{4D\Delta t}{h^2}\sin^2\left(\frac{kh}{2}\right)}, \tag{6.32}$$

whose norm is always less than unity, that is,

$$|\xi| \leq 1. \tag{6.33}$$

This means that this implicit scheme is unconditionally stable for any size of time steps. This is the main reason why implicit methods are desirable in simulation. However, the step sizes cannot be too large in practice because the accuracy of this scheme is related to the step size.

In addition, there is a disadvantage associated with the implicit scheme: this scheme requires the inverse of a large (usually sparse) matrix, which increases the computational costs and also requires more sophisticated programming. In practice, to avoid the inverse of a large sparse matrix, some iteration methods are commonly used, such as the Gauss–Seidel iteration method and the relaxation method.

6.4. Second-order PDEs: elliptical equation

In general, the mathematical model for a heat transfer problem or a diffusion problem is governed by a parabolic PDE in 3D with constant coefficient κ, that is,

$$\frac{\partial u}{\partial t} = \kappa \nabla^2 u + f, \quad \nabla^2 u = \frac{\partial^2 u}{\partial x^2} + \frac{\partial^2 u}{\partial y^2} + \frac{\partial^2 u}{\partial z^2}, \tag{6.34}$$

where f is the source term.

6.4.1 Poisson's equation

When the time is sufficiently long, the time derivative $u_t = \partial u/\partial t \to 0$ because the system will approach to a steady state, which is no longer changing with time. In this case, we have

$$\nabla^2 u = q, \quad q = \frac{-f}{\kappa}, \tag{6.35}$$

which is the well-known Poisson equation. There are methods available to solve this type of problem, such as the boundary integral method, relaxation method, multigrid method, and iteration method.

For problems in the two-dimensional space

$$\frac{\partial^2 u}{\partial x^2} + \frac{\partial^2 u}{\partial y^2} = q, \tag{6.36}$$

the second-order central difference schemes are used for approximating both spatial derivatives. Thus we have

$$\frac{u_{i+1,j} - 2u_{i,j} + u_{i-1,j}}{(\Delta x)^2} + \frac{u_{i,j+1} - 2u_{i,j} + u_{i,j-1}}{(\Delta y)^2} = q. \tag{6.37}$$

Here we have used $u_{i,j}$ to denote the value of function $u(x, y)$ at nodal point (i, j), which corresponds to $x_i = i\Delta x$ and $y_j = j\Delta y$ where $i = 0, 1, 2, \ldots, m$ and $j = 0, 1, \ldots, n$. In general, the grid sizes Δx and Δy can be different. However, for simplicity, we use $\Delta x = \Delta y = h$, and then Eq. (6.37) simply becomes

$$(u_{i,j+1} + u_{i,j-1} + u_{i+1,j} + u_{i-1,j}) - 4u_{i,j} = h^2 q, \tag{6.38}$$

which can be written more compactly as a matrix equation

$$\mathbf{Au} = \mathbf{b}. \tag{6.39}$$

This equation can be solved using various methods such as the Gauss–Seidel iteration method.

6.4.2 A worked example

The steady-state temperature distribution of a 1D heat transfer problem through a thin plate can be approximated as

$$\frac{d^2 u}{dx^2} = q, \quad 0 \le x \le w, \tag{6.40}$$

where w is the thickness, and q is a constant. The boundary conditions are

$$u(x = 0) = u_0, \quad u(x = w) = 0. \tag{6.41}$$

Integrating the equation twice and using the boundary conditions, we get the analytical solution

$$u = \frac{q}{2}x^2 - \frac{qw}{2}x + u_0\left(1 - \frac{x}{w}\right). \tag{6.42}$$

Let us now solve this problem using the finite difference method that we discussed earlier. For simplicity, we assume that $q = 1$, $u_0 = 1$, and $w = 1$.

In practice, we usually use a very fine grid. Here, for the illustration purpose, we use only five points $i = 0, 1, \ldots, 4$, so that $h = \Delta x = w/4 = 0.25$. Now the second-order central difference scheme becomes

$$\frac{u_{i+1} - 2u_i + u_{i-1}}{h^2} = q, \tag{6.43}$$

or

$$u_{i-1} - 2u_i + u_{i+1} = h^2 q. \tag{6.44}$$

At $x_0 = 0$, the initial condition can be applied, which gives

$$u_0 = 1. \tag{6.45}$$

For the points at $i = 1, 2, 3$, we have

$$u_0 - 2u_1 + u_2 = h^2 q, \tag{6.46}$$

$$u_1 - 2u_2 + u_3 = h^2 q, \tag{6.47}$$

$$u_2 - 2u_3 + u_4 = h^2 q. \tag{6.48}$$

Again, at $x_4 = w = 1$, the other boundary condition is applied, which gives

$$u_4 = 0. \tag{6.49}$$

Combining the above five equations into a matrix equation $\boldsymbol{Au} = \boldsymbol{b}$, we have

$$\begin{pmatrix} 1 & 0 & 0 & 0 & 0 \\ 1 & -2 & 1 & 0 & 0 \\ 0 & 1 & -2 & 1 & 0 \\ 0 & 0 & 1 & -2 & 1 \\ 0 & 0 & 0 & 0 & 1 \end{pmatrix} \begin{pmatrix} u_0 \\ u_1 \\ u_2 \\ u_3 \\ u_4 \end{pmatrix} = \begin{pmatrix} 1 \\ 0.0625 \\ 0.0625 \\ 0.0625 \\ 0 \end{pmatrix}. \tag{6.50}$$

We obtain the solution

$$\boldsymbol{u} = \boldsymbol{A}^{-1}\boldsymbol{b} = \begin{pmatrix} 1.0000 \\ 0.6563 \\ 0.3750 \\ 0.1562 \\ 0.0000 \end{pmatrix},$$

which is almost the same as the true solution

$$\boldsymbol{u}_{\text{true}} = \begin{pmatrix} 1.00000 \\ 0.65625 \\ 0.37500 \\ 0.15625 \\ 0.00000 \end{pmatrix}.$$

This simple example is very small scale with only five points. For large-scale problems or problems with complex geometry, the number of grid or nodal points can be very large. In this case the inverse of matrices should not be used. Iteration methods are preferred for solving large, sparse systems.

From the numerical analysis point of view, the accuracy of any finite difference scheme depends on many factors, such as the way of approximating relevant derivatives, and thus their accuracy can be described by $O(h)$ (first-order scheme), $O(h^2)$ (second-order scheme), or $O(h^s)$ in general. To design higher-order schemes, we have to use elaborate approximations for derivatives.

6.5. Spectral method

Other methods can also provide higher-order accuracy for spatial derivatives. For example, spectral methods are among the widely used.

In essence, the main idea of spectral methods (and their variants) is to approximate the solutions by a linear combination of some basis functions, very similar to the widely used finite element methods to be introduced later in this book. Spectral methods often transform a PDE into a set of ODEs, and these ODEs can in turn be solved using a wide range of techniques for solving ODEs.

To show how the spectral method work, let us consider the diffusion problem in the one-dimensional space or interval $[0, L]$. We have

$$\frac{\partial u}{\partial t} = D\frac{\partial^2 u}{\partial x^2}, \quad x \in [0, L]. \tag{6.51}$$

First, we approximate the solution $u(x, t)$ by using a finite sum of N terms

$$u(x, t) \approx u_N = \sum_{k=0}^{N-1} \alpha_k(t)\psi_k(x), \tag{6.52}$$

where the unknown coefficients $\alpha_k(t)$ are amplitudes that depend only on time t. However, the basis functions $\psi_k(x)$ are known, representing spectral modes that may vary with spatial coordinates x only, not with time t. Here N is the number of terms in the approximation, which is often related to the number of spectral modes.

There are many different basis functions. They can be any orthogonal set of functions, such as Chebyshev or Legendre polynomials. The simplest basis functions are probably the trigonometric functions, as used in Fourier transforms.

Substituting approximation (6.52) into (6.51), we have

$$\frac{\partial}{\partial t}\left[\sum_{k=0}^{N-1} \alpha_k(t)\psi_k(x)\right] = D\frac{\partial^2}{\partial x^2}\left[\sum_{k=0}^{N-1} \alpha_k(t)\psi_k(x)\right], \tag{6.53}$$

which leads to

$$\sum_{k=0}^{N-1} \frac{\mathrm{d}\alpha_k(t)}{\mathrm{d}t} \psi_k(x) = D \sum_{k=0}^{N-1} \alpha_k(t) \frac{\mathrm{d}^2 \psi_k(x)}{\mathrm{d}x^2}. \tag{6.54}$$

If we use the basis functions

$$\psi_k(x) = e^{-i\omega_k x}, \quad \omega_k = \frac{2\pi k}{L} \quad (k = 1, 2, \ldots), \tag{6.55}$$

then we have

$$\frac{\mathrm{d}^2 \psi_k(x)}{\mathrm{d}x^2} = -\omega_k^2 e^{-i\omega_k x}. \tag{6.56}$$

Now we finally get

$$\sum_{k=0}^{N-1} \frac{\mathrm{d}\alpha_k(t)}{\mathrm{d}t} e^{-i\omega_k x} = -\sum_{k=0}^{N-1} D\omega_k^2 \alpha_k(t) e^{-i\omega_k x}. \tag{6.57}$$

Multiplying both sides by $e^{-i\omega_j x}$ and integrating from 0 to L together with the orthogonality condition

$$\int_0^L e^{-i\omega_k x} e^{-i\omega_j x} dx = \begin{cases} 0 & \text{if } (k \neq j), \\ L & \text{if } (k = j), \end{cases} \tag{6.58}$$

we have the following set of N first-order ODEs:

$$\frac{\mathrm{d}\alpha_k(t)}{\mathrm{d}t} = -D\omega_k^2 \alpha_k(t) \quad (k = 1, 2, \ldots, N). \tag{6.59}$$

This set of equations can be solved using any efficient time-stepping methods, such as the RK4 scheme.

Essentially, the spectral method transforms a PDE problem into a set of ODE problems. In practice, numerical methods using the fast Fourier transforms (FFT) can be very efficient to implement. A major advantage of the spectral method is that its spatial accuracy is very high, as we have not used any approximation for the spatial derivatives in the original equation. The only error is the truncated error in (6.52). However, the spectral method does have some disadvantages because it may increase the computational costs in time-stepping due to multiple ODEs involved in the scheme. In addition, boundary conditions cannot be applied naturally because we have to transform them in some way so that they can be related to the coefficients α_k. Other methods with improved accuracy exist in the literature, and the interested readers can refer to more specialized textbooks.

6.6. Notes on software

Finite difference methods are relatively easy to implement by using any programming language. Matlab®, Octave, Scilab, Python, C++, R, and many others all have different levels of numerical functionalities. For example, a few dozen lines of codes would be sufficient to deal with most finite difference problems on a regular domain.

Though finite difference methods work well, however, the ease of implementation only applies to regular domains, such as 1D intervals, 2D rectangular domains, or 3D cubic domains. If the geometry of a domain is irregular, then the applications of boundary conditions and the handling of approximations at the boundaries can be challenging from a programming perspective. In practice, for solving problems in regular domains, other methods such as finite element and finite volume methods are more widely used.

For software packages on finite elements and finite volumes, we will outline them briefly in later chapters.

CHAPTER SEVEN

Finite volume method

Though finite difference methods (FDM) work well in practice, however, they are usually used for problems in regular domains. If irregular domains are involved, then other methods such as finite volume methods and finite elements may be preferable. In many ways, finite volume methods (FVMs) resemble the key features of finite difference methods. However, the starting point for FVMs is the integral formulation of the problem under consideration, rather than the differential form or derivatives of the PDEs for FDMs. This will usually ensure that the integral quantities such as the total mass and energy are conserved. FVMs can deal well with the conservation laws, surface and boundary integrals, and flow or flux through boundaries. Therefore they are widely used in computational fluid dynamics (CFD), engineering simulation, chemical engineering, and many other applications.

7.1. Finite volumes and volume integrals

Let us start with a diffusion–reaction problem in the domain Ω with boundary $\partial\Omega$,

$$\frac{\partial u}{\partial t} - \nabla \cdot (\kappa \nabla u) = q, \tag{7.1}$$

where u depends on time t and spatial coordinates x, y, z in general. Here κ is a constant, q is the source term, and ∇u is the gradient of u. In the three-dimensional space with three unit vectors $\boldsymbol{i}, \boldsymbol{j}, \boldsymbol{k}$ along the x-, y-, and z-axes, respectively, the gradient of a scalar function u is defined as

$$\text{grad} u = \nabla u = \boldsymbol{i}\frac{\partial u}{\partial x} + \boldsymbol{j}\frac{\partial u}{\partial y} + \boldsymbol{k}\frac{\partial u}{\partial z}. \tag{7.2}$$

The divergence of a vector

$$\boldsymbol{F} = F_x\boldsymbol{i} + F_y\boldsymbol{j} + F_z\boldsymbol{k} \tag{7.3}$$

can be calculated by

$$\text{div}\boldsymbol{F} = \nabla \cdot \boldsymbol{F} = \frac{\partial F_x}{\partial x} + \frac{\partial F_y}{\partial y} + \frac{\partial F_z}{\partial z}. \tag{7.4}$$

Since the gradient is a vector, its divergence can be calculated by

$$\text{div}(\text{grad}\, u) = \nabla^2 u = \nabla \cdot (\nabla u) = \frac{\partial^2 u}{\partial x^2} + \frac{\partial^2 u}{\partial y^2} + \frac{\partial^2 u}{\partial z^2}, \tag{7.5}$$

Engineering Simulation and its Applications
https://doi.org/10.1016/B978-0-44-314084-6.00014-0

which is the well-known Laplacian operator.

By defining the flux function

$$\boldsymbol{F} = \boldsymbol{F}(u) = -\kappa \nabla u \tag{7.6}$$

we can rewrite Eq. (7.1) as

$$\frac{\partial u}{\partial t} + \nabla \cdot \boldsymbol{F} = q, \tag{7.7}$$

whose integral form can be obtained by integrating both sides of the equation over the whole domain:

$$\int_{\Omega} \frac{\partial u}{\partial t} d\Omega + \int_{\Omega} \nabla \cdot \boldsymbol{F} d\Omega = \int_{\Omega} q d\Omega. \tag{7.8}$$

Though it may be difficult to evaluate these integrals over a large domain, however, the domain of the integrals can be decomposed into many small finite control volumes so that the domain is the union of many small volumes, that is,

$$\Omega = \bigcup_{i=1}^{N} \Omega_i, \quad \Omega_i \bigcap \Omega_j = \emptyset. \tag{7.9}$$

In principle, we can assume that quantities do not change dramatically in each volume cell, and we can define the average or mean over the control volume cell such that

$$u_i = \frac{1}{V_i} \int_{\Omega_i} u d\Omega_i, \quad q_i = \frac{1}{V_i} \int_{\Omega_i} q d\Omega_i, \tag{7.10}$$

where $V_i = |\Omega_i|$ is the volume of the small control volume Ω_i. Now we can rewrite the equation using the volume cell means:

$$\frac{\partial u_i}{\partial t} + \sum_{i=1}^{N} \frac{1}{V_i} \int_{\Omega_i} \nabla \cdot \mathbf{F}(u_i) d\Omega_i = q_i. \tag{7.11}$$

By the divergence theorem we can relate the volume integral of the divergence to a surface integral, that is,

$$\int_{V} \nabla \cdot \boldsymbol{F} = \int_{\Gamma} \mathbf{F} \cdot \mathbf{n} \, dA, \tag{7.12}$$

where $\mathbf{dS} = \boldsymbol{n} dA$ is the surface element, and $\boldsymbol{n}$ is the outward pointing unit vector on the surface enclosing the finite volume cell. Therefore we can rewrite (7.11) as

$$\frac{\partial u_i}{\partial t} + \sum_{i=1}^{N} \frac{1}{V_i} \int_{\Gamma_i} \mathbf{F} \cdot \mathbf{dS} = q_i. \tag{7.13}$$

Here the integral can be further approximated or evaluated by using various numerical integration schemes.

For example, in the simplest one-dimensional case, the integral

$$u_i = \frac{1}{h}\int_{(i-1/2)h}^{(i+1/2)h} u dx, \quad h = \Delta x, \tag{7.14}$$

is a vertex-centered finite volume scheme.

In the rest of this chapter, we will introduce different discretization schemes for three types of PDEs.

7.2. Finite volumes for Laplace equation

In the two-dimensional (2D) space, Laplace's equation can be written as

$$\nabla^2 u = 0, \quad \text{or} \quad \frac{\partial^2 u}{\partial x^2} + \frac{\partial^2 u}{\partial y^2} = 0, \tag{7.15}$$

where $u(x, y)$ is a function of $(x, y) \in \Omega$.

Integrating the preceding equation and using the divergence theorem, we have

$$\int_\Omega \nabla^2 u d\Omega = \int_\Omega \nabla \cdot (\nabla u) d\Omega = \int_\Gamma \frac{\partial u}{\partial \boldsymbol{n}} \cdot \mathbf{dS} = 0. \tag{7.16}$$

In the case of regular grid points $(i\Delta x, j\Delta y)$, the control volume element is a cell, centered at $(i\Delta x, j\Delta y)$ with a size of Δx (along the x-axis) and Δy (along the y-axis). Thus the boundary integral on each cell consists of four parts, and each part is the integral on each of the four sides.

Now we can approximate the partial derivatives by

$$\frac{\partial u}{\partial x} = \frac{(u_{i+1,j} - u_{i,j})}{\Delta x}, \quad \frac{\partial u}{\partial y} = \frac{(u_{i,j+1} - u_{i,j})}{\Delta y}, \tag{7.17}$$

where $u_{i,j}$ is the value of $u(x, y)$ at location $(x_i = i\Delta x, y_j = j\Delta y)$ or node (i, j).

Assuming that the quantities do not change inside the cell, we can evaluate the integral as a simple constant multiplied by the area $\Delta x \Delta y$:

$$\begin{aligned}\int_{\Omega_{i,j}} \frac{\partial u}{\partial \mathbf{n}} d\Omega &= (\Delta x \Delta y)\frac{(u_{i+1,j} - 2u_{i,j} + u_{i-1,j})}{(\Delta x)^2} + (\Delta x \Delta y)\frac{(u_{i,j+1} - 2u_{i,j} + u_{i,j-1})}{(\Delta y)^2} \\ &= \frac{\Delta y}{\Delta x}(u_{i+1,j} + u_{i-1,j} - 2u_{i,j}) + \frac{\Delta x}{\Delta y}(u_{i,j+1} + u_{i,j-1} - 2u_{i,j}) = 0.\end{aligned} \tag{7.18}$$

For regular grids with equal spacing $\Delta x = \Delta y = h$, we have the discrete form of the Laplace equation

$$(u_{i+1,j} + u_{i,j+1} + u_{i-1,j} + u_{i,j-1}) - 4u_{i,j} = 0. \tag{7.19}$$

In many ways, this formula is quite similar to the formulas in the finite difference methods. To be specific, this is exactly the five-point difference scheme for the Laplace operator.

7.3. Finite volumes for 1D heat conduction

Let us now use the 1D heat conduction problem as an example to see how its finite volume scheme works. From the 1D heat equation

$$\frac{\partial u}{\partial t} = k\frac{\partial^2 u}{\partial x^2} + q(u, x, t) \tag{7.20}$$

we can first integrate it with respect to x and then integrate it with respect to t:

$$\int_t \left[\int_\Omega \left(\frac{\partial u}{\partial t} - k\frac{\partial^2 u}{\partial x^2} - q\right) dx\right] dt = 0. \tag{7.21}$$

For simplicity, we now use a node-centered or vertex-centered control volume from $(i-1/2)h$ to $(i+1/2)h$, where $h = \Delta x$. For the time-stepping, we then integrate from step time $t = n$ to $n+1$:

$$\int_{n\Delta t}^{(n+1)\Delta t} \left[\int_{(i-1/2)h}^{(i+1/2)h} \left(\frac{\partial u}{\partial t} - k\frac{\partial^2 u}{\partial x^2} - q\right) dx\right] dt = 0. \tag{7.22}$$

We can approximate the integral of any function $\psi(x)$ using the midpoint approximation

$$\int_a^b \psi(x) dx \approx \psi\left[\frac{(a+b)}{2}\right](b-a), \tag{7.23}$$

where $x_0 = (a+b)/2$ is the midpoint of the integration interval. Now let us introduce the DuFort–Frankel scheme, which first approximates the gradient by the central difference scheme

$$\frac{\partial^2 u}{\partial x^2} = \frac{u_{i+1}^n - 2u_i^n + u_{i-1}^n}{h^2} \tag{7.24}$$

and then replaces $-2u_i^n$ with the values at the two different time levels $-(u_j^{n+1} + u_j^{n-1})$. For the time-stepping, the central scheme is also used. Therefore the DuFort–Frankel scheme becomes

$$\frac{u_i^{n+1} - u_i^{n-1}}{2\Delta t} = \frac{[(u_{i+1}^n - (u_i^{n+1} + u_i^{n-1}) + u_{i-1}^n)]}{h^2} + q_i^n, \tag{7.25}$$

which is exactly the explicit scheme in the finite difference method, but the starting point here is different.

In principle, we can carry out its stability analysis using the similar procedure for FDMs, which requires $|\xi| < 1$. In fact, this condition is always true, and thus the Dufort–Frankel scheme is unconditionally stable for all Δt and Δx.

Though some of the discrete equations in the FVMs may be exactly the same as those in the FDMs, the finite volume scheme is in general more versatile in dealing with irregular geometry and more natural in applying boundary conditions.

7.4. Flows and conservation law

The heat equation we considered in the previous section is a parabolic PDE. Now we can discretize a hyperbolic PDE. The conservation law of flows in the one-dimensional case can be written as

$$\frac{\partial u}{\partial t} + \frac{\partial \Phi(u)}{\partial x} = 0, \tag{7.26}$$

where $\Phi(u)$ is the flux, which is a function of $u(x, t)$. Let us first integrate it from x_a to x_b:

$$\int_{x_a}^{x_b} \left[\frac{\partial u}{\partial t} + \frac{\partial \Phi(u)}{\partial x} \right] dx = 0. \tag{7.27}$$

Interchanging the order of integration and differentiation, we have

$$\int_{x_a}^{x_b} \frac{\partial u}{\partial t} dx = \frac{\partial}{\partial t} \int_{x_a}^{x_b} u \, dx = -\left\{ \Phi[u(x_b)] - \Phi[u(x_a)] \right\} = 0. \tag{7.28}$$

Using the midpoint rule with the value u^* at the midpoint to approximate the integral, we get

$$(x_b - x_a) \frac{\partial u^*}{\partial t} = -\{\Phi[u(x_b)] - \Phi[u(x_a)]\}. \tag{7.29}$$

For the control volume $[(i - 1/2)\Delta x, (i + 1/2)\Delta x]$ centered at the nodal point $x_i = i\Delta x = ih$, we can approximate $u_i \approx u_i^*$ in each interval using the midpoint value u_i^*. Using a forward difference scheme for the time derivative, we obtain

$$u_i^{n+1} - u_i^n = -\frac{\Delta t}{h} \left[\Phi(x_{i+1/2}) - \Phi(x_{i-1/2}) \right], \tag{7.30}$$

where $\Phi(x_{i+1/2})$ and $\Phi(x_{i-1/2})$ are the values of $\Phi(u)$ at $x_{i+1/2}$ and $x_{i-1/2}$, respectively. Further approximating the flux $\Phi(x_{i+1/2})$ using the value at the grid or nodal point, we have $\Phi(x_{i+1/2}) \approx \Phi(x_i)$ or, more specifically, $\Phi(x_{i+1/2} \approx \Phi(u_i)$. Now the explicit forward scheme for the flow equation becomes

$$u_i^{n+1} - u_i^n = -\frac{\Delta t}{h}\left[\Phi(u_i) - \Phi(u_{i-1})\right]. \tag{7.31}$$

It is straightforward to show that this scheme is conditionally stable because we know this from the corresponding FDM.

As a simple example, using the flux function $\Phi(u) = cu$, where c is a constant, we have

$$u^{n+1} = u_i^n - \frac{c\Delta t}{h}\left(u_i^n - u_{i-1}^n\right). \tag{7.32}$$

We leave it as an exercise to show that its stability requires

$$0 < \frac{c\Delta t}{h} \le 1. \tag{7.33}$$

The literature on finite volume methods is vast, and software becomes very powerful for solving various problems, including solving the Navier–Stokes equations numerically. The interested readers can refer to more advanced literature.

7.5. Notes on software

There are many software packages that implemented FVMs comprehensively. It is estimated that there are more than 200 FVM-related software packages. Powerful packages include *Ansys Fluent*, *Star-CCM+*, *SolidWorks*, *Visual-CFD*, *simFlow*, *COMSOL/CFD*, *Autodesk CFD*, *Converge*, *OpenFOAM*, *SimScale*, and many others.

CHAPTER EIGHT

Finite element methods

For engineering simulation, especially simulation of structures, the finite element method (FEM) is widely used. In the FEM the main idea is dividing the domain of interest into many small blocks or elements. However, the mathematical formulations are based on the weak form or integral form of the PDE, and functions or quantities are approximated based on shape functions.

Loosely speaking, the small elements are characterized by nodes, edges, and surfaces, and the whole domain can be considered as if all these blocks or elements are glued together at these nodes and along the element boundaries. Essentially, the PDE problem on a continuous domain with infinite degrees of freedom is transformed into a discrete system with finite degrees of freedom, typically, as algebraic equations or at most ODEs in the matrix forms.

8.1. Fundamentals of finite elements

The main advantage of the FEM is that the differential equation for a continuum system is transformed into a set of simultaneous algebraic equations as a discrete system with a finite number of elements. We can then use computational linear algebra to solve such equations.

8.1.1 Differential operators

Many problems in engineering and science can be formulated as PDEs. For example, the Laplace equation

$$\nabla^2 u = \frac{\partial^2 u}{\partial x^2} + \frac{\partial^2 u}{\partial y^2} + \frac{\partial^2 u}{\partial z^2} = 0 \tag{8.1}$$

models the steady-state behavior of heat conduction and diffusion problems. For simplicity, we can use a differential operator $\mathcal{L}$ to write PDEs more compactly. For example, we can write the preceding PDE as

$$\mathcal{L}u = 0 \tag{8.2}$$

with the differential operator

$$\mathcal{L} = \nabla^2 = \frac{\partial^2}{\partial x^2} + \frac{\partial^2}{\partial y^2} + \frac{\partial^2}{\partial z^2}. \tag{8.3}$$

Here $\mathcal{L}u$ means the differential operator $\mathcal{L}$ applied to the function $u(x, y, z)$.

Engineering Simulation and its Applications
https://doi.org/10.1016/B978-0-44-314084-6.00015-2

As another example, the 1D heat conduction equation with a source

$$\frac{\partial u}{\partial t} = \kappa \frac{\partial^2 u}{\partial x^2} + \alpha u \tag{8.4}$$

can be written compactly as

$$\mathcal{L}u = 0, \quad \mathcal{L} = \frac{\partial}{\partial t} - \kappa \frac{\partial^2}{\partial x^2} - \alpha. \tag{8.5}$$

8.1.2 Weak forms

For simplicity in the discussion of finite element formulations, we can write any linear PDEs in the form

$$\mathcal{L}(u) = 0, \quad \boldsymbol{x} \in \Omega, \tag{8.6}$$

where $\mathcal{L}$ is a generalized linear differential operator.

The full problem definition also requires to impose appropriate boundary conditions. The essential boundary condition, which means that u is prescribed with fixed values $\bar{u}$, can be applied by

$$\mathcal{E}(u) = u - \bar{u} = 0, \quad \boldsymbol{x} \in \partial\Omega_E. \tag{8.7}$$

The natural boundary condition can be described by a known function such that

$$\mathcal{B}(u) = 0 \quad \forall \boldsymbol{x} \in \partial\Omega_N. \tag{8.8}$$

In practice, natural boundary conditions are usually related to flux or force at boundaries. Overall, the whole boundary $\partial\Omega$ is the union of the essential boundary part $\partial\Omega_E$ and the natural boundary part $\partial\Omega_N$.

Suppose that we can approximate the true solution u by u_h over a finite element whose average size is h, which is the mean distance between two adjacent nodes. Then the original PDE in the form of $\mathcal{L}(u) = 0$ becomes an approximate equation

$$\mathcal{L}(u_h) \approx 0. \tag{8.9}$$

Now the main question is how to find the approximation solution u_h? Obviously, we would like to find an efficient method to construct u_h such that the overall error $|u_h - u|$ is minimized. In general, the errors will depend on both space and time.

There are several methods for minimizing such approximation errors, depending on the shape functions and details of the approximation schemes, including the weighted residual method, the method of least squares, the Galerkin method, and others.

Let us try to multiply both sides of Eq. (8.9) by a weighting function w_i, called a test function, and then integrate it over the domain. After applying the boundary conditions

(8.7) and (8.8), we have the following general weak form:

$$\int_{\Omega} \mathcal{L}(u_h) w_i d\Omega + \int_{\partial\Omega_N} \mathcal{B}(u_h)\bar{w}_i d\Gamma + \int_{\partial\Omega_E} \mathcal{E}(u_h)\tilde{w}_i d\Gamma_E \approx 0, \tag{8.10}$$

where $i = 1, 2, \ldots, M$, and $\bar{w}_i$ and $\tilde{w}_i$ are the values of w_i on the natural and essential boundaries. This formulation is also called the Zienkiewicz–Taylor formulation in some literature. It worth pointing out that this weak formulation is very generic. Different schemes depend on the actual choice of the test function w and shape functions N_i.

For a given shape function N_i that is a function of space only (not time), we can approximate the solution u_h by

$$u_h(x, t) = \sum_{i=1}^{M} u_i(t) N_i(x) = \sum_{j=1}^{M} u_j N_j, \tag{8.11}$$

where $u_i(t)$ is a function of time t, not space, and u_j is the value of $u(t)$ at node j. It is worth pointing out that it does not matter whether i or j is used in the summation. With this form of approximating u_h, it requires that $N_i = 0$ on the essential boundary $\partial\Omega_E$. Therefore we can choose the form of w so that its values on the essential boundary are zero, that is, $\tilde{w}_i = 0$ on $\partial\Omega_E$. This means that essential boundary conditions are automatically satisfied and no longer need to be considered.

Therefore only the natural boundary conditions need to be considered. Mathematically, there is no specific constraint on the choice of w_i and $\bar{w}_i$. Naturally, a good choice would simplify the weak formulation further. For example, if we choose $\bar{w}_i = -w_i$ on the natural boundary, then we get

$$\int_{\Omega} \mathcal{L}(u_h) w_i d\Omega \approx \int_{\partial\Omega_N} \mathcal{B}(u_h) w_i d\Gamma, \tag{8.12}$$

which involves a volume integral on the left-hand side and a boundary integral on the right-hand side.

8.2. The Galerkin method

Since there are different ways for choosing test functions w_i and shape functions N_i, the most popular method uses $w_i = N_i$, which means that the test function is the same as its shape function. The Galerkin formulation becomes

$$\int_{\Omega} \mathcal{L}(u_h) N_i d\Omega \approx \int_{\partial\Omega_N} \mathcal{B}(u_h) N_i d\Gamma, \quad w_i = N_i. \tag{8.13}$$

The beauty of this formulation is that its discretization usually leads to an algebraic matrix equation.

Other forms of test functions can have different formulations. For example, the so-called collocation method uses the Dirac delta function as its test function, that is,

$$w_i = \delta(\boldsymbol{x} - \boldsymbol{x}_i), \tag{8.14}$$

where

$$\delta(\boldsymbol{x} - \boldsymbol{x}_i) = \begin{cases} 1, & \boldsymbol{x} = \boldsymbol{x}_i, \\ 0, & \boldsymbol{x} \neq \boldsymbol{x}_i. \end{cases} \tag{8.15}$$

This method uses the useful property of the Dirac function for dealing with integrals:

$$\int_\Omega f(\boldsymbol{x})\delta(\boldsymbol{x} - \boldsymbol{x}_i)d\Omega = f(\boldsymbol{x}_i). \tag{8.16}$$

8.3. Shape functions

As we have briefly seen earlier, shape functions can be very useful in approximating solution u_h, which somehow can allow us to decouple the spatial coordinates $\boldsymbol{x}$ (as a vector) from time t. One of the main tasks in the FEM is to use a good set of shape functions so as to provide better approximations.

Let us assume that we can approximate the exact solution u by $u_h(\boldsymbol{x}, t)$ on some nodal points

$$u_h(\boldsymbol{x}, t) = \sum_{i=1}^{M} u_i(t) N_i(\boldsymbol{x}), \tag{8.17}$$

where u_i $(i = 1, 2, \ldots, M)$ are unknown coefficients or the values of u at the discrete nodal points i. The shape functions N_i $(i = 1, 2, \ldots, M)$ are linearly independent functions that vanish on the part of the essential boundary (i.e., $N_i = 0$ on $\partial\Omega_E$). To make it consistent, it also requires that $N_i = 1$ at node i, but $N_i = 0$ at any other nodes. Mathematically speaking, this means that

$$\sum_{i=1}^{M} N_i = 1, \quad N_i(\boldsymbol{x}_j) = \delta_{ij}, \tag{8.18}$$

where δ_{ij} is the Kronecker function

$$\delta_{ij} = \begin{cases} 1 & \text{if } i = j, \\ 0 & \text{if } i \neq j. \end{cases} \tag{8.19}$$

Sometimes, the shape functions $N_i(\boldsymbol{x})$ are also referred to as basis functions or trial functions in some textbooks and FEM literature.

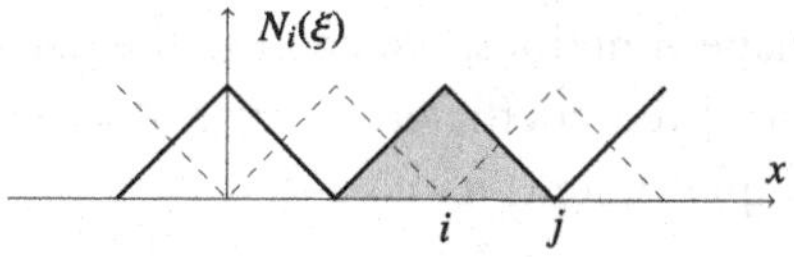

Figure 8.1 Linear shape functions for 1D elements.

8.3.1 Linear shape functions

There are many different ways of designing shape functions that can satisfy condition (8.18). Probably, the simplest shape function for a 1D element with two nodes i and j is the linear shape function

$$N_i = \frac{x_j - x}{L} = \frac{1-\xi}{2}, \quad N_j = \xi = \frac{x - x_i}{L} = \frac{1+\xi}{2}, \tag{8.20}$$

where ξ is the natural coordinate defined by

$$\xi = \frac{x - x_o}{L/2}. \tag{8.21}$$

Here $L = |x_j - x_i|$ is the length of the element, and

$$x_o = \frac{x_i + x_j}{2} \tag{8.22}$$

is the midpoint of the element. Using the natural coordinate, we have $\xi_i = -1$ at $x = x_i$ and $\xi_j = 1$ at $x = x_j$. Linear shape functions are shown in Fig. 8.1.

In general, a linear shape function spans only two adjacent nodes i and j, which can be written in the generic form

$$N(\xi) = a + b\xi, \tag{8.23}$$

where a and b are two coefficients.

8.3.2 Quadratic shape functions

Linear shape functions are first-order functions, which may limit their approximation capabilities. To get better approximations to solutions, higher-order approximations are desirable.

The next order of approximations is using a quadratic shape function, which spans three adjacent nodes i, j, and k with three coefficients. Now let us assume that the displacement u can be approximated by

$$u(\xi) = a + b\xi + c\xi^2, \tag{8.24}$$

where a, b, and c are the coefficients to be determined.

Similarly to the linear shape functions, we can use the natural coordinate and nodal conditions to determine the three coefficients. From $\xi_i = -1$ at $x = x_i$ and $\xi_j = 1$ at $x = x_j$, we use the known displacements u_i, u_j, and u_k:

$$u_i = a + b(-1) + c(-1)^2, \tag{8.25}$$

$$u_j = a, \tag{8.26}$$

$$u_k = a + b(1) + c(1)^2. \tag{8.27}$$

It is straightforward to obtain the solutions

$$\begin{pmatrix} a \\ b \\ c \end{pmatrix} = \begin{pmatrix} u_j \\ \frac{1}{2}(u_i - 2u_j + u_k) \\ \frac{1}{2}(u_k - u_i) \end{pmatrix}. \tag{8.28}$$

Substituting the above results for coefficients into Eq. (8.24) and carrying out some algebraic rearrangements, we have

$$u = \frac{\xi(\xi - 1)}{2} u_i + (1 - \xi^2) u_j + \frac{\xi(\xi + 1)}{2} u_k. \tag{8.29}$$

Since the displacement u over an element should be a linear combination of shape functions and nodal values, we can rewrite the preceding equation as

$$u = N_i u_i + N_j u_j + N_k u_k, \tag{8.30}$$

which corresponds to the quadratic shape functions

$$N_i = \frac{\xi(\xi - 1)}{2}, \quad N_j = (1 - \xi^2), \quad N_k = \frac{\xi(\xi + 1)}{2}. \tag{8.31}$$

Higher-order shape functions can be obtained by using Lagrange polynomials, which can be easily extended to 2D and 3D elements.

8.3.3 2D shape functions

Shape functions for 1D elements are curves in terms of a single independent variable x or a natural coordinate ξ. Shape functions for 2D elements are surfaces in terms of two independent variables x and y or their corresponding natural coordinates ξ and η, respectively. The two natural coordinates ξ and η are shown in Fig. 8.2.

With the above notations, for a bilinear quadrilateral (Q4) element, we can also use bilinear approximations for the displacement field: u (the x-component) and v (the y-component). In general, we can assume that the displacements can be written as

$$u = \alpha_0 + \alpha_1 x + \alpha_2 y + \alpha_3 xy, \tag{8.32}$$

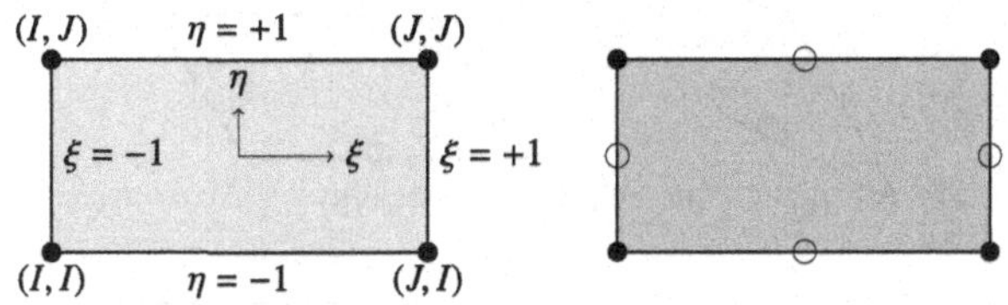

Figure 8.2 Quadrilateral elements: bilinear (left) and quadratic (right).

$$v = \beta_0 + \beta_1 x + \beta_2 y + \beta_3 xy, \tag{8.33}$$

which can also be expressed in terms of shape functions N_i:

$$u = \sum N_i u_i, \quad v = \sum N_j v_j. \tag{8.34}$$

Following the same procedure for deriving the quadratic shape functions earlier, we can obtain (after some lengthy algebra) the following 2D shape functions:

$$N_1 = \frac{(1-\xi)(1-\eta)}{4}, \quad N_2 = \frac{(1+\xi)(1-\eta)}{4}, \tag{8.35}$$

$$N_3 = \frac{(1+\xi)(1+\eta)}{4}, \quad N_4 = \frac{(1-\xi)(1+\eta)}{4}, \tag{8.36}$$

which have a regular structure. In fact, the 2D shape functions can be formulated by multiplying linear shape functions. Similarly, higher-order shape functions for 2D and 3D elements can be systematically derived by using a similar procedure.

For example, for a quadratic quadrilateral (Q8) element shown in Fig. 8.2, eight nodes (four finite element nodes and four midpoints) are needed to form a set of more complicated shape functions.

Finite elements can be of various types, from triangular elements to higher-order hexahedron elements. Several commonly used elements are shown in Fig. 8.3.

8.4. Approximations to derivatives and integrals

Shape functions are useful to approximate displacements. Since the governing equations are PDEs, we can have to approximate derivatives and integrals properly.

8.4.1 Derivatives and shape functions

In the FEM the displacement field $u(\boldsymbol{x}, t)$ is approximated by

$$u = \sum_{i=1}^{M} u_i(t) N(\boldsymbol{x}), \tag{8.37}$$

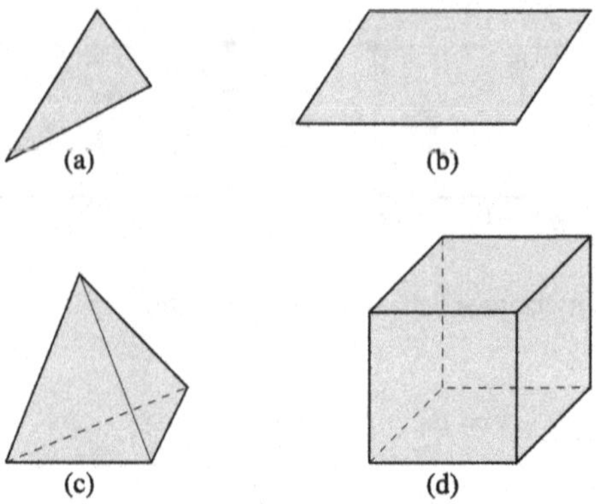

Figure 8.3 Common elements: (a) triangular element; (b) quadrilateral element; (c) tetrahedron; and (d) hexahedron.

where $u_i(t)$ does not depend on space $\boldsymbol{x}$, and the shape function $N_i(\boldsymbol{x})$ does not depend on time. Thus the spatial derivative of u can be obtained by direct differentiation of $N_i(\boldsymbol{x})$ with respect to $\boldsymbol{x}$, that is,

$$\frac{\partial u}{\partial \boldsymbol{x}} \approx \frac{\partial u_h}{\partial \boldsymbol{x}} = \sum_{i=1}^{M} u_i(t) N'(\boldsymbol{x}), \tag{8.38}$$

where $N' = dN/d\boldsymbol{x}$. Similarly, its time derivative can be obtained by

$$\frac{\partial u}{\partial t} \approx \frac{\partial u_h}{\partial t} = \sum_{i=1}^{M} \dot{u}_i N(\boldsymbol{x}), \quad \dot{u} = \frac{\mathrm{d}u}{\mathrm{d}t}. \tag{8.39}$$

From the above we expect that the first derivative of a linear shape function is constant in each interval or element, which may lead to discontinuity in u'. Similarly, the second derivative of a quadratic shape function is constant, which may lead to discontinuity for u'' between elements. Thus, to ensure smoothness of certain derivatives, higher-order shape functions should be used.

8.4.2 Integrals and Gauss quadrature

For integration, there are many different numerical integration formulas and rules, such as the midpoint rule, Simpson's rule, Newton–Cotes formulas, and Gauss quadrature formulas.

In the FEM, it is more common to use Gauss quadrature to save computational costs. Gauss integration has relatively high accuracy, and its formulas are written in terms of the natural coordinates ξ and η.

For a one-dimensional integral of $f(\xi)$, the n-point Gauss–Legendre quadrature is given by

$$I = \int_{-1}^{1} f(\xi)d\xi \approx \sum_{i=1}^{n} w_i f_i(\xi_i), \tag{8.40}$$

which is a weighted sum with weights w_i. Here n is the number of sample points, and $f_i = f(\xi_i)$ is the functional value at ξ_i where ξ_i $(i = 1, 2, \ldots, n)$ are the roots of the nth-order Legendre polynomial $P_n(x)$.

There are several ways for generating Legendre polynomials, and one straightforward way is to use differentiation

$$P_n(x) = \frac{1}{n!2^n}\frac{d^n[(x^2-1)^n]}{dx^n}, \tag{8.41}$$

where $n \geq 1$ is an integer.

The first five Legendre polynomials are

$$P_1(x) = x, \quad P_2(x) = \frac{1}{2}(3x^2 - 1), \tag{8.42}$$

$$P_3(x) = \frac{1}{2}(5x^3 - 3x), \quad P_4(x) = \frac{(35x^4 - 30x^2 + 3)}{8}, \tag{8.43}$$

$$P_5(x) = \frac{(63x^5 - 70x^3 + 15x)}{8}. \tag{8.44}$$

For example, the three roots of the cubic Legendre polynomial $P_3(x)$ are

$$\xi_1 = -\sqrt{3/5}, \quad \xi_2 = 0, \quad \xi_3 = +\sqrt{3/5}. \tag{8.45}$$

The weight coefficients w_i can be obtained by

$$w_i = \frac{2}{(1-\xi_i^2)}\frac{1}{[P_n'(\xi_i)]^2}, \tag{8.46}$$

where the values of $P_n'(\xi_i) = dP/d\xi$ are evaluated at roots ξ_i. For $n = 3$, the three weights are

$$w_1 = \frac{5}{9}, \quad w_2 = \frac{8}{9}, \quad w_3 = \frac{5}{9}. \tag{8.47}$$

For the Gauss quadrature when $n = 3$, it becomes

$$\int_{-1}^{1} f(\xi)d\xi \approx \sum_{i=1}^{3} w_i f_i = \frac{5f_1}{9} + \frac{8f_2}{9} + \frac{5f_3}{9}, \tag{8.48}$$

where the location of the three points are $\xi_1 = -\sqrt{3/5}$, $\xi_2 = 0$, and $\xi_3 = \sqrt{3/5}$. This is shown schematically in Fig. 8.4.

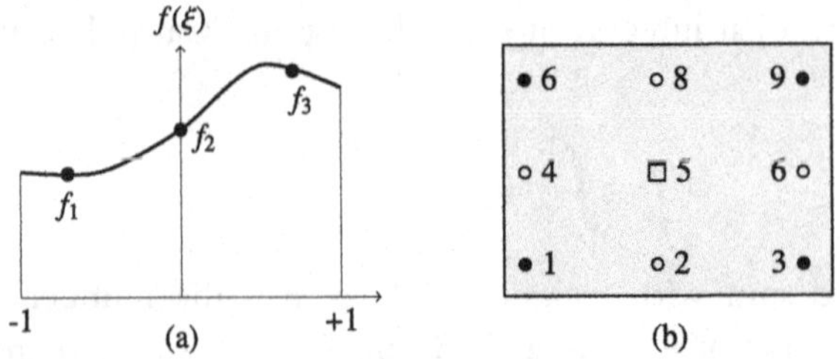

Figure 8.4 Gauss integration: (a) 1D quadrature and (b) 2D quadrature with a nine-point element.

Example 8.1. As an example, let us evaluate

$$J=\int_{-1}^{1} e^{-x^2}\,dx. \tag{8.49}$$

Using the three-point quadrature formula (8.48), we have

$$f_1=e^{-\xi_1^2}=e^{-3/5}\approx 0.5488116, \quad f_2=e^{-0^2}=1, \quad f_3=e^{-3/5}=f_1. \tag{8.50}$$

Thus the integral is estimated by

$$J=\frac{5f_1}{9}+\frac{8f_2}{9}+\frac{5f_3}{9}\approx 1.49867, \tag{8.51}$$

which is within 0.3% from the true value of the integral $J=1.4936482656$.

In this simple example, we only used three points, but the estimate is still far better in accuracy than that obtained by other numerical integration methods such as the rectangular rule. Obviously, higher accuracy can be achieved by using five-point or seven-point formulas.

For a two-dimensional integral of $f(\xi,\eta)$, the general formula for the n^2-point Gauss quadrature of order n is given by

$$I=\int_{-1}^{1}\int_{-1}^{1} f(\xi,\eta)\,d\xi\,d\eta=\sum_{i=1}^{n}\sum_{j=1}^{n} w_i w_j f_{i,j}, \tag{8.52}$$

where $f_{i,j}=f(\xi_i,\eta_j)$. For example, when $n=3$, it needs nine points (shown in Fig. 8.4), which leads to

$$I=\int_{-1}^{1}\int_{-1}^{1} f(\xi,\eta)\approx\sum_{i=1}^{3}\sum_{j=1}^{3} w_i w_j f_{i+3*(j-1)}(\xi_i,\eta_j)$$
$$=[25(f_1+f_3+f_7+f_9)+64f_5+40(f_2+f_4+f_6+f_8)]/81. \tag{8.53}$$

It is worth pointing out that the points used for Gauss quadrature are not on the regular grid points. For the 1D quadrature, three points are used in an element with $|\xi_1 - \xi_2| = |\xi_2 - \xi_3| = \sqrt{3/5}$. For the 2D quadrature in a nine-point quadrilateral element, the location of the points are shown in Fig. 8.4 where point 3 is at $(\xi_3, \eta_1) = (\sqrt{3/5}, -\sqrt{3/5})$, and point 9 is at $(\xi_3, \eta_3) = (\sqrt{3/5}, \sqrt{3/5})$.

Gauss quadrature formulas are based on the roots of Legendre orthogonal polynomials. There are many variants and forms that are based on other polynomials such as Jacobi and Hermite polynomials. The interested readers can refer to more advanced literature on Gauss integration.

8.5. Finite elements for Poisson's equation

In many engineering applications, heat transfer problems often involved irregular geometry with complex shapes. Thus the FEM is widely used to carry out such modeling and simulation.

8.5.1 Weak formulation

As heat transfer problems involve both space and time, we will deal with time-dependent FEM in the next section. Here let us start with the steady-state heat transfer using Poisson's equation

$$\nabla \cdot (k \nabla u) + Q = 0, \tag{8.54}$$

where k is a constant, and the source term Q is a known function of spatial coordinates $\boldsymbol{x} = (x, y, z)$.

The boundary conditions are the essential boundary condition

$$u = \bar{u}, \quad \boldsymbol{x} \in \partial\Omega_E, \tag{8.55}$$

and the natural boundary condition

$$k\frac{\partial u}{\partial n} - q = 0, \quad \boldsymbol{x} \in \partial\Omega_N. \tag{8.56}$$

Following a similar formulation (8.13) in terms of $u \approx u_h$, we can multiply both sides of Eq. (8.54) by a shape function N_i and obtain

$$\int_\Omega [\nabla \cdot (k\nabla u) + Q] N_i d\Omega - \int_{\partial\Omega_N} \left[k\frac{\partial u}{\partial n} - q\right] N_i d\Gamma = 0, \tag{8.57}$$

where we have used the boundary conditions.

Using integration by parts and Green's theorem, we have

$$\int_{\Omega}(\nabla u_h \cdot k \cdot \nabla N_i)d\Omega - \int_{\Omega} QN_i d\Omega - \int_{\partial\Omega_N} qN_i d\Gamma = 0. \tag{8.58}$$

This weak formulation is still very general.

As usual in the FEM, u_h is now approximated by

$$u_h = \sum_{j=1}^{M} u_j N_j(\boldsymbol{x}). \tag{8.59}$$

Substituting it into (8.58), we have

$$\sum_{j=1}^{M} u_j \left[\int_{\Omega}(k\nabla N_i \cdot \nabla N_j)d\Omega\right] - \int_{\Omega} QN_i d\Omega - \int_{\partial\Omega_N} qN_i d\Gamma = 0. \tag{8.60}$$

Since all the integrals are functions of only $\boldsymbol{x}$ via shape functions, we can in principle calculate all these integrals numerically. Thus we can rewrite the preceding equation in a compact matrix form

$$\sum_{j=1}^{M} K_{ij} U_j = f_i, \tag{8.61}$$

or

$$\boldsymbol{KU} = \boldsymbol{f}, \tag{8.62}$$

where $\mathbf{K} = [K_{ij}]$ is the stiffness matrix with $i, j = 1, 2, \ldots, M$. The two vectors are

$$\boldsymbol{U} = \begin{pmatrix} u_1 \\ u_2 \\ \vdots \\ u_M \end{pmatrix}, \quad \boldsymbol{f} = \begin{pmatrix} f_1 \\ f_2 \\ \vdots \\ f_M \end{pmatrix}. \tag{8.63}$$

More specifically, the matrix $\boldsymbol{K}$ and vector $\boldsymbol{f}$ can be calculated by

$$K_{ij} = \int_{\Omega} k\nabla N_i \nabla N_j d\Omega \tag{8.64}$$

and

$$f_i = \int_{\Omega} QN_i d\Omega + \int_{\partial\Omega_N} qN_i d\Gamma. \tag{8.65}$$

With a proper selection of elements and shape functions, we can solve this problem numerically in terms of a linear system with a sparse matrix.

8.5.2 A worked example

Using the formulation earlier for the heat transfer problem, let us solve the 1D steady-steady heat conduction problem

$$ku''(x) + Q(x) = 0 \tag{8.66}$$

with two-point boundary conditions

$$u(0) = p, \quad u'(1) = q. \tag{8.67}$$

For simplicity, we use only four elements with five nodes. This essentially splits the domain interval [0, 1] into four elements. In practice, it is not required that the elements or lengths of intervals are the same.

For each element with i and j nodes, we use the shape functions

$$N_i = 1 - \xi, \quad N_j = \xi, \tag{8.68}$$

where

$$\xi = \frac{x}{L}, \tag{8.69}$$

and L is the size or length of element n. For each element $n = 1, 2, 3, 4$, we have

$$K_{ij}^{(n)} = \left[\int_0^L kN_i'N_j'dx\right] = \frac{k}{h_n}\begin{pmatrix} 1 & -1 \\ -1 & 1 \end{pmatrix} \tag{8.70}$$

and

$$f_i^{(n)} = \frac{Qh_n}{2}\begin{pmatrix} 1 \\ 1 \end{pmatrix}. \tag{8.71}$$

Using the notations $h_i = x_{i+1} - x_i$ for $i = 1, 2, 3, 4$, $a = k/h_1$, $b = k/h_2$, $c = k/h_3$, and $d = k/h_4$, we can rewrite the stiffness matrices for the first two elements as

$$K^{(1)} = \begin{pmatrix} a & -a & 0 & 0 & 0 \\ -a & a & 0 & 0 & 0 \\ 0 & 0 & 0 & 0 & 0 \\ 0 & 0 & 0 & 0 & 0 \\ 0 & 0 & 0 & 0 & 0 \end{pmatrix}, \quad f^{(1)} = \frac{Q}{2}\begin{pmatrix} h_1 \\ h_1 \\ 0 \\ 0 \\ 0 \end{pmatrix},$$

and

$$K^{(2)} = \begin{pmatrix} 0 & 0 & 0 & 0 & 0 \\ 0 & b & -b & 0 & 0 \\ 0 & -b & b & 0 & 0 \\ 0 & 0 & 0 & 0 & 0 \\ 0 & 0 & 0 & 0 & 0 \end{pmatrix}, \quad f^{(2)} = \frac{Q}{2}\begin{pmatrix} 0 \\ h_2 \\ h_2 \\ 0 \\ 0 \end{pmatrix}.$$

Following exactly the same process, the global stiffness matrix can be assembled by adding all the stiffness matrices (of each element) together. Now we have

$$\boldsymbol{K} = \begin{pmatrix} a & -a & 0 & 0 & 0 \\ -a & a+b & -b & 0 & 0 \\ 0 & -b & b+c & -c & 0 \\ 0 & 0 & -c & c+d & -d \\ 0 & 0 & 0 & -d & d \end{pmatrix} \tag{8.72}$$

and

$$\mathbf{U} = \begin{pmatrix} u_1 \\ u_2 \\ u_3 \\ u_4 \\ u_5 \end{pmatrix}, \quad \boldsymbol{f} = \begin{pmatrix} Qh_1/2 \\ Q(h_1+h_2)/2 \\ Q(h_2+h_3)/2 \\ Q(h_3+h_4)/2 \\ Qh_4/2+q \end{pmatrix}, \tag{8.73}$$

where we have applied the natural boundary condition $u'(1) = q$ to the last element on the right, which changes the last entry of $\boldsymbol{f}$.

To apply the essential boundary condition $u_1(0) = p$ at $x = 0$ on the first element, we have to modify the first row of $\boldsymbol{K}$. Conveniently, we can replace the first row by $K_{1j} = (1\,0\,0\,0\,0)$ and $f_1 = p$. Therefore the finite element formulation with four elements now becomes

$$\boldsymbol{K} = \begin{pmatrix} 1 & 0 & 0 & 0 & 0 \\ -a & a+b & -b & 0 & 0 \\ 0 & -b & b+c & -c & 0 \\ 0 & 0 & -c & c+d & -d \\ 0 & 0 & 0 & -d & d \end{pmatrix}, \tag{8.74}$$

and

$$\boldsymbol{f} = \begin{pmatrix} p \\ Q(h_1+h_2)/2 \\ Q(h_2+h_3)/2 \\ Q(h_3+h_4)/2 \\ Qh_4/2+q \end{pmatrix}. \tag{8.75}$$

For the case of $k = 1$, $Q = -2$, $h_1 = h_2 = h_3 = h_4 = 0.25$, $p = 1$, and $q = -0.5$, we have

$$\boldsymbol{K} = \begin{pmatrix} 1 & 0 & 0 & 0 & 0 \\ -4 & 8 & -4 & 0 & 0 \\ 0 & -4 & 8 & -4 & 0 \\ 0 & 0 & -4 & 8 & -4 \\ 0 & 0 & 0 & -4 & 4 \end{pmatrix}, \quad \boldsymbol{f} = \begin{pmatrix} 1 \\ -0.5 \\ -0.5 \\ -0.5 \\ -0.75 \end{pmatrix}. \tag{8.76}$$

A simple inverse gives the solution

$$\boldsymbol{U} = \boldsymbol{K}^{-1}\boldsymbol{f} = \begin{pmatrix} 1.00 & 0.4375 & 0.0000 & -0.3125 & -0.5000 \end{pmatrix}^T. \tag{8.77}$$

The true solution can be obtained by integrating twice with respect to x and using the boundary conditions, which gives

$$u(x) = -\frac{Q}{2k}x^2 + \left(\frac{Q}{k} + q\right)x + p. \tag{8.78}$$

For $p = 1$, $q = -1/2$, $k = 1$, and $Q = -2$, we have

$$u(x) = x^2 - 2.5x + 1. \tag{8.79}$$

For the simple five nodes, the true values are

$$\boldsymbol{u}_{\text{true}} = \begin{pmatrix} 1 & 0.4375 & 0 & -0.3125 & -0.5 \end{pmatrix}^T. \tag{8.80}$$

The true and estimated values from FEM are exactly the same. It is worth pointing out that this is a rare case that two solutions are exactly the same. In general, higher-order shape functions and fine mesh or elements should be used so as to obtain more accurate results.

8.6. Finite elements for time-dependent problems

The beauty of the FEM is that a well-posed PDE problem is converted into a linear algebra problem in terms of a matrix equation. This is true for steady-state problems or nontransient problems. For time-dependent problems, time-stepping schemes are needed because the FEM will lead to an ODE in terms of matrices. In the rest of the chapter, we will discuss transient problems and time-stepping schemes.

8.6.1 General weak formulation

Different formulations exist for handling time-dependent problems, depending on the type of problem. For example, for the transient heat transfer problems, one straightforward way is to replace the source term Q in (8.54) with a time-dependent term $Q(t)$. For example, the Zienkiewicz–Taylor formulation uses

$$\tilde{Q} = Q - a\frac{du}{dt} - b\frac{d^2u}{dt^2} = Q - a\dot{u} - b\ddot{u} \tag{8.81}$$

as the new source term with two constants a and b.

With this new source, the heat transfer problem (8.54) becomes a time-dependent problem

$$\nabla \cdot (k\nabla u) + (Q - a\dot{u} - b\ddot{u}) = 0. \tag{8.82}$$

For boundary conditions, we can use the similar essential and natural boundary conditions. However, since now we are dealing with time-dependent problems, initial conditions are needed.

The initial condition and boundary conditions become

$$u(\boldsymbol{x}, 0) = \phi(\boldsymbol{x}), \quad \text{initial condition as a known function,} \tag{8.83}$$

$$u(\boldsymbol{x}, t) = \bar{u}, \quad \boldsymbol{x} \in \partial\Omega_E, \quad \text{essential boundary condition,} \tag{8.84}$$

and

$$k\frac{\partial u}{\partial n} - q = 0, \quad \boldsymbol{x} \in \partial\Omega_N, \quad \text{natural boundary condition.} \tag{8.85}$$

Using the approximation

$$u_h = \sum_{j=1}^{M} u_j(t) N_j(\boldsymbol{x}) \tag{8.86}$$

and applying integration by parts, we obtain

$$\sum_{j=1}^{M} \left[\int_\Omega (k\nabla N_i \nabla N_j) d\Omega \right]$$

$$+ \sum_{j=1}^{M} \int_\Omega \left[(N_i a N_j)\dot{u}_j + (N_i b N_j)\ddot{u}_j \right] d\Omega - \int_\Omega N_i Q d\Omega - \int_{\partial\Omega_N} N_i q d\Gamma = 0. \tag{8.87}$$

Using compact matrix notations

$$K_{ij} = \int_\Omega \left[(k\nabla N_i \nabla N_j) \right] d\Omega, \quad f_i = \int_\Omega N_i Q d\Omega + \int_{\partial\Omega_N} N_i q d\Gamma, \tag{8.88}$$

and

$$C_{ij} = \int_\Omega N_i \alpha N_j d\Omega, \quad M_{ij} = \int_\Omega N_i \beta N_j d\Omega, \tag{8.89}$$

we can rewrite (8.87) compactly as

$$M\ddot{u} + C\dot{u} + Ku = f. \tag{8.90}$$

Comparing with the matrix equation for steady-state problems, now we have two extra terms with mass matrix M and damping matrix C. This is an ODE for matrices.

It is worth pointing out that all three matrices K, M, and C are symmetric. However, before the boundary conditions are imposed, the stiffness matrix is usually singular, which may imply many solutions. With proper boundary and initial conditions, the problem can become well posed with unique solutions.

Since the final form (8.90) is a matrix ODE, we can use any efficient numerical scheme for solving ODEs to solve this type of problem.

8.6.2 Simplified case with time-stepping

As an example, let us try to use time-stepping to solve (8.90). In the case $C = 0$, it corresponds to the wave equation, and its matrix formulation becomes

$$M\ddot{u} + Ku = f, \tag{8.91}$$

which is a second-order matrix ODE.

One way is using the central difference scheme for time-stepping

$$\ddot{u} = \frac{u^{n+1} - 2u^n + u^{n-1}}{(\Delta t)^2}, \tag{8.92}$$

where n is for time step. With this time-stepping scheme, Eq. (8.91) becomes

$$u^{n+1} = (\Delta t)^2 M^{-1} f + [2I - (\Delta t)^2 M^{-1} K]u^n - u^{n-1}, \tag{8.93}$$

where $\mathbf{I}$ is the identity matrix. Once the initial condition u^0 is given, solutions can be obtained by iteration.

The literature on FEMs and their variants is vast, and new methods are also become widely used, such as the extended finite element method and element-free methods. The interested readers can refer to more specialized literature.

8.7. Notes on software

A vast spectrum of software packages are available to carry out extensive finite element analysis and simulation with diverse capabilities. A comprehensive list can be found on the web, such as the wikipedia list of finite element software packages at https://en.wikipedia.org/wiki/List_of_finite_element_software_packages.

Examples of powerful FEM packages are *Abaqus/CAE*, *ANSYS*, *COMSOL Multiphysics*, *Nastran*, *OpenFORAM*, *DIANA FEA*, and others, such as *Matlab*® PDE toolbox.

CHAPTER NINE

Modeling and simulation by Simulink®

For engineering systems governed by ODEs and PDEs, suitable numerical methods can be used to carry out simulation. However, in the special case where the systems under consideration have linear and time-invariant properties, such systems are called linear time-invariant (LTI) systems. Special techniques using transfer functions are powerful for solving LTI systems in signal processing and control systems. This chapter introduces the fundamentals of Laplace transforms, transfer functions, and block diagrams using Simulink®.

9.1. System models

Most LTI systems in engineering (either mechanical or electrical) can be modeled by ODEs or a set of ODEs.

- First-order systems: Mathematical models of first-order systems are usually written as the first-order ODEs. The main characteristics of such systems are either exponential decay or exponential increase without any oscillations. For example, the charge and discharge of an ideal capacitor and the response of a thermometer are all first-order responses.
- Second-order systems: The mathematical models of second-order systems require a second-order ODE or a set of two first-order ODEs. Such systems can have oscillations; however, there can be no oscillations at all in certain special cases, and thus a system may behave like a first-order one. For example, a car suspension system and a fire-door mechanism are second-order systems.
- Higher-order systems: Higher systems can have complex behavior because they require higher-order ODEs or a set of more than two ODEs. They tend to be highly nonlinear. For example, the Lorenz model for the simplified weather system has three coupled nonlinear first-order ODEs, which can lead to complex chaotic behavior. Higher-order nonlinear systems are not part of this chapter.

9.2. Laplace transforms

The simulation models and ODEs we have discussed so far in this book are mainly in the time domain (t) or in the original independent variable (x) domain; though, mathematically speaking, either t or x can be considered as exactly the same thing. However, sometimes, it is more convenient to use another domain that has been trans-

Engineering Simulation and its Applications
https://doi.org/10.1016/B978-0-44-314084-6.00016-4

formed from time t. This is true in signal processing, image processing, and the linear time-invariant (LTI) systems.

The Laplace transform is such a useful technique that transforms a function/signal $f(t)$ in the time domain t into a corresponding function $F(s)$ in the s-domain. Mathematically, this transformation is defined by then integral

$$F(s) \equiv \mathcal{L}[f(t)] = \int_0^{\infty} e^{-st} f(t) dt, \quad s > 0. \tag{9.1}$$

Strictly speaking, s should be a complex number, though we implicitly assume that its real part should be nonnegative.

Example 9.1. The Laplace transform of the Heaviside function

$$H(t) = u(t) = \begin{cases} 1 & \text{if } t \geq 0, \\ 0 & \text{if } t < 0, \end{cases} \tag{9.2}$$

can be calculated directly:

$$\begin{aligned} F(s) &= \mathcal{L}[u(t)] = \int_0^{\infty} u(t) e^{-st} dt = \int_0^{\infty} e^{-st} dt \\ &= \left[-\frac{1}{s} e^{-st} \right]_0^{\infty} = 0 - \left(-\frac{1}{s} \right) = \frac{1}{s}. \end{aligned} \tag{9.3}$$

For $f(t) = e^{at}$ with $a \in \mathbb{R}$, we have

$$\begin{aligned} F(s) &= \int_0^{\infty} e^{-st} e^{at} dt = \int_0^{\infty} e^{-(s-a)t} dt \\ &= \left[-\frac{1}{s-a} e^{-(s-a)t} \right]_0^{\infty} = \frac{1}{s-a} \quad (s > a). \end{aligned} \tag{9.4}$$

For many basic functions, we can find their Laplace transforms directly. For example, for $f(t) = \sin(\omega t)$, we have

$$\begin{aligned} F(s) &= \int_0^{\infty} e^{-st} \sin(\omega t) dt \\ &= \left[\frac{1}{s^2 + \omega^2} e^{-st} (-s \sin \omega t - \omega \cos \omega t) \right]_0^{\infty} \\ &= 0 - \left[\frac{1}{s^2 + \omega^2} (-0 - \omega) \right] = \frac{\omega}{s^2 + \omega^2}. \end{aligned} \tag{9.5}$$

9.2.1 Laplace transform properties

We now state some useful properties of Laplace transforms without rigorous proofs.

- Integration becomes division
  If $F(s) = \mathcal{L}[f(t)]$, we have

$$\mathcal{L}\left[\int_0^t f(t)dt\right] \Longrightarrow \frac{F(s)}{s}. \tag{9.6}$$

  That is, the integration in the t-domain becomes division in the s-domain, which is also equivalent to the multiplication by $1/s$. That is why the integrator in Simulink is denoted by

$$\int dt \quad \Longrightarrow \quad \frac{1}{s}. \tag{9.7}$$

- Differentiation becomes multiplication

$$\mathcal{L}[f'(t)] = sF(s) - f(0), \tag{9.8}$$

  where $f(0)$ is the initial condition/value at $t = 0$. Similarly,

$$\mathcal{L}[f''(t)] = s^2F(s) - sf(0) - f'(0). \tag{9.9}$$

  That is, the nth-order derivative in the t-domain becomes the multiplication by s^n, which is an nth-order polynomial.
- Shift properties
  The shift in time leads to the multiplication by an exponential factor:

$$\mathcal{L}[f(t-\tau)H(t-\tau)] = e^{-s\tau}F(s), \quad \tau > 0. \tag{9.10}$$

  The multiplication by an exponential factor leads to a shift in s:

$$\mathcal{L}[e^{-at}f(t)] = F(s+a). \tag{9.11}$$

- Convolution integral
  For $\mathcal{L}[f(t)] = F(s)$ and $\mathcal{L}[g(t)] = G(s)$, we have

$$\mathcal{L}\left[\int_0^t f(\tau)g(t-\tau)d\tau\right] = F(s)G(s), \tag{9.12}$$

  which means that the convolution integral in the t-domain becomes the product of the corresponding Laplace transforms in the s-domain.

By using the above properties, together with the direct integration of the basic functions, we can easily obtain the Laplace transforms of various complex functions. The commonly used Laplace transforms, called Laplace pairs, are listed in Table 9.1.

There are some detailed tables of Laplace transform pairs in many mathematical handbooks. In addition, many software packages can do Laplace transforms, such as

Table 9.1 Some common Laplace transform pairs.

Function	$f(t)$	Laplace $F(s)$	Function	$f(t)$	$F(s)$
Step	$H(t)$	$\frac{1}{s}$	Power	t^n	$\frac{n!}{s^{n+1}}$
Ramp	t	$\frac{1}{s^2}$	Exp. decay	e^{-at} $(a > 0)$	$\frac{1}{s+a}$
Exp.	e^{at}	$\frac{1}{s-a}$	Freq. shift	te^{-at}	$\frac{1}{(s+a)^2}$
Sine	$\sin(\omega t)$	$\frac{\omega}{s^2+\omega^2}$	Cosine	$\cos(\omega t)$	$\frac{s}{s^2+\omega^2}$
	$e^{-at}\sin(\omega t)$	$\frac{\omega}{(s+a)^2+\omega^2}$		$e^{-at}\cos(\omega t)$	$\frac{s+a}{(s+a)^2+\omega^2}$
...	...	...	...	...	...

Mathematica, Maple, Maxima, and Matlab®. For example, Matlab can do Laplace transforms using its Symbolic Maths Toolbox. In Matlab, we can use

```
»syms t s
»laplace(sin(t),t,s)
```

to find the Laplace transform of sin(t).

9.2.2 Solving ODEs by Laplace transforms

From the discussion of the Laplace transforms and commonly used Laplace pairs, we have the following observations:

- A complicated form of signal $f(t)$ in the t-domain is usually transformed to a rational fraction of polynomials.
- Integration of $f(t)$ becomes the division of $F(s)$ by s.
- Differentiation of $f(t)$ becomes the multiplication of $F(s)$ by s (plus a term of the initial value).

This means that a differential equation in terms of t becomes an algebraic equation in terms of s. Thus this provides a useful technique to solve ODEs by using Laplace transform pairs and their properties.

Let us use a first-order ODE to show how this method works.

Example 9.2. Using $V(s) = \mathcal{L}[v(t)]$, the differential equation

$$\tau v'(t) + v(t) = v_0, \quad v(0) = 0,$$

can be transformed into

$$\tau[sV(s) - v(0)] + V(s) = \frac{v_0}{s},$$

where we have used the Laplace pair "$1 \Longrightarrow 1/s$" and the differentiation property. The solution $V(s)$ can be obtained by simple algebra:

$$V(s) = \frac{v_0/s}{\tau s + 1} = \frac{v_0}{s(\tau s + 1)}$$
$$= v_0 \left[\frac{1}{s} - \frac{\tau}{\tau s + 1} \right] = v_0 \left[\frac{1}{s} - \frac{1}{s + 1/\tau} \right]. \tag{9.13}$$

This gives an expression with input v_0 and output $V(s)$:

$$H(s) = \frac{V(s)}{v_0} = \frac{1}{s(\tau s + 1)}.$$

The solution $v(t)$ can be obtained by inversely transforming $V(s)$ back to $v(t)$ in the time domain. We first rewrite $H(s)$ as the partial fraction

$$H(s) = \frac{1}{s(\tau s + 1)} = \frac{1}{s} - \frac{1}{s + 1/\tau}.$$

Using the Laplace pairs

$$\frac{1}{s} \to 1, \quad \frac{1}{(s + a)} \to e^{-at}, \quad a = 1/\tau,$$

and transforming from the s-domain back to the t-domain, we have

$$v(t) = \mathcal{L}^{-1} \left\{ v_0 \left[\frac{1}{s} - \frac{1}{s + 1/\tau} \right] \right\} = v_0 \left[1 - e^{-t/\tau} \right].$$

This is the solution in the time domain.

9.2.3 Transfer function

Transfer functions are commonly used for describing system behavior, especially for LTI systems. There are different ways of representing the input and output/response of a system. For a given signal, we can represent it as a function $f(t)$ in the time domain. Equally, we can represent the same signal in the s-domain by Laplace transforming it to a different function form $F(s)$, as shown in Fig. 9.1.

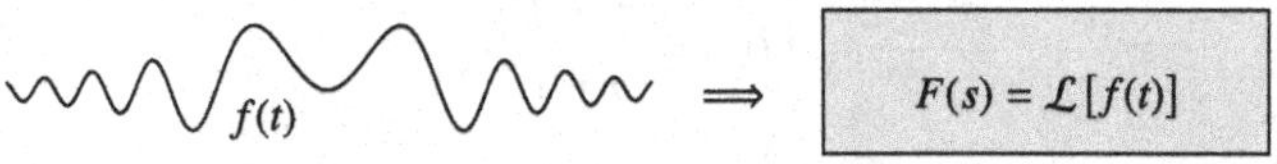

Figure 9.1 The transformation of a signal in the time domain (left) to the s-domain (right).

For different ways of representing system inputs and outputs, the calculations of the output will also be different. In the t-domain representations, the output $g(t)$ for a corresponding input $f(t)$ for a given system requires the convolution integral in the

t-domain

$$g(t) = \int_{-\infty}^{\infty} f(\tau)h(t-\tau)d\tau, \tag{9.14}$$

where function h is a model for the system under consideration.

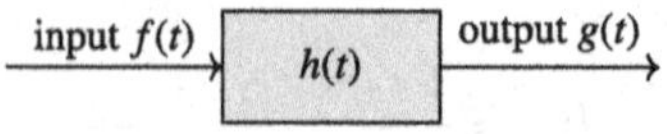

Figure 9.2 The representation of a system model in the time (t) domain.

If both $f(t)$ and $g(t)$ are transformed into the Laplace domain, then we have

$$F(s) = \mathcal{L}[f(t)] = \int_0^{\infty} f(t)e^{-st}dt, \quad G(s) = \mathcal{L}[g(t)] = \int_0^{\infty} g(t)e^{-st}dt. \tag{9.15}$$

The same system in the time domain, shown in Fig. 9.2, can be represented in the s-domain, shown in Fig. 9.3.

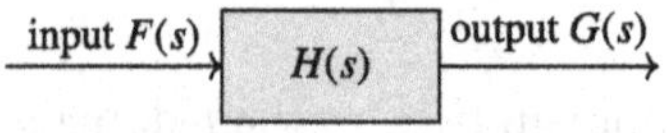

Figure 9.3 The representation of a system model in the s-domain.

Since $f(t) = 0$ and $g(t) = 0$ for $t < 0$, the convolution integral is transformed into the multiplication in the s-domain as

$$\mathcal{L}[g(t)] = \mathcal{L}\left[\int_0^t f(\tau)g(t-\tau)d\tau\right] = \mathcal{L}[f(t)]\mathcal{L}[h(t)], \tag{9.16}$$

that is,

$$G(s) = F(s)H(s), \tag{9.17}$$

or

$$H(s) = \frac{G(s)}{F(s)}, \tag{9.18}$$

where $H(s)$ is the transfer function.

The transfer function $H(s)$ describes the main behavior of a linear system. Interestingly, $H(s)$ can typically be represented as a ratio of two polynomials of s.

If the input $f(t)$ to a system is an impulse $\delta(t)$ (the Dirac δ function), then its Laplace transform is $F(s) = \mathcal{L}[\delta(t)] = 1$. We have $H(s) = G(s) \times 1$. Thus the transfer function is the system response/output for an impulse input.

For a given linear ODE, it is usually straightforward to write out its transfer function. For example, for a 4th-order LTI system with an input $x(t)$ and an output $y(t)$, governed by an ODE

$$a_4 \ddddot{y} + a_3 \dddot{y} + a_2 \ddot{y} + a_1 \dot{y} + a_0 y = b_2 \ddot{x} + b_1 \dot{x} + b_0 x,$$

we can convert it into a transfer function $H(s)$ as

$$H(s) = \frac{Y(s)}{X(s)} = \frac{b_2 s^2 + b_1 s + b_0}{a_4 s^4 + a_3 s^3 + a_2 s^2 + a_1 s + a_0}.$$

Here we have implicitly assumed that all initial conditions and initial derivatives are zeros, that is, $y(0) = \dot{y}(0) = \ddot{y}(0) = \dddot{y}(0) = 0$ and $x(0) = \dot{x}(0) = 0$.

Sometimes, from the simulation point of view, it may be easier to treat the whole right-hand side of the ODE as the input signal.

Example 9.3. For the ODE with the step input $u(t)$

$$\ddot{y} + 3\dot{y} + 2y = 5u(t), \quad u(t) = \begin{cases} 1 & \text{if } t \geq 0, \\ 0 & \text{if } t < 0, \end{cases} \tag{9.19}$$

its transfer function can be written as

$$H(s) = \frac{5}{s^2 + 3s + 2} \tag{9.20}$$

with input $u(t)$. The transfer function can also be written as

$$H(s) = \frac{1}{s^2 + 3s + 2} \tag{9.21}$$

with input $5u(t)$.

For the ODE

$$3\ddot{y} + 7\dot{y} + y = 2\sin(t), \tag{9.22}$$

its transfer function is

$$H(s) = \frac{1}{3s^2 + 7s + 1} \tag{9.23}$$

with input $f(t) = 2\sin(t)$.

Once the transfer function for a system is known, it is relatively straightforward to do some analysis and numerical simulation. Some software packages such as Matlab's Simulink use s-domain representations to do simulation. Simulink is a graphical block-based modeling system, which uses mainly the s-domain for modeling and simulation of LTI systems.

Some features of Simulink:

- Transfer functions are part of the built-in models;
- Inputs are in the time domain;
- Simulation outputs are converted directly into responses in the time domain.

It is worth pointing out that there are ways for dealing with cases where the initial conditions are not zero, including modifying the transfer function and more commonly using state-space equations. The state-space approach can deal with multiple inputs and outputs. In addition, if some of the coefficients may be nonconstant, then a varying transfer function can be used to simulate such systems. The interested readers can refer to more advanced literature on control systems, signal processing, and Simulink documents.

9.3. Simulink model

Since Simulink uses the *s*-domain transfer functions as its basic building blocks, we usually first have to convert the model based on differential equations into the model in terms of transfer functions. The main steps for Simulink simulation are as follows:

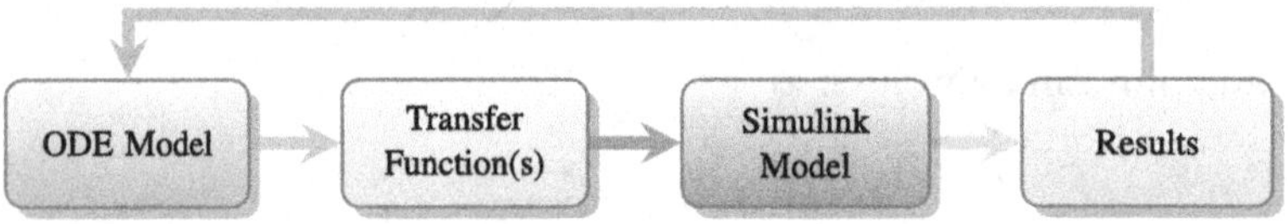

To launch the `Simulink` tool, either type in the Matlab command window

`»simulink` [enter]

or click the icon. Once it is open, click `File` and open a new model (or use `Ctr+N`).

Then click the `Model Library` icon to go to different modules. Find the function as a block diagram you want to use and then drag and drop it into the workspace. Once in the model mode, click on the icon to launch an interactive interface to set or change parameters.

For a simple ODE model

$$\tau v'(t) + v(t) = v_0 u(t), \tag{9.24}$$

where $u(t)$ is the Heaviside unit step function, its transfer function can be written as

$$H(s) = \frac{1}{\tau s + 1} \tag{9.25}$$

with step input $v_0 u(t)$. This input can be simulated by using either a unit step with a gain or a step function with the final value of v_0. The corresponding Simulink model

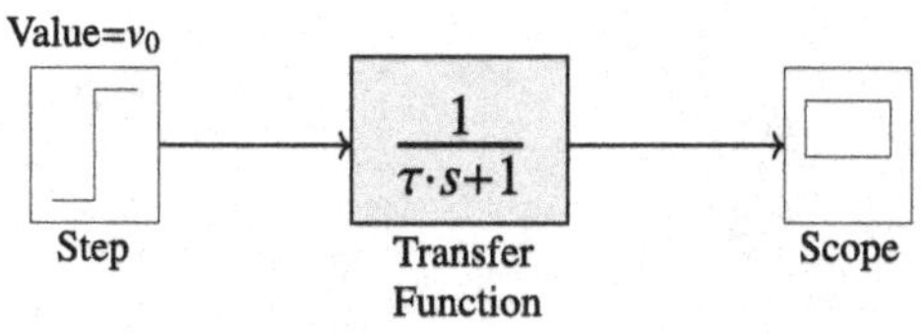

Figure 9.4 The layout of a simple Simulink model.

for this simple ODE model should look like the layout shown in Fig. 9.4, where the Step is the input, and the Scope is the display for the simulation output. The Step input essentially simulates input as the Heaviside step function. The three block diagrams can be edited interactively.

Though the Simulink transfer functions are in the s-domain, the outputs from the simulation will be converted automatically into the time domain.

9.4. Notes on software

There are a few software packages that can simulate LTI systems using the s-domain representations. Obviously, Matlab's *Simulink* is among the most widely used with powerful functionalities. In addition, *Simscape* and its add-on toolboxes are also closely related to *Simulink*, which can simulate physical systems such as mechanical rigid-body systems, electrical systems, and fluid–gas systems.

There are other good software packages. For example, the free *XCOS* package of *Scilab* also has some similar functionalities, which can be used to construct a proper simulation model. For ODEs and Laplace transforms, Matlab has a symbolic mathematics toolbox. In addition, Mathematica, Maple, Maxima, Geogebra, Python's SymPy, and many others symbolic mathematics packages are also very useful.

CHAPTER TEN

Optimization in engineering applications

Many problems in engineering and industry can be formulated as optimization problems with the objectives to maximize performance, energy efficiency and sustainability, or to minimize costs, environmental impact, and wastage. This chapter introduces the fundamentals of optimization and some optimization techniques.

10.1. Introduction to optimization

The simplest optimization task is probably the function optimization of $f(x) = x^2$ in the domain of $x \in \mathbb{R}$. Since x^2 is always nonnegative in the whole domain of real numbers, its minimum occurs at $x = 0$ with $f_{\min} = 0$. This simple optimization problem is unconstrained because there is no constraint imposed on the variable x. The objective is the function itself. From the calculus point of view, the minimum or maximum for a smooth function $f(x)$ will have the property that

$$f'(x) = \frac{\mathrm{d}f}{\mathrm{d}x} = 0. \tag{10.1}$$

This stationary condition or critical condition can help to find the location of the optimality. In this case, $f'(x) = 2x = 0$, which gives $x = 0$ as the location or solution to this optimization problem. However, the simple condition $f'(x) = 0$ may not give a simple answer if the function is highly nonlinear. For example, it is not straightforward to find the optima of $f(x) = \sin(x)/x$ because

$$f'(x) = \left[\frac{\sin(x)}{x}\right]' = \frac{(x\cos x - \sin x)}{x^2} = 0 \tag{10.2}$$

has infinitely many solutions. In fact, the global optimality of $\sin(x)/x$ occurs at $x = 0$ with $f_{\max} = 1$, which is not easily obtained by $f'(x) = 0$. This highlights one of the challenges of nonlinear optimization.

Whatever an engineering optimization problem is, it is usually possible to formulate it in a generic form in an n-dimensional space:

$$\text{Maximize/Minimize } f(\mathbf{x}), \quad \mathbf{x} = (x_1, x_2, \ldots, x_n)^T \in \mathbb{R}^n, \tag{10.3}$$

subject to M equalities

$$\phi_j(\mathbf{x}) = 0 \quad (j = 1, 2, \ldots, M) \tag{10.4}$$

Engineering Simulation and its Applications
https://doi.org/10.1016/B978-0-44-314084-6.00017-6

and N inequalities

$$\psi_k(\boldsymbol{x}) \leq 0 \ (k = 1, \ldots, N), \tag{10.5}$$

where $f(\boldsymbol{x})$, $\phi_i(\boldsymbol{x})$, and $\psi_j(\boldsymbol{x})$ are scalar functions of the design vector $\boldsymbol{x}$. Here the components x_i of $\boldsymbol{x} = (x_1, \ldots, x_n)^T$ are called design or decision variables, which can be continuous, discrete, or a mixture of the two types.

The vector $\boldsymbol{x}$ is often called the decision vector, which varies in an n-dimensional space $\mathbb{R}^n$. It is worth pointing out that we use a column vector here for $\boldsymbol{x}$ (thus with a transpose T when displayed in a horizontal row). We can also use a row vector $\boldsymbol{x} = (x_1, \ldots, x_n)$, and the results will be the same. Different textbooks may use slightly different formulations; once we are aware of such minor variations, it causes no difficulty or confusion.

The function $f(\boldsymbol{x})$ is often referred to as the objective function or cost function. The space spanned by all the possible values of objective functions is called the objective space or landscape space (or simply the landscape). The space spanned by all the decision variables is an n-dimensional search space, also called the decision space, parameter space, or solution space. There are $M + N$ constraints in total. The optimization problem formulated here is a nonlinear constrained problem.

All the functions $f(\boldsymbol{x})$, $\phi_i(\boldsymbol{x})$, and $\psi_j(\boldsymbol{x})$ can be linear or nonlinear. In the particular case that all these functions are linear, it becomes a linear programming (LP) problem, and we will deal with this case in a later chapter in this book.

Whatever the objective is, we have to evaluate it many times. In most cases the evaluations of the objective functions consume a substantial amount of computational power (which costs money) and design time. Any efficient algorithms that can reduce the number of objective evaluations will save both time and money.

10.2. Feasibility and optimality

For an optimization problem with an objective function and multiple constraints, a point $\boldsymbol{x}$ or a solution that satisfies all the constraints is called a feasible point and thus is a feasible solution to the optimization problem. The set of all feasible points forms the feasible domain or region.

An optimization problem without any objective function (but with many constraints) is called a feasibility problem.

A solution or a point $\boldsymbol{x}_*$ is called a local maximum of $f(\boldsymbol{x})$ if $f(\boldsymbol{x}_*) \geq f(\boldsymbol{x})$ for $\boldsymbol{x} \neq \boldsymbol{x}_*$ in a neighborhood $N(\boldsymbol{x}_*, \delta)$, where $\delta > 0$. If this maximum holds in the whole feasible domain, then it becomes the global maximum. Similarly, a solution or a point $\boldsymbol{x}_*$ is called a local minimum if $f(\boldsymbol{x}_*) \leq f(\boldsymbol{x})$ for $\boldsymbol{x} \neq \boldsymbol{x}_*$ in a neighborhood $N(\boldsymbol{x}_*.\delta)$, where $\delta > 0$. If this minimum holds for the whole domain of feasible solutions, it is called the

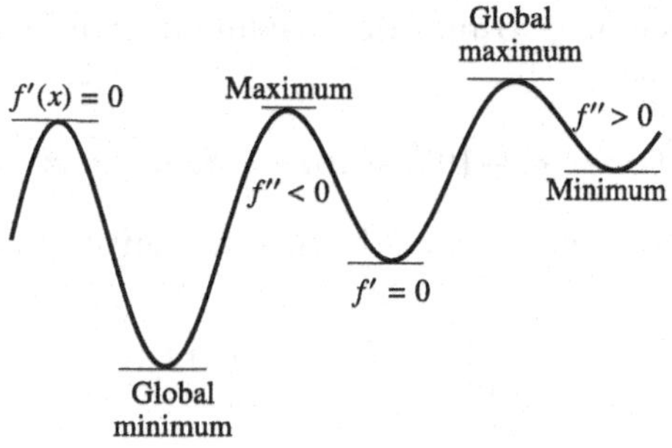

Figure 10.1 Minima and maxima of a univariate function.

global minimum. For nonlinear functions, there may be multiple local optima (maxima or minima), and multiple global optima may also exist (see Fig. 10.1).

For the present discussion, we will assume that both $f(\mathbf{x})$ and $f'(\mathbf{x})$ are everywhere continuous or that $f(\mathbf{x})$ is everywhere twice continuously differentiable. In practice, this condition may not be satisfied, but many concepts and properties may still hold.

10.2.1 Unconstrained optimization

To find the maxima or minima of a univariate function $f(x)$ is an unconstrained optimization problem. For univariate functions, the optimality occurs at either boundary or more often at the critical points given by the stationary condition

$$f'(x) = 0, \tag{10.6}$$

which is shown in Fig. 10.1. This condition is just a necessary condition, but it is not a sufficient condition. Whether it is a maximum or minimum, it is determined by the second derivative.

- If $f'(x_*) = 0$ and $f''(x_*) > 0$, it is a local minimum.
- If $f'(x_*) = 0$ and $f''(x_*) < 0$, it is a local maximum.

Among all the minima, there is a global minimum in the whole domain. Similarly, among all the maxima, there is a global maximum. In addition, multiple global optima (maxima or minima) with the same objective value may exist in some problems.

If $f'(x_*) = 0$ and $f''(x_*) = 0$, then it is not possible to determine whether it is a maximum or minimum. Higher-order derivatives are needed. For example, $f(x) = x^4$ gives $f'(x) = 4x^3 = 0$ and $f''(x) = 12x^2 = 0$ at $x = 0$. Obviously, $x = 0$ corresponds to the global minimum of x^4. However, if $f'(x_*) = 0$ but $f''(x)$ is indefinite (both positive and negative) as $x \to x_*$, then x_* corresponds to a saddle point. For example, $f(x) = x^3$ has a saddle point at $x_* = 0$ because $f'(0) = 0$ and $f''(0) = 0$, but f'' changes sign from $f''(0+) > 0$ to $f''(0-) < 0$.

Example 10.1. For example, to find the maximum or minimum of the univariate function

$$f(x) = x^4 - 10x^2 + 16, \quad -\infty < x < \infty, \tag{10.7}$$

we first find its stationary point x_* when the first derivative $f'(x)$ is zero, that is,

$$\frac{df}{dx} = 4x^3 - 20x = 0, \tag{10.8}$$

which gives three solutions

$$x_* = 0, \quad +\sqrt{5}, \quad -\sqrt{5}. \tag{10.9}$$

The signs of the second derivative $f''(x) = 12x^2 - 20$ are, respectively,

$$f''(0) < 0, \quad f''(\pm\sqrt{5}) > 0. \tag{10.10}$$

Thus, the solution $x = 0$ is a local maximum, whereas the two global minima occur at $x = \pm\sqrt{5}$.

The maximization of a function $f(x)$ can be converted into the minimization of $-f(x)$. For example, we know that the maximum of $f(x) = e^{-x^2}$ is 1 at $x_* = 0$. This problem can be converted to a minimization problem for $-f(x)$. Therefore in the optimization literature, some books formulate all the optimization problems in terms of maximization, whereas others use formulations in terms of minimization.

10.2.2 Function optimization

For univariate functions, optimality conditions are related to $f'(x)$ and $f''(x)$. However, for multivariate functions, there are no simple rules, though the definiteness of the Hessian matrix is required.

To find the optima of a multivariate function $f(\boldsymbol{x})$ where $\boldsymbol{x} = (x_1, \ldots, x_n)^T$, we can express it as an optimization problem concerning a decision vector $\boldsymbol{x}$:

$$\text{Minimize/maximize } f(\boldsymbol{x}), \quad \boldsymbol{x} \in \mathbb{R}^n. \tag{10.11}$$

The optimality is determined by the stationary or critical condition

$$\mathbf{G} = \nabla f = \begin{pmatrix} \partial f / \partial x_1 \\ \partial f / \partial x_2 \\ \vdots \\ \partial f / \partial x_n \end{pmatrix} = 0, \tag{10.12}$$

which means that

$$\frac{\partial f}{\partial x_1} = 0, \quad \frac{\partial f}{\partial x_2} = 0, \quad \ldots, \quad \frac{\partial f}{\partial x_n} = 0. \tag{10.13}$$

The solution to this set of equations gives the critical points. The Hessian matrix is defined by

$$\boldsymbol{H} = \begin{pmatrix} \frac{\partial^2 f}{\partial {x_1}^2} & \frac{\partial^2 f}{\partial x_1 \partial x_2} & \cdots & \frac{\partial^2 f}{\partial x_1 \partial x_n} \\ \frac{\partial^2 f}{\partial x_2 \partial x_1} & \frac{\partial^2 f}{\partial {x_2}^2} & \cdots & \frac{\partial^2 f}{\partial x_2 \partial x_n} \\ \vdots & \vdots & \ddots & \vdots \\ \frac{\partial^2 f}{\partial x_n \partial x_1} & \frac{\partial^2 f}{\partial x_n \partial x_2} & \cdots & \frac{\partial^2 f}{\partial {x_n}^2} \end{pmatrix}. \tag{10.14}$$

If the Hessian matrix is positive definite at the critical point, then the point is a local minimum. If the Hessian matrix is negative definite at the critical point, then the point is a local maximum. Otherwise, the critical point is neither a maximum nor a minimum, which can be something else, such as a saddle point.

Example 10.2. For the function

$$f(x, y, z) = 2x^2 + y^2 + z^2 - 2xy - 2x + 1, \tag{10.15}$$

its critical condition gives zero gradient:

$$\frac{\partial f}{\partial x} = 4x - 2y - 2 = 0, \quad \frac{\partial f}{\partial y} = -2x + 2y = 0, \quad \frac{\partial f}{\partial z} = 2z = 0. \tag{10.16}$$

The critical point is thus at

$$x_* = 1, \quad y_* = 1, \quad z_* = 0. \tag{10.17}$$

It is straightforward to show that its Hessian matrix is

$$\boldsymbol{H} = \begin{pmatrix} 4 & -2 & 0 \\ -2 & 2 & 0 \\ 0 & 0 & 2 \end{pmatrix}, \tag{10.18}$$

and its eigenvalues are

$$\lambda = 3 - \sqrt{5}, \quad 2, \quad 3 + \sqrt{5}. \tag{10.19}$$

Since all three eigenvalues are positive, $\boldsymbol{H}$ is positive definite. Thus the point (1,1,0) corresponds to a minimum. In fact, it is the global minimum of this function because the Hessian matrix is independent of x, y, z and is positive definite in the whole domain $x, y, z \in \mathbb{R}$.

Alternatively, we can rewrite the above function as

$$f(x, y, z) = (x - 1)^2 + (y - x)^2 + z^2. \tag{10.20}$$

All its terms are nonnegative, and it is easy to see that its global minimum occurs at $x = 1$, $y = 1$, and $z = 0$.

This is a relatively simple example. In most cases, it is not possible to determine the definiteness of the Hessian matrix. Some local approximations using Taylor expansions are usually needed to figure out the local behavior of the function in the neighborhood of critical points.

10.2.3 Constrained optimization

Unconstrained optimization is rarely relevant in engineering applications because real-world applications have various constraints. In general, we can formulate a constrained optimization problem as

$$\text{Minimize } f(\boldsymbol{x}), \quad \boldsymbol{x} = (x_1, \ldots, x_n)^T \in \mathbb{R}^n, \tag{10.21}$$

subject to M equalities

$$\phi_i(\boldsymbol{x}) = 0 \quad (i = 1, \ldots, M) \tag{10.22}$$

and N inequalities

$$\psi_j(\boldsymbol{x}) \le 0 \quad (j = 1, \ldots, N). \tag{10.23}$$

Now the question is how to deal with the constraints.

There are many ways of dealing with constraints. A commonly used method is the penalty method, which is also easy to implement. Its main idea is to incorporate the constraints into the penalty function so that the constrained problem is transformed into an unconstrained problem

$$P(\boldsymbol{x}, \mu_i, \nu_j) = f(\boldsymbol{x}) + \sum_{i=1}^{M} \mu_i \phi_i^2(\boldsymbol{x}) + \sum_{j=1}^{N} \nu_j \max\left\{0, \psi_j(\boldsymbol{x})\right\}^2, \tag{10.24}$$

where $\mu_i > 0$ and $\nu_j > 0$ are the penalty coefficients or parameters. In practice, the single penalty parameter μ is used in the form of

$$P(\boldsymbol{x}, \mu) = f(\boldsymbol{x}) + \mu \left[\sum_{i=1}^{M} \phi_i^2(\boldsymbol{x}) + \sum_{j=1}^{N} \max\left\{0, \psi_j(\boldsymbol{x})\right\}^2 \right], \tag{10.25}$$

and $\mu \gg 1$. In most cases, a smaller μ, such as $\mu = 1$ or $\mu = 10$, is used, and its value increases gradually during iteration. This is the so-called dynamic penalty method.

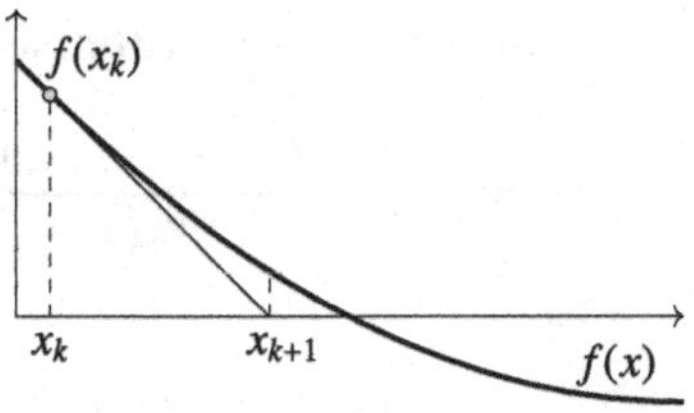

Figure 10.2 Newton's method and iterations.

10.3. Gradient-based methods

There are many techniques for solving optimization problems, including the gradient-based methods, gradient-free method, quadratic programming, interior-point method, evolutionary algorithms, nature-inspired algorithms, as well as many hybrid techniques. In this section, we introduce the basic gradient-based methods.

Gradient-based methods are a class of iterative methods that extensively use the gradient information of the objective function during iterations. The essence of this method is to start with a random initial solution or an educated guess $\boldsymbol{x}_0 = \boldsymbol{x}^{(0)}$, and then an improved solution is sought iteratively.

For the minimization of a function $f(\boldsymbol{x})$, the iteration equation can be written as

$$\boldsymbol{x}^{(k+1)} = \boldsymbol{x}^{(k)} + \alpha g(\nabla f, \boldsymbol{x}^{(k)}), \tag{10.26}$$

where α is the step size or learning rate, which can vary during iterations, and $g(\nabla f, \boldsymbol{x}^{(k)})$ is a known function of the gradient ∇f and the current location $\boldsymbol{x}^{(k)}$. Different methods use different forms of $g(\nabla f, \boldsymbol{x}^{(k)})$.

10.3.1 Newton's root-finding algorithm

Before we introduce Newton's method for optimization, let us review the basic idea for finding roots of a univariate function $f(x) = 0$ in the interval $[a, b]$. In fact, Newton's root-finding algorithm is widely used for solving nonlinear equations of functions. Sometimes, Newton's method is also referred to as the Newton–Raphson method.

The task is to solve $f(x) = 0$ to find the root(s) of f. In most cases, analytical solutions are not possible, and thus we have to use iterative methods to approximate the roots. Suppose we start with an initial guess x_0 and then try to improve it iteratively.

At any given point x_k shown in Fig. 10.2, during the iteration, we can approximate the function by a Taylor series

$$f(x_{k+1}) = f(x_k + \Delta x) \approx f(x_k) + f'(x_k)\Delta x, \tag{10.27}$$

where $\Delta x = x_{k+1} - x_k$. This equation can be also written as

$$x_{k+1} - x_k = \Delta x \approx \frac{f(x_{k+1}) - f(x_k)}{f'(x_k)}, \tag{10.28}$$

or

$$x_{k+1} \approx x_k + \frac{f(x_{k+1}) - f(x_k)}{f'(x_k)}. \tag{10.29}$$

Since the aim is to find an approximation to $f(x) = 0$ with $f(x_{k+1})$, we can expect that the right steps should give a new solution that is close to the true solution. Then a very crude approximation $f(x_{k+1}) \approx 0$ can be used in the above expression. Therefore the preceding equation becomes the standard Newton iterative formula

$$x_{k+1} = x_k - \frac{f(x_k)}{f'(x_k)}. \tag{10.30}$$

The iteration procedure starts from an initial guess value x_0 and continues until a predefined criterion is met. A good initial guess will use fewer steps; however, if there is no obvious initial good starting point, then the iteration can start at any point on the interval $[a, b]$. But if the initial value is too far from the true zero, then the iteration process may fail. So it is a good idea to limit the number of iterations.

Example 10.3. To find the root of

$$f(x) = x - e^{-x} = 0,$$

we use Newton's method starting from $x_0 = 0$. We know that

$$f'(x) = \left(x - e^{-x}\right)' = 1 + e^{-x},$$

and thus the iteration formula becomes

$$x_{k+1} = x_k - \frac{x_k - e^{-x_k}}{1 + e^{-x_k}}.$$

Since $x_0 = 0$, we have

$$x_1 = 0 - \frac{0 - e^{-0}}{1 + e^{-0}} = 0.5, \tag{10.31}$$

$$x_2 = 0.5 - \frac{0.5 - e^{-0.5}}{1 + e^{-0.5}} \approx 0.566311003, \tag{10.32}$$

$$x_3 \approx 0.56714317, \quad x_4 \approx 0.56714329. \tag{10.33}$$

We can see that x_3 (only three iterations) is very close (to the 6th decimal place) to the true root $x_* \approx 0.5671432904$, and x_4 is accurate to the 8th decimal place.

Sometimes, we can use a linear interpolation of two consecutive values to approximate $f'(x)$, and we have the alternative Newton formula

$$x_{k+1} = x_k - \frac{f(x_k)}{[f(x_k) - f(x_{k-1})]/(x_k - x_{k-1})} = x_k - \frac{(x_k - x_{k-1})f(x_k)}{f(x_k) - f(x_{k-1})}, \tag{10.34}$$

which can be more convenient in certain applications.

We have seen that Newton's method is very efficient, and that is why it is so widely used. Using this method, we can virtually solve almost all root-finding problems, though care should be taken when dealing with multiple roots, and proper initial starting points should be chosen sufficiently close to the root of interest and also avoid $f'(x_0) = 0$.

10.3.2 Newton's method for optimization

We know that Newton's method is a popular iterative method for finding the zeros of a nonlinear univariate function of $f(x)$ on the interval $[a, b]$. It can be modified for solving optimization problems because it is equivalent to finding the zeros or roots of the first derivative $f'(\boldsymbol{x})$ once the objective function $f(\boldsymbol{x})$ is given.

For a given continuously differentiable function $f(\boldsymbol{x})$, we have the Taylor expansion about a known point $\boldsymbol{x} = \boldsymbol{x}_k$ (with $\Delta\boldsymbol{x} = \boldsymbol{x} - \boldsymbol{x}_k$)

$$f(\boldsymbol{x}) = f(\boldsymbol{x}_k) + (\nabla f(\boldsymbol{x}_k))^T \Delta\boldsymbol{x} + \frac{1}{2}\Delta\boldsymbol{x}^T \nabla^2 f(\boldsymbol{x}_k)\Delta\boldsymbol{x} + \cdots,$$

which is minimized near a critical point when $\Delta\boldsymbol{x}$ is the solution of the linear equation

$$\nabla f(\boldsymbol{x}_k) + \nabla^2 f(\boldsymbol{x}_k)\Delta\boldsymbol{x} = 0, \tag{10.35}$$

that is,

$$\Delta\boldsymbol{x} = -\frac{\nabla f(\boldsymbol{x}_k)}{\nabla^2 f(\boldsymbol{x}_k)}. \tag{10.36}$$

This leads to

$$\boldsymbol{x} = \boldsymbol{x}_k - \boldsymbol{H}^{-1}\nabla f(\boldsymbol{x}_k), \tag{10.37}$$

where $\boldsymbol{H} = \nabla^2 f(\boldsymbol{x}_k)$ is the Hessian matrix. If the iteration procedure starts from the initial vector $\boldsymbol{x}^{(0)}$ (usually taken to be a guessed point in the domain), then Newton's iteration formula for the kth iteration is

$$\boldsymbol{x}^{(k+1)} = \boldsymbol{x}^{(k)} - \boldsymbol{H}^{-1}(\boldsymbol{x}^{(k)})f(\boldsymbol{x}^{(k)}). \tag{10.38}$$

It is worth pointing out that if $f(\boldsymbol{x})$ is quadratic, then the optimal solution can be found exactly in a single step. However, this method is not efficient for nonquadratic functions.

To speed up the convergence, we can use a smaller step size $\alpha \in (0, 1]$, so that we have the modified Newton method

$$x^{(k+1)} = x^{(k)} - \alpha H^{-1}(x^{(k)}) f(x^{(k)}). \tag{10.39}$$

It can usually be time-consuming to calculate the Hessian matrix for second derivatives. A good alternative is to use an identity matrix to approximate the Hessian by using $H^{-1} = I$, and we have the quasi-Newton method

$$x^{(k+1)} = x^{(k)} - \alpha I \nabla f(x^{(k)}), \tag{10.40}$$

which is essentially the steepest descent method.

10.3.3 Steepest descent method

The essence of this method is to find the lowest possible objective function $f(x)$ from the current point $x^{(k)}$. From the Taylor expansion of $f(x)$ about $x^{(k)}$ we have

$$f(x^{(k+1)}) = f(x^{(k)} + \Delta s) \approx f(x^{(k)}) + (\nabla f(x^{(k)}))^T \Delta s, \tag{10.41}$$

where $\Delta s = x^{(k+1)} - x^{(k)}$ is the increment vector. Since we try to find a lower (better) approximation to the objective function, it requires that the second term on the right hand is negative, that is,

$$f(x^{(k)} + \Delta s) - f(x^{(k)}) = (\nabla f)^T \Delta s < 0. \tag{10.42}$$

From vector analysis we know that the inner product $u^T v$ of two vectors u and v is largest negative when they are parallel but in opposite directions. Therefore $(\nabla f)^T \Delta s$ becomes the largest when

$$\Delta s = -\alpha \nabla f(x^{(k)}), \tag{10.43}$$

where $\alpha > 0$ is the step size. This is the case where the direction Δs is along the steepest descent in the negative gradient direction. As we have seen earlier, this method is a quasi-Newton method.

The choice of the step size α is very important. A very small step size means slow movement toward the local minimum, whereas a large step may overshoot and subsequently make it move far away from the local minimum. In each iteration the gradient and step size will be calculated. Again, a good initial guess of both the starting point and the step size is useful.

There are many variations of the steepest descent methods. For maximization problems, this method becomes the *hill-climbing* method because the aim is to climb up the hill to the highest peak.

The standard steepest descent method works well for convex functions and near a local peak (valley) of most smooth multimodal functions, though this local peak is not necessarily the global best. However, for some tough functions, it is not a good method. In this case, other methods can be used, such as genetic algorithms, particle swarm optimization, the firefly algorithm, the cuckoo search algorithm, the bat algorithm, and differential evolution. The interested readers can refer to more specialized literature on nature-inspired algorithms.

10.4. Design optimization in engineering

Design optimization is a vast area concerning optimal designs of key components, products, and systems. Here we only briefly introduce a few case studies as benchmarks to show how design problems can be formulated as standard optimization problems in different context. The interested readers can refer to more advanced literature on engineering design optimization.

10.4.1 Design of a spring

Design of a spring under tension or compression from a metal wire is a good example for nonlinear constrained optimization. There are three design variables: the wire diameter r, the mean coil diameter d, and the number N of turns/coils. The objective is to minimize the overall weight of the spring

$$\text{minimize } f(\boldsymbol{x}) = (2+N)r^2 d, \tag{10.44}$$

subject to nonlinear constraints

$$g_1(\boldsymbol{x}) = 1 - \frac{Nd^3}{71785r^4} \le 0, \tag{10.45}$$

$$g_2(\boldsymbol{x}) = \frac{d(4d-r)}{12566r^3(d-r)} + \frac{1}{5108r^2} - 1 \le 0, \tag{10.46}$$

$$g_3(\boldsymbol{x}) = 1 - \frac{140.45r}{d^2 N} \le 0, \tag{10.47}$$

$$g_4(\boldsymbol{x}) = (d+r) - 1.5 \le 0. \tag{10.48}$$

Some simple bounds or limits for the design variables are

$$0.05 \le r \le 2.0, \quad 0.25 \le d \le 1.3, \quad 2.0 \le N \le 15.0. \tag{10.49}$$

In principle, we can solve this problem using any efficient algorithm, together with proper handling of constraints. Different algorithms may performance differently, and the computational costs may also be different. Most algorithms can find the best or optimal solution. The best solution found so far in the literature is

$$\boldsymbol{x} = (0.051690,\ \ 0.356750,\ \ 11.28716) \tag{10.50}$$

with

$$f_{\min} = 0.012665. \tag{10.51}$$

One possible variant of this optimization problem is to ensure that N is an integer, which becomes a mixed integer programming problem. In this case the branch-and-bound approach can be used to deal with the integer constraint. We will introduce this type of mixed integer programming in the next chapter.

We leave it as an exercise for the readers to solve this problem using a chosen software package. We will briefly outline some of the optimization software packages in the final section of this chapter.

10.4.2 Pressure vessel design

The pressure vessel design problem is a well-known benchmark, which has been used by many researchers. The design objective for this pressure vessel problem is to minimize the overall cost of materials, subject to stress and volume requirements. There are four design variables: the thicknesses d_1 and d_2 for the head and body, respectively, the inner radius r, and the length W of the cylindrical section.

The main objective is

$$\text{minimize } f(\boldsymbol{x}) = 0.6224rWd_1 + 1.7781r^2 d_2 + 19.64rd_1^2 + 3.1661\,Wd_1^2, \tag{10.52}$$

subject to four constraints

$$g_1(\boldsymbol{x}) = -d_1 + 0.0193r \leq 0, \tag{10.53}$$

$$g_2(\boldsymbol{x}) = -d_2 + 0.00954r \leq 0, \tag{10.54}$$

$$g_3(\boldsymbol{x}) = -\frac{4\pi r^3}{3} - \pi r^2 W - 1296000 \leq 0, \tag{10.55}$$

$$g_4(\boldsymbol{x}) = W - 240 \leq 0. \tag{10.56}$$

The inner radius and length are limited to $10.0 \leq r,\ W \leq 200.0$. However, due to manufacturing requirements, the thicknesses d_1 and d_2 can only be integer multiples of a basic thickness of 0.0625 inches. Thus the simple bounds for thicknesses are

$$1 \times 0.0625 \leq d_1, d_2 \leq 99 \times 0.0625. \tag{10.57}$$

This means that the vessel can have multiple layers of thin sheet of thickness of 0.0625 inches. With such integer multiples of thicknesses in terms of multiple layers, the optimization problem essentially becomes a mixed integer programming with two discrete variables and two continuous variables.

The best solution found so far in the literature is

$$\boldsymbol{x} = (0.8125, 0.4375, 42.0984456, 176.6366) \tag{10.58}$$

with

$$f_{\min} = 6059.714. \tag{10.59}$$

The first two variable values (0.8125 and 0.4375) are 13 layers and 7 layers, respectively, of the basic sheet with a thickness of 0.0625 inches.

10.4.3 Speed reducer design

A more complicated design problem with seven design variables is the speed reducer design problem. The main design variables are the face width of the gear, number of teeth, and diameter of the shaft and others. All these variables can take continuous values, except for x_3, which is an integer (e.g., the number of teeth).

The objective is to minimize the cost function

$$\begin{aligned}\text{minimize } f(\boldsymbol{x}) = 0.7854\Big[x_1x_2^2(3.3333x_3^2 + 14.9334x_3 - 43.0934) + (x_4x_6^2 + x_5x_7^2)\Big]\\ -1.508x_1(x_6^2 + x_7^2) + 7.4777(x_6^3 + x_7^3),\end{aligned} \tag{10.60}$$

subject to 11 constraints

$$g_1(\boldsymbol{x}) = \frac{27}{x_1x_2^2x_3} - 1 \le 0, \tag{10.61}$$

$$g_2(\boldsymbol{x}) = \frac{397.5}{x_1x_2^2x_3^2} - 1 \le 0, \tag{10.62}$$

$$g_3(\boldsymbol{x}) = \frac{1.93x_4^3}{x_2x_3x_6^4} - 1 \le 0, \tag{10.63}$$

$$g_4(\boldsymbol{x}) = \frac{1.93x_5^3}{x_2x_3x_7^4} - 1 \le 0, \tag{10.64}$$

$$g_5(\boldsymbol{x}) = \frac{1.0}{110x_6^3}\sqrt{(\frac{745.0x_4}{x_2x_3})^2 + 16.9 \times 10^6} - 1 \le 0, \tag{10.65}$$

$$g_6(\boldsymbol{x}) = \frac{1.0}{85x_7^3}\sqrt{(\frac{745.0x_5}{x_2x_3})^2 + 157.5 \times 10^6} - 1 \le 0, \tag{10.66}$$

$$g_7(\boldsymbol{x}) = x_2x_3 - 40 \le 0, \tag{10.67}$$

$$g_8(\boldsymbol{x}) = 5x_2 - x_1 \le 0, \tag{10.68}$$

$$g_9(\boldsymbol{x}) = x_1 - 12x_2 \leq 0, \tag{10.69}$$

$$g_{10}(\boldsymbol{x}) = (1.5x_6 + 1.9) - x_4 \leq 0, \tag{10.70}$$

$$g_{11}(\boldsymbol{x}) = (1.1x_7 + 1.9) - x_5 \leq 0. \tag{10.71}$$

In addition, the simple bounds for the variables are

$$2.6 \leq x_1 \leq 3.6, \quad 0.7 \leq x_2 \leq 0.8, \tag{10.72}$$

$$17 \leq x_3 \leq 28, \quad x_3 \in \mathbb{I}, \tag{10.73}$$

$$7.3 \leq x_4 \leq 8.3, \quad 7.8 \leq x_5 \leq 8.4, \tag{10.74}$$

$$2.9 \leq x_6 \leq 3.9, \quad 5.0 \leq x_7 \leq 5.5. \tag{10.75}$$

The best solution found so far in the literature is

$$\boldsymbol{x} = (3.5, 0.7, 17, 7.3, 7.8, 3.34336449, 5.285351) \tag{10.76}$$

with

$$f_{\min} = 2993.749589. \tag{10.77}$$

10.4.4 Inverse problems and parameter identification

Many problems in engineering simulation can be considered as inverse problems or parameter estimation problems. The main task is to estimate or identify the key parameter values for a given set of observations under a given configuration of a physical, chemical, or biological system.

As an example to show how this type of problem works, we now look at a simple vibration problem with two unknown parameters μ and ν. For a given set of the measurements of vibration amplitudes, estimation of the two parameters can be carried out by minimizing the differences between the predicted responses and the actual measured responses.

The governing equation of the vibration displacement $y(t)$ is

$$\frac{d^2y(t)}{dt^2} + \mu\frac{dy(t)}{dt} + \nu y(t) = 40\cos(3t), \tag{10.78}$$

which is a damped harmonic motion problem, and its general solution can be quite complex. However, for the fixed values of $\mu = 4$ and $\nu = 5$ with initial values of $y(0) = 0$ and $y'(0) = 0$, its analytical solution can be simplified as

$$y(t) = e^{-2t}[\cos(t) - 7\sin(t)] + 3\sin(3t) - \cos(3t). \tag{10.79}$$

For a real system with a forcing term $40\cos(3t)$, we do not know the parameters, but its vibrations can be measured. For example, in an experiment, there are $N = 11$ measurements as shown in Table 10.1.

Table 10.1 Measured response of a simple vibration system.

t	0	0.20	0.40	0.60	0.80	1.00	1.20	1.40	1.60	1.80	2.00
$\tilde{y}$	0	0.59	1.62	2.21	1.89	0.69	−0.99	−2.53	−3.36	−3.15	−1.92

The task is to estimate the values of the two parameters. However, one of the challenges is that the calculation of the objective function defined as the sum of errors squared, that is,

$$f(\boldsymbol{x}) = \sum_{i=1}^{N} (y_{i,\text{predicted}} - \tilde{y}_i)^2, \tag{10.80}$$

where the predicted $y(t)$ has to be obtained by solving the second-order ordinary differential equation (10.78) numerically and iteratively for every given set of μ and ν. This becomes a series of optimization problems.

By using a proper optimization technique such as Newton's method, the mean values of the two parameters obtained from the measured data are $\mu_* = 4.05$ and $\nu_* = 4.93$, which are very close to the true values of $\mu = 4.000$ and $\nu = 5.000$. It is worth pointing out that the measurements have some noise or errors, and thus it is not possible to obtain the exact values of μ and ν whatever algorithms we may use.

10.5. Notes on software

There are a vast spectrum of optimization software tools that can solve various optimization problems. It is not possible to list even a good fraction of the available software packages. A quite comprehensive list can be found in wikipedia at https://en.wikipedia.org/wiki/List_of_optimization_software.

Many programming languages and software packages include various optimization toolboxes or packages. *Matlab*®, *Excel Solver, Python, R, Mathematica, Maple, Scilab, Octave*, C++, and Java all have optimization functionalities. For example, Matlab's global optimization toolbox and Python's *Gekko* package are capable of solving many engineering optimization problems.

In addition, there are many software libraries such as COIN-OR (Computational Infrastructure for Operations Research), IPOPT (Interior Point Optimizer), SCIP (Solving Constraint Integer Programs), NAG (Numerical Algorithm Group) numerical library, and HiGHS (open-source software to solve linear programming, mixed-integer programming, and quadratic programming). Many software packages use these libraries as their engines to solve optimization problems. Other powerful optimization tools include AMPL, CPLEX, LINDO, LIONsolver, MINTO, OptiStruct, SNOPT, and others.

CHAPTER ELEVEN

Linear programming and its applications

Some problems in engineering simulation and applications are related to optimization and planning as well as scheduling. One class of such problems is the design optimization we introduced in the previous chapter. Another class of such problems is linear programming. This chapter introduces the fundamentals of both linear programming and integer programming.

11.1. Introduction

Linear programming (LP) is a mathematical programming technique widely used in transport, logistics, manufacturing, scheduling, business planning, and many other areas.

All the functions in LP, including the objective function and all constraints, are linear functions. The optimality occurs at the boundary, typically at a corner point. LP is routinely used by airlines, logistic companies, and many industries. There are many software packages, such as Matlab®, Excel Solver, and OpenSolver, that can solve LP tasks on a desktop computer.

11.1.1 An illustrative example

The main idea in LP is finding the maximum or minimum of a linear objective under linear constraints. Let us explain the essence of LP by an example.

A company has two different services x and y. The first service has a fixed monthly price with a monthly profit of 2 pounds, whereas the second service has a higher subscription monthly price with a profit of 3 pounds per month. Due to staff and capacity constraints, the company can provide at most $n_1 = 16$ million of the first service and at most $n_2 = 10$ million of the second service. In addition, the total number of both services is limited to $n = 20$ million. The main objective for this company is to maximize its profit by formulating a proper service portfolio.

Let x and y be the numbers of the first and second services, respectively. The objective is the overall profit

$$P = 2x + 3y \tag{11.1}$$

Engineering Simulation and its Applications
https://doi.org/10.1016/B978-0-44-314084-6.00018-8

to be maximized. The total number of service constraints at most $n = 20$ million is represented by

$$x + y \leq 20. \tag{11.2}$$

The capacity constraints of at most $n_1 = 16$ for the first service and at most $n_2 = 10$ for the second service can be written as the following inequalities:

$$x \leq 16, \quad y \leq 10. \tag{11.3}$$

In addition, an implicit constraint is that the numbers of customers must be nonnegative, that is,

$$x \geq 0, \quad y \geq 0. \tag{11.4}$$

This problem becomes an optimization problem:

$$\text{Maximize} \quad P(x, y) = 2x + 3y, \tag{11.5}$$

subject to the constraints

$$x + y \leq 20, \tag{11.6}$$

$$x \leq 16, \tag{11.7}$$

$$y \leq 10, \tag{11.8}$$

$$x \geq 0, \tag{11.9}$$

$$y \geq 0. \tag{11.10}$$

Since all the functions (left-hand sides of the inequalities) are all linear, this optimization problem is a linear programming problem, often called a *linear program*. Furthermore, since the numbers of customers or units of service must be integers, this LP is in fact an *integer linear programming* (ILP) problem, or simply an integer program.

11.1.2 Solution by graphic method

From problem (11.5) we can first look at their constraints to figure out the feasible region. A solution is said to be feasible if it satisfies all the constraints. All the feasible solutions form the feasible domain or region of the LP problem. The feasible region for the present problem is shown as the shaded region in Fig. 11.1.

For this simple LP, the feasible region is formed by satisfying all the constraints. Each constraint forms a line if we let an inequality become a tight equality. For example, line AB corresponds to $y = 10$ from $y \leq 10$, whereas line CD corresponds to $x = 16$ from $x \leq 16$. Line BC comes from equality $x + y = 20$ from the corresponding inequality $x + y \leq 20$. Lines OA and OD are the nonnegative constraints. The feasible region, also

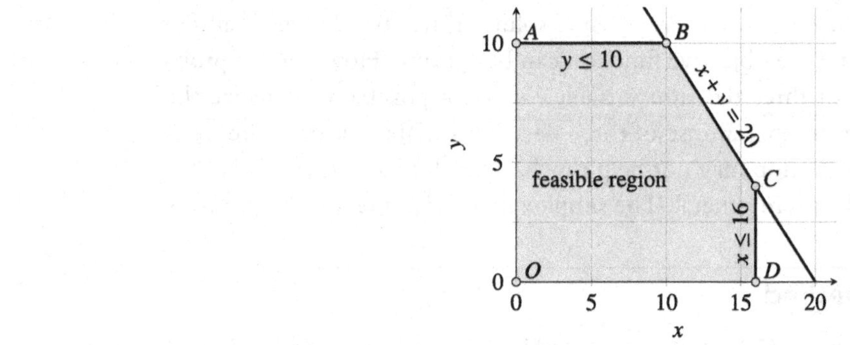

Figure 11.1 The feasible domain is a convex polygon with five corners at O(0,0), A(0,10), B(10,10), C(16,4), and D(16,0).

called the feasible domain, is the inside of a polygon with five sides determined from five constraints (11.6)–(11.10).

The vertices or corners of the polygon are the points that two equalities (from their corresponding inequalities) are satisfied simultaneously. For example, corner B at (10,10) is found by solving the system of two equations $y = 10$ and $x + y = 20$. All the five corner points are shown in Fig. 11.1.

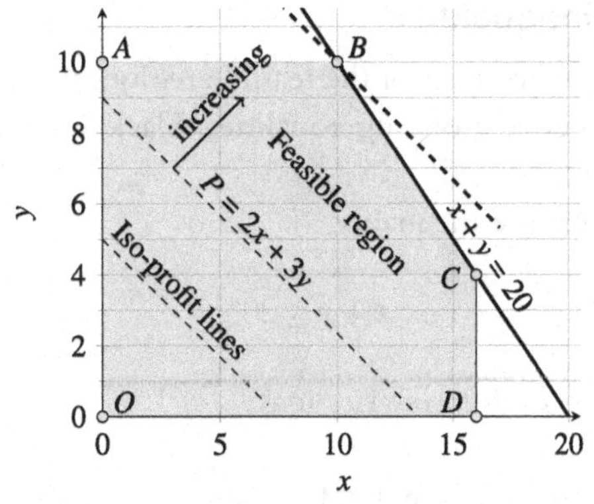

Figure 11.2 Linear programming with corners O(0,0), A(0,10), B(10,10), C(16,4), and D(16,0). The optimal solution occurs at B with $x = y = 10$ and $P = 50$.

For the objective function $P(x, y)$, we can plot it as a family of parallel lines, shown as dashed lines, for a given value of P. There are many solutions on a line with the same P, and thus such lines are called isoprofit lines. Now the aim for solving the LP problem is to move up the isoprofit line (to maximize the profit) such that it is still within the feasible region. Clearly, the best solution will occur at a corner point, which is B(10,10) in this case, as shown in Fig. 11.2.

This illustrative example shows that the optimal solution may be obvious if all the constraints are visualized and the objective function can be varying. However, for problems with more than two or three decision variables, it is not possible to visualize the problem properly. Even in the special case of three decision variables, if there are multiple constraints, then visualization may not help much. Therefore a formal approach is needed for solving LP problems in general. The simplex method just serves this purpose.

11.2. Simplex method

The widely used simplex method was developed by George Dantzig in 1947. This method has solid mathematical background, and its implementation can be done using matrices and linear algebra.

Loosely speaking, the simplex method has the following main steps: 1) formulate the LP properly and convert to its standard form; 2) find the extreme points or vertices of the feasible region; 3) start with an initial guess or solution and move to adjacent vertex or corner point as a new solution to see if the objective value improves (increase for maximization); 4) accept the new solution if the objective improves and continue in the same manner to other adjacent vertices; 5) stop if the new solution starts to get worse (decrease for maximization).

11.2.1 Dealing with inequalities

To find the corner points or vertices of the feasible region, we have to convert or transform all inequalities into corresponding equalities. Slack variables are used to achieve such transformations.

For example, to convert the inequality

$$x+y \leq 20, \tag{11.11}$$

we can use a slack variable $s \geq 0$ to rewrite it as

$$x+y+s=20. \tag{11.12}$$

If $s=0$, then it becomes the equality $x+y=20$. If $s>0$, then it corresponds to the inequality $x+y<20$. Either way, $x+y+s=0$ corresponds to $x+y \leq 20$ if $s \geq 0$.

The advantage of this transformation using slack variables is that inequalities now becomes equalities; however, the dimensionality of the problem or the number of decision variables increases. In general, for every independent inequality, an extra slack variable is needed. Mathematically speaking, this conversion technique transforms the LP with inequality constraints into a corresponding LP with equality constraints in a higher-dimensional space.

As the number of decision variables and slack variables increases, it is more convenient to use subscript notations x_1, x_2, and x_3 rather than x, y, and z. For the above illustrative example, we can use $x_1 = x$ and $x_2 = y$ and rewrite the LP as

$$\text{Maximize} \quad P = 2x_1 + 3x_2, \tag{11.13}$$

subject to

$$x_1 + x_2 \leq 20, \tag{11.14}$$

$$x_1 \leq 16, \tag{11.15}$$

$$x_2 \leq 10, \tag{11.16}$$

$$x_1 \geq 0, \tag{11.17}$$

$$x_2 \geq 0. \tag{11.18}$$

Using three slack variables $s_1 \geq 0$, $s_2 \geq 0$, and $s_3 \geq 0$, we can rewrite the first three inequalities as

$$x_1 + x_2 + s_1 = 20, \tag{11.19}$$

$$x_1 + s_2 = 16, \quad x_2 + s_3 = 10. \tag{11.20}$$

In the simplex method and many software packages, the nonnegative conditions are dealt with using different techniques, such as simply imposing all the variables are nonnegative in the programming. Thus we can leave the nonnegativeness as

$$x_i \geq 0 \ (i = 1, 2), \quad s_j \geq 0 \ (j = 1, 2, 3). \tag{11.21}$$

In addition, the objective function P can be written as a dot product of the coefficient vector (2, 3, 0, 0, 0) with the decision variable vector $\boldsymbol{x}$, that is,

$$P = \boldsymbol{a}^T \boldsymbol{x} = \boldsymbol{a} \cdot \boldsymbol{x} = 2x_1 + 3x_2 + 0s_1 + 0s_2 + 0s_3, \tag{11.22}$$

where

$$\boldsymbol{a} = \begin{pmatrix} 2 \\ 3 \\ 0 \\ 0 \\ 0 \end{pmatrix}, \quad \boldsymbol{x} = \begin{pmatrix} x_1 \\ x_2 \\ s_1 \\ s_2 \\ s_3 \end{pmatrix}. \tag{11.23}$$

Now the original problem (11.5) can be written as

$$\text{Maximize} \quad P(\boldsymbol{x}) = \boldsymbol{a}^T \boldsymbol{x}, \tag{11.24}$$

subject to

$$\begin{pmatrix} 1 & 1 & 1 & 0 & 0 \\ 1 & 0 & 0 & 1 & 0 \\ 0 & 1 & 0 & 0 & 1 \end{pmatrix} \begin{pmatrix} x_1 \\ x_2 \\ s_1 \\ s_2 \\ s_3 \end{pmatrix} = \begin{pmatrix} 20 \\ 16 \\ 10 \end{pmatrix} \tag{11.25}$$

and

$$x_i \geq 0 \quad (i = 1, 2, \ldots, 5). \tag{11.26}$$

The equality constraints can be written more compactly as

$$\boldsymbol{Ax} = \boldsymbol{b}, \tag{11.27}$$

where

$$\boldsymbol{A} = \begin{pmatrix} 1 & 1 & 1 & 0 & 0 \\ 1 & 0 & 0 & 1 & 0 \\ 0 & 1 & 0 & 0 & 1 \end{pmatrix}, \quad \boldsymbol{b} = \begin{pmatrix} 20 \\ 16 \\ 10 \end{pmatrix}. \tag{11.28}$$

This transformed LP is a five-dimensional LP problem with two control variables (x_1, x_2) and three slack variables $x_3 = s_1$, $x_4 = s_2$, $x_5 = s_3$.

11.2.2 Standard formulation

In the simplex method, the standard form is preferred because it provides a unified notation and problem formulation. For the decision variable $\boldsymbol{x} = (x_1, x_2, \ldots, x_n)^T$ (including all the slack variables) and the profit or objective coefficients a_i, $i = 1, 2, \ldots, n$, an LP problem can be written in the following standard form:

$$\text{Maximize } f(\boldsymbol{x}) = Z = \sum_{i=1}^{n} a_i x_i = \boldsymbol{a}^T \boldsymbol{x}, \quad \boldsymbol{x} \in \mathbb{R}^n, \tag{11.29}$$

subject to

$$\boldsymbol{Ax} = \boldsymbol{b}, \qquad x_i \geq 0 \ (i = 1, \ldots, n), \tag{11.30}$$

which is an n-dimensional LP problem with m equalities. Here $\boldsymbol{A}$ is an $m \times n$ matrix, and $\boldsymbol{b} = (b_1, \ldots, b_m)^T$ is a column vector.

In the context of LP, a basic solution to the linear system $\boldsymbol{Ax} = \boldsymbol{b}$ in terms of m basic variables in the standard form can be obtained by setting other $n - m$ variables equal to zero and subsequently solving the resulting $m \times n$ linear system to get a unique solution of the remaining m variables. These m variables are called the basic variables of the basic solution. Any basic solution to $\boldsymbol{Ax} = \boldsymbol{b}$ is called a basic feasible solution (BFS) if all its variables are nonnegative. Two corner points are said to be adjacent if their corresponding BFS vectors have $m-1$ basic variables in common.

The key property of a BFS is that it corresponds to a unique corner point or vertex. Conversely, each corner on the edges of the feasible region corresponds to at least one BFS.

Sometimes, it is useful to rewrite the LP (11.29) as the following canonical form or augmented form:

$$\begin{pmatrix} 1 & -\boldsymbol{a}^T \\ 0 & \boldsymbol{A} \end{pmatrix} \begin{pmatrix} Z \\ \boldsymbol{x} \end{pmatrix} = \begin{pmatrix} 0 \\ \boldsymbol{b} \end{pmatrix}, \tag{11.31}$$

which includes the objective Z. The first row comes from $Z - \boldsymbol{a}^T\boldsymbol{x} = 0$. All the constraints are expressed as equalities for all nonnegative variables in this form. In addition, each constraint equation has a single basic variable.

The main reason for transforming the LP into this canonical form is to find BFSs and then move from one BFS to another by a pivot operation of relevant matrices.

Though the illustrative example is easy to solve with only a small number of BFSs, in practice, the number of BFSs can be huge. For example, for $m = 100$ basic variables taking only binary values 0 or 1, simple equalities such as $x_i + x_j = 1$ where $i, j = 1, 2, \ldots, 100$ give a huge number of combinations $2^{100} \approx 1.27 \times 10^{30}$. Therefore it is not possible to go through all the corner points. The essential idea of the simplex method is that only a small fraction of the corner points or BFSs need to be evaluated to find the optimality of the LP.

11.3. Steps for simplex method

The mathematical foundations for the simplex method and its duality theory are rigorous and complicated, which is not the focus of this chapter. Now we can focus on the solution procedure or steps for solving an LP, and thus we will use the illustrative example that we solved earlier to demonstrate these steps.

The main solution steps are as follows:

1. Find a BFS to start the algorithm. If it is not possible to find a BFS, then some minor reformulation may be necessary.
2. Test if the current BFS can be improved by increasing the nonbasic variables from zero to nonnegative values.
3. Move to an adjacent BFS to see if the objective can be improved.
4. Stop the process if the latest BFS cannot be improved. In this case the optimal solution is found.

In linear algebra, pivot manipulations work because a linear system will remain an equivalent system by multiplying a nonzero constant with a row and adding it to the other row. The above procedure continues by going to Step 2 and repeating the evaluation of the objective function.

Let us revisit our earlier example by writing it in the canonical form

$$\begin{pmatrix} 1 & -2 & -3 & 0 & 0 & 0 \\ 0 & 1 & 1 & 1 & 0 & 0 \\ 0 & 1 & 0 & 0 & 1 & 0 \\ 0 & 0 & 1 & 0 & 0 & 1 \end{pmatrix} \begin{pmatrix} Z \\ x_1 \\ x_2 \\ s_1 \\ s_2 \\ s_3 \end{pmatrix} = \begin{pmatrix} 0 \\ 20 \\ 16 \\ 10 \end{pmatrix}. \tag{11.32}$$

Obviously, all the variables x_1, x_2, s_1, s_2, s_3 are nonnegative.

Step 1 is to figure out a corner point or a BFS. We first set $x_1 = 0$ and $x_2 = 0$, and thus now the basic variables are s_1, s_2, and s_3. From Eq. (11.32) with $x_1 = x_2 = 0$ we can easily obtain

$$s_1 = 20, \; s_2 = 16, \; s_3 = 10. \tag{11.33}$$

In this case the objective function $Z = 0$. This BFS corresponds to the origin O at (0,0), as shown Fig. 11.2.

The beauty of the canonical form is that the column corresponding to each basic variable has only one nonzero entry (marked by a box) associated with each constraint equality. All other entries in the same column are zero. In most cases the nonzero value is not unity. The convention is that the nonzero value is converted into 1 by dividing this value. Thus the matrix form has a nice structure, as shown below as an example:

$$\begin{matrix} Z & x_1 & x_2 & s_1 & s_2 & s_3 \end{matrix}$$
$$\begin{pmatrix} 1 & -2 & -3 & 0 & 0 & 0 \\ 0 & 1 & 1 & \boxed{1} & 0 & 0 \\ 0 & 1 & 0 & 0 & \boxed{1} & 0 \\ 0 & 0 & 1 & 0 & 0 & \boxed{1} \end{pmatrix}. \tag{11.34}$$

It is worth pointing out that two conventions exist for numbering the rows of a matrix. On the one hand, we can refer to the first row [1, −2, −3, 0, 0, 0] as the 0th row, which means that all other rows correspond to their corresponding constraint inequality. On the other hand, we can simply use its order in the matrix, so [1, −2, −3, 0, 0, 0] is simply the first row. For simplicity, we will use the latter as our standard numbering convention.

Step 2 is to see if we can improve the objective by increasing one of the nonbasic variables x_1 and x_2.

From (11.32) the first row gives

$$Z - 2x_1 - 3x_2 + 0s_1 + 0s_2 + 0s_3 = 0. \tag{11.35}$$

The coefficients of x_1 and x_2 are -2 and -3, respectively. If we increase x_1 by one unit, then Z will also increase by two units. But if we increase x_2 by one unit, then Z will increase by three units. Thus, to increase Z most, we should choose to increase x_2 as much as possible. However, the requirement of the nonnegativeness of all variables will impose a limit on x_2.

To increase x_2 while ensuring $x_1 = 0$, we have

$$s_1 = 20 - x_2, \quad s_2 = 16, \quad s_3 = 10 - x_2, \tag{11.36}$$

which implies that the highest possible value of x_2 is $x_2 = 10$ when $s_1 = s_3 = 0$. Further increase of x_2 will lead to negative values of s_1 and s_2.

Step 3 is to try to move to an adjacent corner point. We can either set $x_1 = 0$ and $s_1 = 0$ as nonbasic variables or set $x_1 = 0$ and $s_3 = 0$. Both cases correspond to the point A(0,10) in our example. For simplicity, let us choose $x_1 = 0$ and $s_3 = 0$ as nonbasic variables, and thus the basic variables are x_2, s_1, and s_2.

To carry out some pivot operations, we can replace s_3 by x_2 as a new basic variable. Since each constraint equation has only a single basic variable in the new canonical form, we should ensure that each column corresponding to each basic variable should have only a single nonzero entry, typically unity. To convert the third column for x_2 to the form with only a single nonzero entry 1 while ensuring that all other coefficients in the column are zero, we first multiply the fourth row by 3 and add it to the first row, which means that the first row now becomes

$$Z - 2x_1 + 0x_2 + 0s_1 + 0s_2 + 3s_3 = 30. \tag{11.37}$$

Similarly, we can multiply the fourth row by -1 and add it to the second row, and we get

$$0Z + x_1 + 0x_2 + s_1 + 0s_2 - s_3 = 10. \tag{11.38}$$

Using the above results, the new canonical form can be written as

$$\begin{pmatrix} 1 & -2 & 0 & 0 & 0 & 3 \\ 0 & 1 & 0 & 1 & 0 & -1 \\ 0 & 1 & 0 & 0 & 1 & 0 \\ 0 & 0 & 1 & 0 & 0 & 1 \end{pmatrix} \begin{pmatrix} Z \\ x_1 \\ x_2 \\ s_1 \\ s_2 \\ s_3 \end{pmatrix} = \begin{pmatrix} 30 \\ 10 \\ 16 \\ 10 \end{pmatrix}, \tag{11.39}$$

where the third, fourth, and fifth columns (for x_2, s_1, and s_2, respectively) have only one nonzero coefficient. All the values on the right-hand side are nonnegative.

Based on this new canonical form, we can find a BFS by setting nonbasic variables equal to zero, that is, setting $x_1 = 0$ and $s_3 = 0$. So we have the new BFS

$$x_2 = 10, \; s_1 = 10, \; s_2 = 16, \tag{11.40}$$

which corresponds to the corner point A. The objective $Z = 30$.

The next question is if we can improve the objective by increasing the nonbasic variables. Since the objective

$$Z = 30 + 2x_1 - 3s_3 \tag{11.41}$$

will increase by 2 units if x_1 is increased by 1, but Z will decrease by 3 if s_3 is increased by 1. Obviously, the best way to improve the objective is to increase x_1. Again, the nonnegativeness will impose a limit on x_1. To find this limit, we hold s_3 at 0, and we have

$$s_1 = 10 - x_1, \; s_2 = 16 - x_1, x_2 = 10. \tag{11.42}$$

Clearly, x_1 can increase up to $x_1 = 10$, since after that s_1 becomes negative. Thus we have $x_1 = 10$ and $s_1 = 0$, which corresponds to corner B. This also suggests that the new adjacent basic feasible solution can be obtained by choosing s_1 and s_3 as the nonbasic variables. So we now replace s_1 with x_1, and the new basic variables are x_1, x_2, and s_2.

To make sure that the second column (for x_1) has only a single nonzero entry, we can multiply the second row by 2 and add it to the first row, and we have the new first row

$$Z + 0x_1 + 0x_2 + 2s_1 + 0s_2 + s_3 = 50. \tag{11.43}$$

Similarly, we multiply the second row by -1 and add it to the third row, and we have

$$0Z + 0x_1 + 0x_2 - s_1 + s_2 + s_3 = 6. \tag{11.44}$$

Now the new canonical form becomes

$$\begin{pmatrix} 1 & 0 & 0 & 2 & 0 & 1 \\ 0 & 1 & 0 & 1 & 0 & -1 \\ 0 & 0 & 0 & -1 & 1 & 1 \\ 0 & 0 & 1 & 0 & 0 & 1 \end{pmatrix} \begin{pmatrix} Z \\ x_1 \\ x_2 \\ s_1 \\ s_2 \\ s_3 \end{pmatrix} = \begin{pmatrix} 50 \\ 10 \\ 6 \\ 10 \end{pmatrix}, \tag{11.45}$$

and its BFS can be found by setting nonbasic variables $s_1 = s_3 = 0$. So we get

$$x_1 = 10, \; x_2 = 10, \; s_2 = 6, \tag{11.46}$$

and this BFS corresponds to the corner point B in Fig. 11.2 with the objective value of $Z = 50$.

Step 4 is to check if we can improve the objective further. Since the objective is expressed as

$$Z = 50 - 2s_1 - s_3, \tag{11.47}$$

any increase of s_1 or s_3 from zero will decrease the objective value. This means that we cannot improve the objective, and thus the current BFS is optimal. In fact, this BFS is the same solution as that obtained earlier from the graphic method. Based on the stopping criterion, we can stop the process and conclude that we have found the best solution or the optimal solution.

As we have clearly seen that the main advantage of the simplex method is that we have found the optimal solution after searching a certain number of corner points. Not all extreme or corners are evaluated. In fact, there is no need to evaluate other extreme points at all. In practice, it needs to go through only a small fraction of corner points to figure out the optimal solution. This is exactly why the simplex method is so efficient and widely used.

The standard LP formulation in terms of matrix representations makes it straightforward to implement in many programming languages. There are a wide spectrum of software packages for solving LP problems, including Matlab, Excel Solver, R, Python, and OpenSolver.

11.4. Integer programming

The variables in the LP problems we have introduced so far can take continuous real values. In our example, we solved it without explicitly imposing the integer values for x and y, and we managed to find the correct integer solutions. This is just a lucky case or a particular case. In general, we may not be able to find integer solutions without explicitly imposing the integer constraints.

An LP problem with all variables being integers is called integer linear programming (ILP) problem or an integer program (IP) for short. The IP problems are a special class of combinatorial optimization problems, and they belong to a class of nondeterministic polynomial-time (NP) hard problems. There are no efficient algorithms for solving large-scale NP-hard problems. Therefore the IP problems we will solve are small-scale problems in the rest of this chapter. For larger problem sizes, special techniques or approximation techniques are needed.

11.4.1 LP in continuous domain

Before we introduce integer programming in general, let us use an example to show the continuous characteristics of standard LP by trying to solve the simple LP

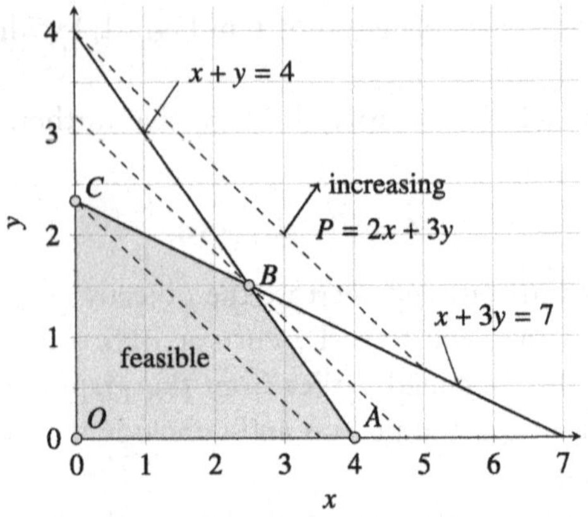

Figure 11.3 A simple linear program.

$$\text{maximize } P = 2x + 3y, \tag{11.48}$$

subject to

$$x + y \leq 4, \tag{11.49}$$

$$x + 3y \leq 7, \tag{11.50}$$

$$x, y \geq 0. \tag{11.51}$$

It is straightforward to solve this problem using either graphic method or the simplex method. For simplicity, the feasible domain and constraints are shown in Fig. 11.3. Dashed lines are isoprofit lines corresponding to fixed values of the objective function P. As the aim is to maximize P, the optimal solution should occur at the corner B with the highest objective value.

The solution at B satisfies both equalities

$$x + y = 4, \quad x + 3y = 7, \tag{11.52}$$

which leads to

$$x = 2.5, \quad y = 1.5. \tag{11.53}$$

Thus the objective value at B is

$$P = 2x + 3y = 2 \times (2.5) + 3 \times 1.5 = 9.5. \tag{11.54}$$

Both x and y are not integers.

11.4.2 Integer linear programming

In many cases, variables such as the number of customers must be integers, so we have to deal with integer programming problems. For the previous LP problem, if both variables x and y are integers ($\mathbb{I}$), it becomes the ILP problem

$$\text{maximize } P = 2x + 3y, \tag{11.55}$$

subject to

$$x + y \le 4, \tag{11.56}$$

$$x + 3y \le 7, \tag{11.57}$$

$$x, y \ge 0, \tag{11.58}$$

$$x, y \in \mathbb{I}. \tag{11.59}$$

It is worth pointing out that $\mathbb{I}$ denotes the set of nonnegative integers and $\mathbb{Z}$ denotes the set of all integers.

In the case of one variable taking only integers and the other variable being any real number, the problem becomes a mixed-integer programming (MIP) problem.

11.4.3 Bounds of optimality by LP relaxation

In general, integer programming problems are difficult to solve because the standard simplex method cannot be used directly. Exact methods such as the branch-and-bound method can be very time consuming with many possible subproblems. If the aim is to estimate the optimality, then the LP relaxation method can give some useful results.

Since the decision variables are integers, the feasible domain becomes a set of a finite number of points (usually a very large number), and the number of possible permutations can be astronomical. Thus a systematical approach is needed.

For the simple problem given in Eq. (11.55), the feasible domain consists of 11 discrete points, marked as gray dots in Fig. 11.4. Since there are only 11 points, it is easy to verify that the global optimal solution is

$$x = 3, \quad y = 1, \qquad P = 2 \times 3 + 3 \times 1 = 9, \tag{11.60}$$

which is marked best in Fig. 11.4.

To understand the role of the integer constraints $x, y \in \mathbb{I}$, let us first ignore the constraint and try to solve the standard LP to see the location of possible optimality. This idea is essentially the LP relaxation method.

Without the integer constraint, the above IP problem becomes the LP problem we solved earlier, and its solution is

$$x_* = 2.5, \quad y_* = 1.5, \qquad P = 9.5. \tag{11.61}$$

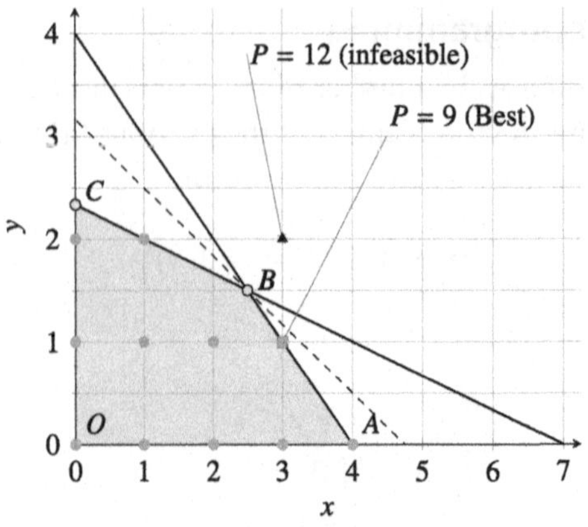

Figure 11.4 Integer programming.

A naive next step is to round this solution to the nearest integers to ensure that x and y are integers. In this case the above solution leads to four possibilities of rounding:

$$x=3, \quad y=1, \tag{11.62}$$

$$x=3, \quad y=2, \tag{11.63}$$

$$x=2, \quad y=1, \tag{11.64}$$

$$x=2, \quad y=2. \tag{11.65}$$

Among the four cases, not all constraints are satisfied. By applying all the constraints, we have

$$x=3, \quad y=1, \quad P=9 \quad \text{(feasible)}, \tag{11.66}$$

$$x=3, \quad y=2, \quad P=12 \quad \text{(infeasible)}, \tag{11.67}$$

$$x=2, \quad y=1, \quad P=7 \quad \text{(feasible)}, \tag{11.68}$$

$$x=2, \quad y=2, \quad P=10 \quad \text{(infeasible)}. \tag{11.69}$$

Here the two infeasible solutions are outside the feasible domain. For two feasible solutions, the point at $x=3$ and $y=1$ corresponds to the global best with $P=9$ (marked with a square in Fig. 11.4).

In this simple case, the LP relaxation method, together with rounding to integers, seems to work well. However, this is a particular or lucky case, but in general the global optimality is not achievable by such LP relaxation.

To show this important point, let us solve a slightly different problem with the same constraints but with a new objective function $Q=x+4y$. So we have

$$\text{maximize } Q=x+4y, \tag{11.70}$$

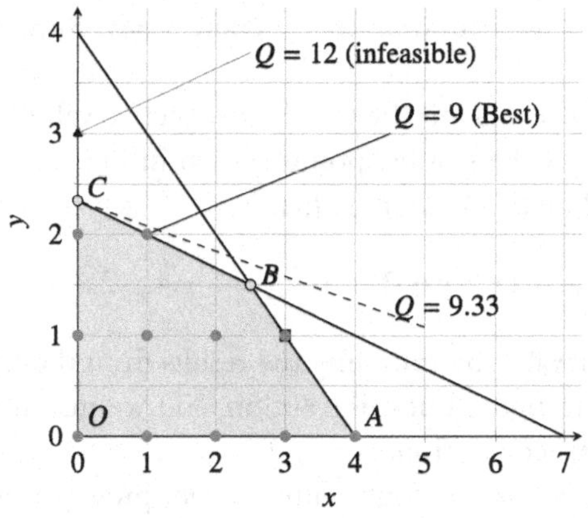

Figure 11.5 Integer programming (with an alternative objective).

subject to

$$x + y \leq 4, \tag{11.71}$$

$$x + 3y \leq 7, \tag{11.72}$$

$$x, y \geq 0, \tag{11.73}$$

$$x, y \in \mathbb{I}. \tag{11.74}$$

As all the constraints are the same, the feasible domain remains the same as before, and the feasible points are shown in Fig. 11.5.

Using LP relaxation by first ignoring the integer constraints, we can solve the corresponding LP

$$\text{maximize } Q = x + 4y, \tag{11.75}$$

subject to

$$x + y \leq 4, \tag{11.76}$$

$$x + 3y \leq 7, \tag{11.77}$$

$$x, y \geq 0. \tag{11.78}$$

It is straightforward to show that the solution is at C with

$$x_* = 0, \quad y_* = 7/3 = 2.333333, \quad Q = x_* + 4y_* = 28/3 = 9.33333. \tag{11.79}$$

Rounding this solution to the nearest integers, we get

$$x = 0, \quad y = 2, \quad Q = 0 + 4 \times 2 = 8. \tag{11.80}$$

A natural question is why not round up to $x=0$ and $y=3$? However, the point at $x=0$ and $y=3$ is not feasible.

Though we obtain $Q=8$, is this the true best objective value (highest for maximization)? If we look closely at the feasible points shown in Fig. 11.5, it is obvious that the point at $x=1$ and $y=2$ gives a higher Q, that is,

$$x=1, \quad y=2, \qquad Q=1+4\times 2=9. \tag{11.81}$$

This solution is not achievable by rounding the results from the LP relaxation. Without the graph, it is not easy to figure out this solution, and we may have to try ever possible combination to reach this conclusion.

In general, there are two issues concerning integer programming:

- The globally optimal solution cannot be achieved by first carrying out LP relaxation and then rounding up.
- It is impractical to try every possible combination in practice because the number of combinations grows exponentially as the problem size increases.

There are different approaches to tackle such integer programs systematically, though not very efficient in most cases, including the branch-and-bound, cut-and-bound, cutting planes, heuristic methods, and others. In the rest of this chapter, we will only introduce the essential branch-and-bound method.

11.5. Branch-and-bound method

The basic idea of the branch-and-bound approach is to divide and conquer. The branch step divides the problem into subproblems (usually smaller problems), whereas the bound step solves relevant subproblems so as to find a better feasible solution. The stop criterion decides if a branch should stop.

Briefly speaking, the branch-and-bound procedure consists of three major steps:

1. Divide the problem into subproblems.
2. Solve each subproblem by LP relaxation.
3. Decide if a branch should be stopped.

For a given problem P_1, the branching division is carried out by choosing a variable with a noninteger solution, first obtained by using LP relaxation to solve P_1. Suppose that the LP relaxation gives variable x a noninteger value of x_*. We can then divide the problem into two subproblems by adding an additional constraint to round x_* to two nearest integers (one above and one below):

- Problem P_2: $x \le \lfloor x_* \rfloor$;
- Problem P_3: $x \ge \lceil x_* \rceil$;

The domains of the two subproblems form two subdomains that split the original feasible domain into two regions or domains. The next step is to solve each of the subproblems.

For example, if $x_* = 3.7$, then we have

$$\lfloor x_* \rfloor = 3, \quad \lceil x_* \rceil = 4, \tag{11.82}$$

which leads to two new subproblems:

- Problem P_2: $x \le 3$;
- Problem P_3: $x \ge 4$.

In essence, this subdivision makes the search domain smaller, which may potentially help to solve these subproblems.

11.5.1 When to stop

In the branch-and-bound method, the following stopping criteria are used for deciding a branching process:

- Stop if the new LP has no feasible solution (e.g., constraints are not all satisfied).
- Stop if the new LP has a lower optimal objective (for maximization problems).
- Stop if the LP problem has an optimal integer solution.

In essence, the branching process can be viewed as a decision tree technique, and each subproblem forms a branch of the decision tree. Mathematically speaking, the LP relaxation of an IP problem will make its feasible domain slightly larger, and thus the optimal solution obtained by solving the relaxed LP provides an upper bound for the original IP (for maximization) because the solution to the IP cannot exceed the optimal solution to its corresponding LP in terms of the objective value in the same feasible domain. Similarly, for minimization problems, the LP relaxation will provide a lower bound.

11.5.2 A worked example

To show how the branch-and-bound process works, let us solve the following IP:

$$\text{Problem} \quad P_0 : \text{maximize } Q = 2x + 3y, \tag{11.83}$$

subject to

$$x + y \le 4, \tag{11.84}$$

$$x + 3y \le 7, \tag{11.85}$$

$$x, y \ge 0, \tag{11.86}$$

$$x, y \in \mathbb{I}. \tag{11.87}$$

The first LP relaxation problem becomes

$$\text{Relaxed LP } P_0 : \text{maximize } Q = 2x + 3y, \tag{11.88}$$

subject to

$$x + y \le 4, \tag{11.89}$$
$$x + 3y \le 7, \tag{11.90}$$
$$x, y \ge 0. \tag{11.91}$$

Using the standard simplex method, as we did earlier, we can find its optimal solution

$$x_* = 2.5, \quad y_* = 1.5, \quad Q = 9.5. \tag{11.92}$$

Since both x_* and y_* are not integers, we have to subdivide in terms of either x or y.

Suppose that we choose to branch x by adding an extra constraint $x \le 2$ or $x \ge 3$. Then we have two subproblems:

$$\text{Subproblem } \ P_1 : \text{maximize } Q = 2x + 3y, \tag{11.93}$$

subject to

$$x + y \le 4, \tag{11.94}$$
$$x + 3y \le 7, \tag{11.95}$$
$$x, y \ge 0, \tag{11.96}$$
$$x, y \in \mathbb{I}, \tag{11.97}$$
$$x \le 2; \tag{11.98}$$

$$\text{Subproblem } \ P_2 : \text{maximize } Q = 2x + 3y, \tag{11.99}$$

subject to

$$x + y \le 4, \tag{11.100}$$
$$x + 3y \le 7, \tag{11.101}$$
$$x, y \ge 0, \tag{11.102}$$
$$x, y \in \mathbb{I}, \tag{11.103}$$
$$x \ge 3. \tag{11.104}$$

It is straightforward to show that both subproblems have feasible solutions, and their graph representations are shown in Fig. 11.6.

The next step is to solve two subproblems along two different branches. For Subproblem P_2, its solution (via LP relaxation) is

$$x_* = 3, \ \ y_* = 1, \quad Q = 2 \times 3 + 3 \times 1 = 9. \tag{11.105}$$

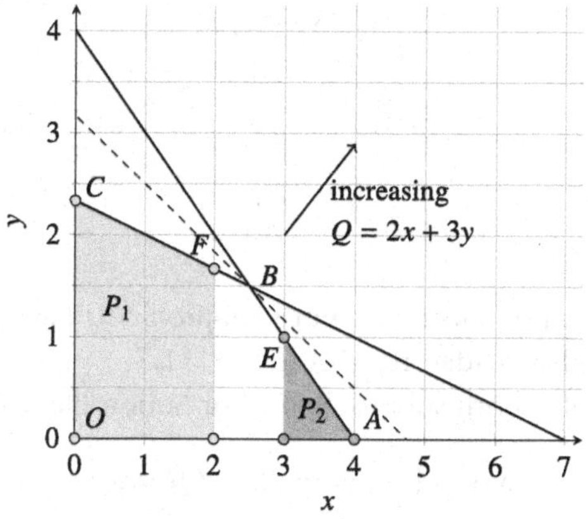

Figure 11.6 Branch and bound with subproblems.

Since this solution is an integer solution, the stopping criterion is met, so there is no need to subdivide it further, and we can consider this branch completed. Thus $Q = 9$ at (3,1) is the best bound we get so far.

For Subproblem P_1, its corresponding relaxed LP gives a solution

$$x_{*1} = 2, \quad y_{*1} = 5/3 = 1.6666, \quad Q = 9, \tag{11.106}$$

which corresponds to point F in Fig. 11.7. However, this solution is not an integer solution, so we have to carry out further branching. By adding a constraint $y \geq 2$ or $y \leq 1$ we have two new subproblems:

$$\text{Subproblem } \; P_3 : \text{maximize } Q = 2x + 3y, \tag{11.107}$$

subject to

$$x + y \leq 4, \tag{11.108}$$
$$x + 3y \leq 7, \tag{11.109}$$
$$x, y \geq 0, \tag{11.110}$$
$$x, y \in \mathbb{I}, \tag{11.111}$$
$$x \leq 2, \tag{11.112}$$
$$y \geq 2, \tag{11.113}$$
$$\text{Subproblem } \; P_4 : \text{maximize } Q = 2x + 3y, \tag{11.114}$$

subject to

$$x + y \leq 4, \tag{11.115}$$

$$x + 3y \le 7, \quad (11.116)$$
$$x, y \ge 0, \quad (11.117)$$
$$x, y \in \mathbb{I}, \quad (11.118)$$
$$x \le 2, \quad (11.119)$$
$$y \le 1. \quad (11.120)$$

Again, it is straightforward to show that both subproblems have feasible solutions, and their domains are marked as shaded regions in Fig. 11.7.

The next task is to solve both subproblems. For Subproblem P_3, its relaxed LP gives

$$x_{*3} = 1, \quad y_{*3} = 2, \quad Q_3 = 8, \quad (11.121)$$

which corresponds to Point D in Fig. 11.7. Since this is an integer solution and its objective value $Q_3 = 8$ is lower than the current best $Q = 9$, we can stop this branch. The stopping criterion is satisfied for this branch, and thus there is no need to continue along this branch.

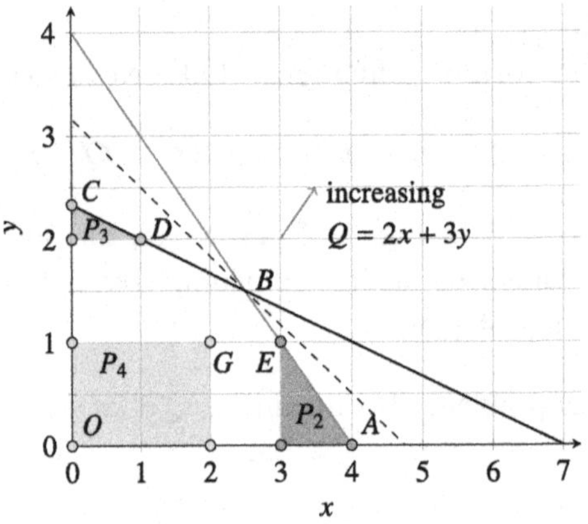

Figure 11.7 Branch and bound (subproblems, continued).

For Subproblem P_4, it is easy to verify that the solution to its relaxed LP is

$$x_{*4} = 2, \quad y_{*4} = 1, \quad Q_4 = 7, \quad (11.122)$$

which corresponds to Point G in the same figure (Fig. 11.7). Since it is an integer solution but its objective value is lower than $Q = 9$, there is need to consider this branch any further, and the stopping criterion is met.

After solving the above four subproblems, we can now conclude that the optimal solution to the original IP problem is

$$x_* = 3, \quad y_* = 1, \quad Q = 9. \quad (11.123)$$

For this simple problem, it is not difficult to find the optimal solution. For large-scale problems, it is not possible to carry out the whole process by solving subproblems with graphs. The essential processes remain the same, and thus computer software should be used to solve multiple subproblems and record the results.

11.5.3 The order of branching

In the previous worked example, we start the branch-and-bound process from the relaxed LP problem with the solution $x_* = 2.5$ and $y_* = 1.5$. We carried out the branching process first in terms of x to give $x \geq 3$ and $x \leq 2$. What happens if we start the branching process in terms of y first (instead of x)?

We leave it as an exercise for the readers to show that only two subproblems need to be evaluated before reaching the same final optimal solution with $Q = 9$. Thus different branching decisions may lead to different branch trees and may potentially save some computational costs, so it may be worth the efforts to seek which way is better. However, there is no universal guide about how to branch at a particular point of branching trees. In practice, most software packages follow a certain rule or simply randomly choose a noninteger variable to start the branching process. As the computer is getting more powerful nowadays, which branch to choose first does not matter much in practice.

11.5.4 Mixed-integer programming

In general, the variables in standard LP problems are real numbers, where variables take only integers values in IP problems. If some of the variables take only integer values while other variables are real numbers, then the LP problem becomes a mixed-integer programming (MIP) problem.

In principle, the branch-and-bound method we have just discussed can be applied to solve such MIP problems without any modification. Clearly, the branch and bound should start with the noninteger solutions of the integer variables and proceed as outlined in the previous section.

For example, in the discussion of the branch-and-bound process, we have the problem

$$\text{maximize} \quad Q = x + 4y, \tag{11.124}$$

subject to

$$x + y \leq 4, \; x + 3y \leq 7, \tag{11.125}$$

and

$$x, y \geq 0, \quad x, y \in \mathbb{I}. \tag{11.126}$$

Table 11.1 Transport problem with m suppliers and n demands.

Supply	Demand (D_1)	D_2	...	Demand (D_n)
S_1	c_{11}	c_{12}	$\cdots$	c_{1n}
S_2	c_{21}	c_{22}	$\cdots$	c_{2n}
$\vdots$	$\vdots$	$\vdots$	$\ddots$	$\vdots$
S_m	c_{m1}	c_{m2}	$\cdots$	c_{mn}

In case that y takes real numbers (no longer integers), it becomes a mixed-integer program. Its LP relaxation gives a solution

$$x_* = 0, \quad y_* = 7/3, \quad Q_* = 28/3. \tag{11.127}$$

Since x_* is an integer and y is real, this solution is the global optimal solution for the MIP. The optimal solution is found without any need for branch and bound.

Obviously, this is an extreme simple example for MIPs. In general, to solve IPs and MIPs, the branch-and-bound method can become computationally extensive, especially the number of integer variables is large. Other methods such as cutting planes, branch and cut, and heuristic methods can be used.

11.6. Applications and problem formulations

The applications of LP are very diverse, ranging from logistic problems to scheduling problems and from manufacturing engineering to industrial planning. In this section, we will briefly explain the basic formulations of different problems in terms of LP and standard forms. It is worth pointing out that for each type of problem such as the transport problems, there are more than one way of formulating a problem as an LP, and some formulations may be easier or simpler than others. Here our emphasis is not on any easier formulations, so we will introduce one popular way of the formulations.

11.6.1 Transport and logistic problem

For a given product or a set of goods, a logistic problem is to transport the supplies to customers so as to minimize the overall transport costs or distances. To transport goods from m suppliers (or manufacturers) to n locations (shops, facilities, demand stations/centers), a transport cost matrix $C = [c_{ij}]$ is usually given, which shows the unit cost for transporting one unit of product from Supplier i to Demand j. The cost matrix and the quantities of supply and demand are shown in Table 11.1.

Since there are m suppliers (S_i, $i = 1, 2, \ldots, m$) and n demand stations (D_j, $j = 1, 2, \ldots, n$), $m \times n$ decision variables are needed. Let $x_{ij} \geq 0$ denote the units to be transported from S_i to D_j. The main objective is to minimize the overall transport cost

$$\text{minimize } f(x) = \sum_{i=1}^{m} \sum_{j=1}^{n} c_{ij} x_{ij}. \tag{11.128}$$

A natural requirement is that the total shipment from each supplier must be smaller than or equal to its own supply quantity, that is,

$$\sum_{j=1}^{n} x_{ij} \leq S_i \quad (i = 1, 2, \ldots, m). \tag{11.129}$$

Similarly, each demand must be met, which means that

$$\sum_{i=1}^{m} x_{ij} \geq D_j \quad (j = 1, 2, \ldots, n). \tag{11.130}$$

In general, the total supply quantity is not the same as the total demand quantity, and this is the unbalanced case. In the special case of balanced supply and demand, the total supplies are equal to the total demands, which leads to

$$\sum_{i=1}^{m} S_i = \sum_{j=1}^{n} D_j. \tag{11.131}$$

If we consider the role of warehouses, then it is always possible to transform an unbalanced case into a balanced case by using a dummy supplier (if the supply is not enough) or dummy demand (if the supply is higher than all demands). For simplicity, a dummy supplier or a demand station can be considered as a warehouse with a flexible capacity. In this case, all the inequality constraints become equality constraints.

11.6.2 Balanced problem

For balanced cases of supply and demand, we have the standard LP formulation for transport problems

$$\text{minimize } \sum_{i=1}^{m} \sum_{j=1}^{n} c_{ij} x_{ij}, \tag{11.132}$$

subject to

$$\sum_{j=1}^{n} x_{ij} = S_i \quad (i = 1, 2, \ldots, m), \tag{11.133}$$

Table 11.2 Product portfolio of a small factory.

Product	Materials	Assembly	Transport	Profit
A	115	14	6	40
B	70	20	10	50
C	60	15	12	60
D	35	5	2	20

$$\sum_{i=1}^{m} x_{ij} = D_j \quad (j = 1, 2, \ldots, n), \tag{11.134}$$

$$\sum_{i=1}^{m} S_i = \sum_{j=1}^{n} D_j, \tag{11.135}$$

and the nonnegativity condition

$$x_{ij} \geq 0. \tag{11.136}$$

This LP problem has mn decision variables with $m + n + 1$ equality constraints. It is worth pointing out that x_{ij} in the above formulation should be integers, whereas for other applications, they can be real numbers.

Many other problems in real-world applications can also be formulated as LP problems, including resource allocation problems, staff assignment, dietary problems, and many others.

11.6.3 Maximization of product portfolios

Another type of optimization is portfolio optimization, which is relevant to many applications such as product mix optimization and financial portfolio optimization. It is not possible to provide a generic formulation for all types of portfolio optimization because the formulations may depend on how to maximize or minimize and various requirements. Therefore we will use a specific example to show one type of formulations.

A small factory produces a portfolio of four different products (A,B,C,D) with different materials costs, assembly costs, and transport costs (all in £) as shown in Table 11.2.

Due to budget and resource constraints, the factory has a maximum budget for daily costs of £7000 for materials, £1500 for assembly, and £600 for transport. To make a marginal profit, it must produce at least 10 units for each product. Now the main objective is to design a product portfolio so that the total profit is maximized on a daily basis.

Since there are four products, four decision variables are needed. Let $x_i \geq 0$ ($i = 1, 2, 3, 4$) be the numbers (or units) of products (A,B,C,D, respectively) to be produced daily. The daily profit is given by

$$P(x) = 40x_1 + 50x_2 + 60x_3 + 20x_4. \tag{11.137}$$

The material costs are limited to £7000, which leads to

$$115x_1 + 70x_2 + 60x_3 + 35x_4 \leq 7000. \tag{11.138}$$

Similarly, the assembly cost is limited to £1500, which gives

$$14x_1 + 20x_2 + 15x_3 + 5x_4 \leq 1500. \tag{11.139}$$

The limit on the overall transport cost means that

$$6x_1 + 10x_2 + 12x_3 + 2x_4 \leq 600. \tag{11.140}$$

In addition, we should also set

$$x_i \in \mathbb{I} \quad (i = 1, 2, 3, 4). \tag{11.141}$$

Using relaxed LP with the branch and bound may take many steps to solve problems with four decision variables. However, this is a particular case because the relaxed LP gives an integer solution. Thus we leave it as an exercise for the readers to show that the optimal portfolio is $A = 10$, $B = 10$, $C = 17$, and $D = 118$ with total daily profit $P = 4280$.

We can extend the above formulation to n different products with c_i $(i = 1, 2, \ldots, n)$ profit per unit. The overall profit becomes

$$P(x) = \sum_{i=1}^{n} c_i x_i, \tag{11.142}$$

where $x_i \geq 0$ are the units/numbers of products to be produced. For each stage $j = 1, 2, \ldots, K$ for producing the products (such as materials or assembly), the resource requirements mean that

$$\sum_{i=1}^{n} a_{ij} x_i \leq b_j \quad (j = 1, 2, \ldots, K), \tag{11.143}$$

where b_j is the budget constraint for stage i, and a_{ij} is the unit cost of product i to be processed at stage j. With these notations, a general product portfolio problem can be written as

$$\text{maximize} \ \sum_{i=1}^{n} c_i x_i, \tag{11.144}$$

Table 11.3 Production scheduling.

Season	Unit Cost	Unit Price
Spring	11	–
Summer	17	23
Autumn	15	19
Winter	–	22

subject to

$$\sum_{i=1}^{n} a_{ij} x_i \le b_j \quad (j = 1, 2, \ldots, K), \tag{11.145}$$

$$x_i \ge 0 \quad (i = 1, 2, \ldots, n). \tag{11.146}$$

In addition, integer constraints $x_i \in \mathbb{I}$ may be necessary, depending on the actual problem under consideration.

11.6.4 Manufacturing scheduling

LP can be used to model scheduling problems. In general, scheduling itself is a class of challenging problems that can be NP-hard in many applications. Formulation of such scheduling problems can be problem-dependent.

The number of decision variables can vary, depending on the formulation, and some of the constraints may not be obvious from the descriptions and requirements. To show the complexity of a simple scheduling problem, let us formulate the scheduling of a simple manufacturing problem.

A company that manufactures a certain type of expensive products such as small aircraft or a batch of seasonal clothes. The manufacturing costs vary with season. For example, the cost of manufacturing one product or a batch is 11 million dollars in spring, whereas this product can be sold at a price of 23 million dollars. The details are shown in Table 11.3, where "–" means no production or sales. The company can have a capacity of producing at most 40 units per season, whereas their warehouse can store up to 5 units at most. Ideally, all the products should be sold by the end of the year (winter) so that nothing is left in the warehouse.

To formulate this scheduling problem as an LP, let x_1, x_2, x_3, x_4 be the numbers of units produced in four seasons, respectively. In the winter, it is required that $x_4 = 0$; otherwise, it cannot be sold by the end of the year. Let s_i $(i = 1, 2, 3, 4)$ be the numbers of sales in each season. Obviously, $s_1 = 0$ because there is nothing yet to sell in spring.

The profit or objective function is the difference between sales income and the production costs

$$P = 23s_2 + 19s_3 + 22s_4 - (11x_1 + 17x_2 + 15x_3). \tag{11.147}$$

To consider the number of units in the warehouse, the numbers of units in the warehouse in each season are denoted by w_1, w_2, w_3, and w_4, respectively. The capacity of the warehouse means that $0 \le w_i \le 5$ for $i = 1, 2, 3, 4$.

If all products must be sold out by the end of the year, then we can set $w_4 = 0$. At the end of each season, the units in the warehouse is the number of units in the previous season plus the production in this season, subtracting the actual sales in that season. Thus we have

$$w_1 = x_1 \text{ (no sales)}, \qquad w_2 = w_1 + x_2 - s_2, \tag{11.148}$$

and

$$w_3 = w_2 + x_3 - s_3, \qquad w_4 = w_3 - s_4 = 0. \tag{11.149}$$

The capacity constraints and nonnegativity condition mean that

$$w_i \le 5, \;\; x_i, s_i \le 40, \tag{11.150}$$

and

$$x_i, s_i, w_i \ge 0 \quad (i = 1, 2, 3, 4). \tag{11.151}$$

In addition, all x_i, s_i, w_i should be integers.

This scheduling problem needs 12 decision variables for four seasons. Though only x_i $(i = 1, 2, 3)$ matter, we have to add other variables to the formulation to account for all the requirements. This shows that scheduling problems such as staff scheduling in airlines and time-tabling for university classes can be a very challenging task.

11.6.5 Traveling salesman problem

Many NP-hard problems can be related to the well-known traveling salesman problem (TSP). The objective of the TSP is to find an optimal tour of visiting n cities once and exactly once starting from a city and returning to the same starting city so that the total distance traveled is minimal.

There are different ways for formulating the TSP, and there is a vast literature on this topic. The version we use here is based on the binary integer LP formulation by G. Dantzig et al. in 1954. Let $i = 1, 2, \ldots, n$ denote city i among n cities, and each city can be considered as a node on a graph. Let x_{ij} denote the decision variable for connecting city i to city j. An edge from node i to node j means that the tour in this part is from node i to node j, which corresponds to $x_{ij} = 1$. Otherwise, $x_{ij} = 0$ means no connection along this edge. Therefore all the cities form the set V of vertices and all the relevant connections form the set E of the edges. The direct distance from city i to city j is denoted by d_{ij}, which means that $d_{ij} = d_{ij}$ due to symmetry. In this case the graph representing the cities is undirected.

The main objective is to minimize the overall distance, that is,

$$\text{minimize} \sum_{i,j\in E, i\neq j} d_{ij}x_{ij}. \tag{11.152}$$

Since x_{ij} is a binary variable, we have

$$x_{ij} = 0 \quad \text{or} \quad 1, \qquad (i,j) \in V. \tag{11.153}$$

As each city i should be visited once and only once, this implies that only one edge enters a city and only one edge leaves the same city. This leads to

$$\sum_{i\in V} x_{ij} = 2 \quad \forall j \in V. \tag{11.154}$$

This can be equivalently written as

$$\sum_{j=1}^{n} x_{ij} = 1 \quad (i \in V, i \neq j) \tag{11.155}$$

and

$$\sum_{i=1}^{n} x_{ij} = 1 \quad (j \in V, j \neq i). \tag{11.156}$$

The whole tour must form a single path connecting all n cities.

To avoid any unconnected subtour, for any nonempty subset $S \subset V$ of n cities, it is required that

$$\sum_{i,j\in S} x_{ij} \leq |S| - 1 \quad (2 \leq |S| \leq n - 2), \tag{11.157}$$

where $|S|$ is the cardinality of the subset S (i.e., the number of elements of the set).

The LP formulation of the TSP essentially becomes a binary integer linear programming (BILP) problem. However, it is an NP-hard problem, and thus there are no efficient algorithms to solve it.

In real-world applications, many problems can be reformulated as LP problems, including the network flow, flow shop scheduling, packaging problems, vehicle routing, coverage problem, graph coloring problem, and others. The interested readers can refer to more advanced literature. Now let us conclude this chapter by commenting on the related software packages.

11.7. Notes on software

The simplex method and its variants have been implemented in many software packages. However, to deal with integer programming, additional constraint handling and techniques are required. In most implementations, both LP and IP problems can be solved successfully.

The simplex method has been implemented in many software packages, including *Matlab*, *Octave*, *Python*, *R*, *Excel Solver*, and *OpenSolver*. In addition, many symbolic mathematics software packages can also deal with linear programs, such as *Mathematica*, *Maple*, *Maxima*, and many others.

For example, we can solve our example using `linprog` in Matlab. For help, type `»doc linprog` to get its detailed usage, such as

```
»[x,fval]=linprog(f,A,b)
```

For example, the solution of the product portfolio problem can be solved by both Matlab and Octave. You can type `»doc intlinprog` to get more information about its usage in the format

```
[x,fmin]=intlinprog(f,intcon,A,b,[],[],Lb,Ub),
```

where `intcon` is the indicator if a variable is an integer.

To solve the product portfolio optimization problem, we can use the following Matlab code:

```
f=[40 50 60 20];
intcon=[1 2 3 4]; % (all 4 variables must be integers)
A=[115 70 60 35; 14 20 15 5; 6 10 12 2];
b=[7000; 1500; 600];
Lb=[10; 10; 10; 10]; Ub=[]; % Lower and upper bounds
[x,fmin]=intlinprog(-f,intcon,A,b,[],[],Lb,Ub)
```

The result is

$$x_1 = 10, \; x_2 = 10, \; x_3 = 17, \; x_4 = 118,$$

with $f_{\min} = -4280$. This means that $P = 4280$. Here we used $-f$ in the objective because Matlab's `linprog` solves the minimization problems by default, but our problem is maximization.

We can also use Octave's glpk package to solve this problem. We have

```
f=[40 50 60 20];              % Coefficients
vartype="IIII";               % All 4 variables must be integers
```

```
A=[115 70 60 35; 14 20 15 5; 6 10 12 2];
b=[7000; 1500; 600];
ctype="UUU";                 % # of U = number of rows in b
Lb=[10; 10; 10; 10]; Ub=[];  % Lower and upper bounds
Stype=-1;                    % Maximum (-1), minimum (+1, default)
[xbest, fmax]=glpk(f, A, b, Lb, Ub, ctype, vartype, Stype)
```

The result should be

$$\boldsymbol{x} = [10, 10, 17, 118], \quad f_{\max} = 4280.$$

Both Matlab and Octave find the same optimal solution with $P = f_{\max} = 4280$.

CHAPTER TWELVE

Probability and distributions

Engineering simulation sometime involves randomness, either due to the intrinsic nature of the processes (such as queueing and noise) or due to uncertainty or errors (such as the faulty components from manufacturing or machine breakdown). Thus it is necessary to study probability and statistic models. In this chapter, we introduce the fundamentals of probability and some commonly used probability distributions.

12.1. Random variables and probabilities

Randomness such as coin-flipping and noise requires the theory of probability to gain some insights. The theory of probability is mainly the studies of random phenomena so as to find nonrandom regularity.

Probability P is a number or an expected frequency assigned to an event A that indicates how likely it is that the event will occur when a random experiment is performed. Obviously, $0 \leq P \leq 1$; $P = 0$ means an impossibility, whereas $P = 1$ means a certainty. The notation $P(A)$ is usually used to show that the probability P is associated with event A.

A random variable is a quantity or a function of all possible outcomes. For example, a flip of a fair coin can have only two outcomes, head (H) or tail (T). A random variable representing this can only take two values, 1 or 0 (or 0 and 1 if appropriate). A random variable that can only take discrete values is called a discrete random variable. For example, the number of cars passing on a road or the number of calls received in a call center are discrete random variables. On the other hand, a random variable that takes continuous values is called a continuous variable, and examples are the noise level, time taken to travel through a traffic jam, and measurement errors of temperature and pressure.

A discrete random variable X takes distinct values x_i, and each occurs with a certain probability $p(x_i)$. In other words, the probability varies and is associated with its corresponding random variable. As an event must occur inside a sample space, the requirement that all the probabilities must be summed to one leads to

$$\sum_{i=1}^{n} p(x_i) = 1. \tag{12.1}$$

For example, the outcomes of tossing a fair coin form a sample space. The outcome of a head (H) is an event with probability $P(H) = 1/2$, and the outcome of a tail (T) is also

https://doi.org/10.1016/B978-0-44-314084-6.00019-X

an event with probability $P(T) = 1/2$. The sum of both probabilities should be one:

$$P(H) + P(T) = \frac{1}{2} + \frac{1}{2} = 1. \tag{12.2}$$

The probability distribution for a discrete random variable is called a probability mass function (PMF), which is a function on the discrete points. In contrast, the probability distribution of a continuous random variable is called a probability density function (PDF), which is a function on an interval.

The total probability of discrete outcomes in an interval can be described by the cumulative probability function (CPF) of X, which is defined by

$$P(X \leq x) = \sum_{x_i < x} p(x_i). \tag{12.3}$$

For a continuous variable, this becomes an integral.

Mathematically speaking, a continuous random variable X takes a continuous range of values, and its probability density function $p(x)$ is defined for a range of values $x \in [a, b]$ with given limits a and b (or even over the whole real axis $x \in (-\infty, \infty)$). Conventionally, we use the interval $(x, x + dx]$ so that the probability that the random variable X takes the value $x < X \leq x + dx$ is

$$\Phi(x) = P(x < X \leq x + dx) = p(x)dx. \tag{12.4}$$

Since all the probabilities of the distribution should be added to unity, we have

$$\int_a^b p(x)dx = 1. \tag{12.5}$$

Similarly to the CPF for discrete variables, the CPF for a continuous random variable is defined by

$$\Phi(x) = P(X \leq x) = \int_a^x p(x)dx, \tag{12.6}$$

which is essentially the integral of the PDF from the lower limit a up to the present value $X = x$.

Example 12.1. For a uniform distribution with the probability density function

$$p(x) = \frac{1}{b-a}, \quad b > a \geq 0, \tag{12.7}$$

its CPF can be calculated by

$$\Phi(x) = \int_a^x p(x)dx = \int_a^x \frac{1}{b-a} dx$$

$$= \frac{1}{b-a}\int_a^x dx = \frac{x-a}{b-a}. \tag{12.8}$$

This is consistent with the fact that $\Phi(a) = 0$ and $\Phi(b) = 1$.

12.2. Mean, variance, and moments

There are several statistical measures related to random variables. For a random variable X with known probability distribution $p(x)$, two most important measures are its mean and variance.

The mean μ or the expectation $\mathbb{E}[X]$ is defined by

$$\mu \equiv \mathbb{E}[X] = \int_a^b xp(x)dx \tag{12.9}$$

for a continuous distribution, where the integration is within the integration limits. If the random variable is discrete, then the integration becomes the weighted sum

$$\mathbb{E}[X] = \sum_i x_i p(x_i). \tag{12.10}$$

The variance of X is denoted by $\text{var}[X] = \sigma^2$, which is the expectation of the deviation squared $(X - \mu)^2$ and is given by

$$\sigma^2 \equiv \text{var}[X] = \mathbb{E}[(X-\mu)^2] = \int (x-\mu)^2 p(x)dx. \tag{12.11}$$

The square root of the variance (i.e., $\sigma = \sqrt{\text{var}[X]}$) is called the standard deviation.

Based on the definitions of mean and variance, it is easy to show the following properties:

$$\mathbb{E}[aX + b] = a\mathbb{E}[X] + b, \quad \mathbb{E}[X^2] = \mu^2 + \sigma^2, \tag{12.12}$$

and

$$\text{var}[aX + b] = a^2\text{var}[X], \tag{12.13}$$

where a and b are constants.

There are other measures that are also frequently used, including the mode and median as well as various moments. The mode of a distribution is defined by the value at which the probability density function $p(x)$ is the maximum. For an even number of data sets, the mode may have two values. The median m of a distribution corresponds to the value at which the cumulative probability function $\Phi(m) = 1/2$. The upper and lower quartiles Q_U and Q_L are defined by $\Phi(Q_U) = 3/4$ and $\Phi(Q_L) = 1/4$.

In general, the nth raw moment of a continuous random variable is defined by

$$M_n = \mathbb{E}[X^n] = \int_{-\infty}^{\infty} x^n p(x) dx, \tag{12.14}$$

where the integral is over the whole real domain or an interval $[a, b]$, depending on the probability distributions. The central moment about the mean μ is defined by

$$\mu_n = \int_{-\infty}^{\infty} (x - \mu)^n p(x) dx, \tag{12.15}$$

where

$$\mu = \mathbb{E}[X] = \int_{-\infty}^{\infty} x p(x) dx. \tag{12.16}$$

It is straightforward to see that the first raw moment is the mean, whereas the second central moment is the variance.

Higher-order moments are also useful. For example, the third central moment is the skewness, which measures the asymmetry of a probability distribution. The fourth central moment is called the kurtosis, which measures the heaviness of the tails of the probability distribution.

12.3. Discrete probability distributions

Because random variables can be discrete or continuous, their distributions fall into two categories, discrete or continuous. We now first introduce some discrete probability distributions.

12.3.1 Bernoulli distribution

For a discrete random variable with binary outcomes, such as a head or a tail of flipping a coin, we can denote the probability of a head (or a "success") as p. Thus the probability of a tail (or a failure) is $q = 1 - p$. For a single trial, its probability distribution is the Bernoulli distribution

$$p(k, p) = p^k q^{1-k} = p^k (1 - q)^{1-k}, \tag{12.17}$$

where k only takes binary values $k = 1$ or $k = 0$, that is, $k \in \{0, 1\}$. In fact, this is a particular case of the binomial distribution.

12.3.2 Binomial distribution

For multiple trials such as flipping a coin n times (or n trials), the probability of x successes (thus $n - x$ failures) obeys the binomial distribution

$$B(n,x,p) = \binom{n}{x} p^x q^{n-x} = \binom{n}{x} p^x (1-p)^{n-x} \quad (x = 0, 1, 2, \ldots, n), \tag{12.18}$$

where

$$\binom{n}{x} = \frac{n!}{x!(n-x)!}. \tag{12.19}$$

As the total probability must be one, the coefficients from the binomial expansions

$$(p+q)^n = \sum_{x=0}^{n} \binom{n}{x} p^x q^{n-x} = 1 \tag{12.20}$$

guarantee this requirement.

As a simple example, tossing a fair coin 10 times, the probability of getting 7 heads is $B(10, 7, 1/2)$, that is,

$$\binom{10}{7} \left(\frac{1}{2}\right)^7 \left(\frac{1}{2}\right)^{(10-3)} = 120 \times \frac{1}{2^{10}} \approx 0.1172. \tag{12.21}$$

For the binomial distribution, its mean is $\mu = \mathbb{E}[X] = np$, and its variance is $\sigma^2 = npq = np(1-p)$.

12.3.3 Geometric distribution

The distribution for the first success is the geometric distribution

$$P(X = n) = pq^{n-1} = p(1-p)^{n-1}, \; n \geq 1. \tag{12.22}$$

This distribution can be used to calculate the first success among n trials (thus first $n-1$ trials must be failures). For this distribution, we have $\mu = 1/p$ and $\sigma^2 = (1-p)/p^2$.

12.3.4 Poisson distribution

The Poisson distribution can be thought of as the limit of the binomial distribution when the number of trials $n \to \infty$ (very large) and the probability $p \to 0$ (very small) with the constraint that $\lambda = np$ is finite. For this reason, it is often called the distribution for small-probability events. Typically, it is concerned with the number of events that occur in a certain time interval (e.g., the number of telephone calls in an hour) or spatial area. The Poisson distribution is

$$P(X = x) = \frac{\lambda^x e^{-\lambda}}{x!}, \quad \lambda > 0, \tag{12.23}$$

where $x = 0, 1, 2, \ldots, n$, and λ is the mean of the distribution.

Many stochastic processes such as the number of phone calls in a call center and the number of cars passing through a junction obey the Poisson distribution. Let us look at a simple example.

Example 12.2. Some electronic components, such as capacitors, supplied by a specific manufacturer, typically have 0.5% probability of defects. In a batch of 500 capacitors, what is the probability of this batch containing at least one defective component?

The parameter λ can be calculated as

$$\lambda = 500 \times 0.5\% = 500 \times 0.005 = 2.5.$$

The probability of getting no defective components at all is

$$P(X = 0) = \frac{2.5^0 e^{-2.5}}{0!} \approx 0.082.$$

The probability of at least one defective component is

$$P(X \geq 1) = 1 - P(X = 0) = 1 - 0.082 = 0.918.$$

It is worth pointing out that the mean and variance of the Poisson distribution are $\mu = \lambda$ and $\sigma^2 = \lambda$, respectively.

12.3.5 Moment-generating functions

In probability theory, sometimes, it may be much easier to use the so-called moment-generating function to prove certain results that may be very difficult to prove otherwise. In general, the moment-generating function is defined as

$$G_X(\nu) = \mathbb{E}[e^{\nu X}] = \mathbb{E}\left[1 + \nu X + \frac{\nu^2 X^2}{2!} + \cdots + \frac{\nu^n X^n}{n!} + \cdots\right], \tag{12.24}$$

where X is a random variable, and $G_X(0) = 1$ when the parameter $\nu = 0$. Using the definition of the moments (12.14), the above equation becomes

$$\begin{aligned} G_X(\nu) = \mathbb{E}[e^{\nu X}] &= \mathbb{E}[1] + \nu \mathbb{E}[X] + \frac{\nu^2 \mathbb{E}[X^2]}{2!} + \cdots + \frac{\nu^n \mathbb{E}[X^n]}{n!} + \cdots \\ &= 1 + \nu M_1 + \frac{\nu^2 M_2}{2!} + \cdots + \frac{\nu^2 M_n}{n!} + \cdots, \end{aligned} \tag{12.25}$$

which means that the nth moment can be calculated by

$$M_n = \mathbb{E}[X^n] = \left.\frac{d^n G_X}{d\nu^n}\right|_{\nu=0}, \tag{12.26}$$

where $n \geq 1$ is an integer.

In general, the mean of a random variable is the first moment, whereas the variance is the second central moment. So we have

$$\mu = M_1 = \mathbb{E}[X] = \frac{dG_X(\nu)}{d\nu}\Big|_{\nu=0} \tag{12.27}$$

and

$$\begin{aligned}\sigma^2 &= M_2 - M_1^2 = \mathbb{E}[X^2] - (\mathbb{E}[X])^2 \\ &= M_2 - \mu^2 = \frac{d^2 G_X(\nu)}{d\nu^2}\Big|_{\nu=1} - \mu^2.\end{aligned} \tag{12.28}$$

Example 12.3. The moment-generating function for the Poisson distribution is given by

$$G_X(\nu) = \exp[\lambda(e^{\nu} - 1)]. \tag{12.29}$$

Thus the mean and variance of the Poisson distribution can be calculated by

$$\mu = \frac{dG_X}{d\nu}\Big|_{\nu=0} = \lambda \exp[\lambda(e^{\nu} - 1) + \nu]\Big|_{\nu=0} = \lambda \tag{12.30}$$

and

$$\begin{aligned}\sigma^2 &= \frac{d^2 G_X}{d\nu^2}\Big|_{\nu=0} - \mu^2 \\ &= \lambda(1 + \lambda e^{\nu})\exp[\lambda(e^{\nu} - 1) + \nu]\Big|_{\nu=0} - \lambda^2 = (\lambda^2 + \lambda) - \lambda^2 = \lambda.\end{aligned} \tag{12.31}$$

12.4. Continuous probability distributions

There are many continuous probability distributions, and good examples are Gaussian, uniform, Student's *t*, and exponential distributions.

12.4.1 Gaussian distribution

The Gaussian distribution or normal distribution is the most important continuous distribution in probability theory and it has a wide range of applications. For a continuous random variable X, the PDF of a Gaussian distribution is given by

$$p(x) = \frac{1}{\sigma\sqrt{2\pi}} e^{-\frac{(x-\mu)^2}{2\sigma^2}}, \tag{12.32}$$

where $\sigma^2 = \text{var}[X]$ is the variance, and $\mu = \mathbb{E}[X]$ is the mean of the Gaussian distribution. The normalization factor $1/\sigma\sqrt{2\pi}$ ensures that the total probability is unity.

The probability density function is shown in Fig. 12.1, where the peak is at the mean μ, and the standard derivation σ controls the spread or width around the mean.

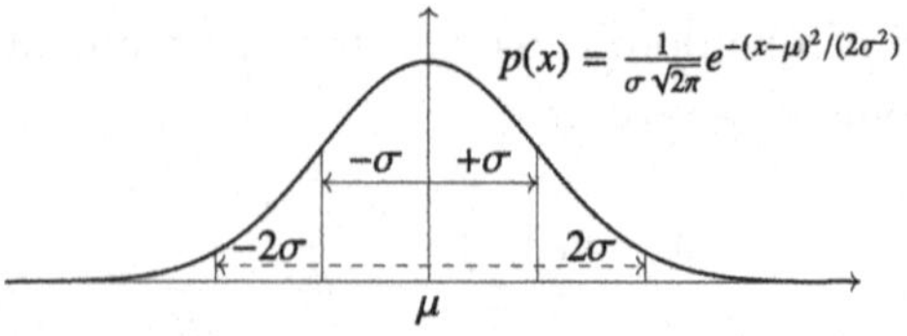

Figure 12.1 Normal distribution and its probability density function.

The total area under the PDF curve is 1, but the area under the curve between $\mu - \sigma$ and $\mu + \sigma$ is 0.6827 or 68.27%, which also corresponds to the probability that the values of the random variable fall between $\mu - \sigma$ and $\mu + \sigma$. In addition, the area under the curve between $\mu - 2\sigma$ and $\mu + 2\sigma$ is 0.9545 or 95.45%. The area between $\mu - 3\sigma$ and $\mu + 3\sigma$ is 0.9973 or 99.73%.

The cumulative probability function (CPF) for a normal distribution is the integral of $p(x)$ from $-\infty$ to x:

$$\Phi(x) = P(X < x) = \frac{1}{\sqrt{2\pi\sigma^2}} \int_{-\infty}^{x} e^{-\frac{(\zeta-\mu)^2}{2\sigma^2}} d\zeta. \tag{12.33}$$

Using the error function, we can write the above equation as

$$\Phi(x) = \frac{1}{\sqrt{2}} \left[1 + \operatorname{erf}\left(\frac{x-\mu}{\sqrt{2}\sigma} \right) \right], \tag{12.34}$$

where

$$\operatorname{erf}(x) = \frac{2}{\sqrt{\pi}} \int_{0}^{x} e^{-\zeta^2} d\zeta. \tag{12.35}$$

The moment-generating function for the Gaussian distribution is given by

$$G_X(v) = \exp\left[\mu v + \frac{1}{2}(\sigma v)^2 \right]. \tag{12.36}$$

The normal distribution is often denoted by $N(\mu, \sigma^2)$ or $N(\mu, \sigma)$ to emphasize that the probability density function depends on two parameters μ and σ.

For n independent random variables X_i $(i = 1, 2, \ldots, n)$, each of which obeys a PDF $p_i(x)$ with corresponding mean μ_i and variance σ_i^2, their sum

$$\Lambda = \sum_{i=1}^{n} X_i, \tag{12.37}$$

is also a random variable. In the limit of large n (i.e., $n \gg 1$), Λ will obey a Gaussian distribution with mean

$$\mu_\Lambda = \sum_{i=1}^{n} \mu_i \tag{12.38}$$

and variance

$$\sigma_\Lambda^2 = \sum_{i=1}^{n} \sigma_i^2. \tag{12.39}$$

This result is guaranteed by the central limit theorem.

In the case of all random variables X_i having the same μ and σ^2, the above results become

$$\mathbb{E}[\Lambda] = n\mu, \quad \text{var}[\Lambda] = n\sigma^2, \tag{12.40}$$

or

$$\mu = \frac{1}{n}\mathbb{E}[\Lambda], \quad \sigma = \frac{1}{\sqrt{n}}\sqrt{\text{var}[\Lambda]}. \tag{12.41}$$

It is worth pointing out that it is not required that X must obey the normal distribution. In fact, this result forms the foundation of Monte Carlo simulation, which means that the estimation of the standard derivation σ becomes more accurate when n is large and that the error decreases as $1/\sqrt{n}$.

12.4.2 Standard normal distribution

The standard normal distribution is the normal distribution $N(0, 1)$ with mean $\mu = 0$ and standard deviation $\sigma = 1$, which is useful to normalize or standardize data for statistical analysis. If we define a normalized z variable or a z-score

$$z = \frac{x - \mu}{\sigma}, \tag{12.42}$$

then it is equivalent to giving a score so as to place the data above or below the mean in the unit of standard deviation. In terms of the area under the probability density function, z sorts where the data falls. In some books, the distribution for $z = (x - \mu)/\sigma$ is also referred to the standard normal distribution as the Z distribution.

Now the probability density function of the standard normal distribution becomes

$$p(z) = \frac{1}{\sqrt{2\pi}} e^{-z^2/2}. \tag{12.43}$$

Its cumulative probability function is

$$\phi(z) = \frac{1}{\sqrt{2\pi}} \int_{-\infty}^{x} e^{-x^2/2} dx = \frac{1}{2}\left[1 + \text{erf}\left(\frac{z}{\sqrt{2}}\right)\right]. \tag{12.44}$$

Table 12.1 Function ϕ defined by (12.44).

z	$\phi(z)$	z	$\phi(z)$
0.0	0.500	1.0	0.841
0.1	0.540	1.1	0.864
0.2	0.579	1.2	0.885
0.3	0.618	1.3	0.903
0.4	0.655	1.4	0.919
0.5	0.692	1.5	0.933
0.6	0.726	1.6	0.945
0.7	0.758	1.7	0.955
0.8	0.788	1.8	0.964
0.9	0.816	1.9	0.971

As the calculations of ϕ and the error function involve numerical integration, it is a traditional practice to tabulate ϕ in a table (see Table 12.1), so that we do not have to calculate their values each time we use this distribution.

There are a number of other important distributions such as the exponential, uniform, χ^2, and Weibull distributions.

12.4.3 Uniform distribution

Many computer simulation packages use random numbers drawn from a uniform distribution. In general, a uniform distribution has a probability density function

$$p = \frac{1}{b-a}, \qquad x = [a, b], \tag{12.45}$$

whose mean is $\mu = \mathbb{E}[X] = (a+b)/2$, and the variance is $\sigma^2 = (b-a)^2/12$. In simulation, $a = 0$ and $b = 1$ are used, which means that $\mu = 1/2$ and $\sigma^2 = 1/12$.

12.4.4 Exponential distribution

The exponential distribution has the probability density function

$$f(x) = \lambda e^{-\lambda x}, \qquad \lambda > 0 \quad (x > 0), \tag{12.46}$$

and $f(x) = 0$ for $x \leq 0$. Its mean and variance are

$$\mu = 1/\lambda, \qquad \sigma^2 = 1/\lambda^2. \tag{12.47}$$

Exponential distributions are widely used in queuing theory and simulating discrete events. For example, the arrival process of customers in a bank is a Poisson process, and the time interval between arrivals (or interarrival time) obeys an exponential distribution.

The service time of a queue typically obeys an exponential distribution

$$P(t) = \begin{cases} \lambda e^{-\lambda t}, & t \geq 0, \\ 0, & t < 0, \end{cases} \tag{12.48}$$

where λ is the average number of customers served per unit time, and thus $\mu = 1/\lambda$ is the mean service time. Thus the service time X less than some time t is the cumulative distribution

$$P(X \leq t) = \int_{-\infty}^{t} \lambda e^{-\lambda \tau} d\tau$$

$$= \int_0^t \lambda e^{-\lambda \tau} d\tau = -e^{-\lambda \tau}\Big|_0^t = 1 - e^{-\lambda t}. \tag{12.49}$$

Example 12.4. If you are in a queue in a coffee shop, you observe that it takes 2 minutes on average to service a customer. The service time obeys the cumulative distribution function

$$P(X \leq t) = 1 - e^{-\lambda t}.$$

What is the probability of taking longer than 5 minutes to the next customer?

From 2 minutes per customer or 0.5 customer per minute, we have $\lambda = 1/2 = 0.5$, and the probability of less than 5 minutes is

$$P(t \leq 5) = 1 - e^{-0.5 \times 5} \approx 0.918.$$

Thus the probability of taking longer than 5 minutes is

$$P(t \geq 5) = 1 - 0.918 = 0.082.$$

12.4.5 Student's t-distribution

Student's t-distribution is the probability distribution for n independent measurements $x_1, x_2, \ldots, x_n$ with sample mean

$$\bar{x} = \frac{x_1 + x_2 + \cdots + x_n}{n} \tag{12.50}$$

and sample variance

$$S^2 = \frac{1}{n-1} \sum_{i=1}^{n} (x_i - \bar{x})^2. \tag{12.51}$$

The t-statistic or t-variable is defined by

$$t = \frac{\bar{x} - \mu}{S/\sqrt{n}}, \tag{12.52}$$

where μ is the population mean or true mean.

Student's t-distribution with $k=n-1$ degrees of freedom can be written as

$$p(t)=\frac{\Gamma((k+1)/2))}{\sqrt{k\pi}\,\Gamma(k/2)}\left[1+\frac{t^2}{k}\right]^{-(k+1)/2}, \tag{12.53}$$

where Γ is the gamma function defined by

$$\Gamma(x)=\int_0^{\infty} t^{x-1}e^{-t}dt \tag{12.54}$$

and the following basic properties:

$$\Gamma(x+1)=x\Gamma(x), \quad \Gamma(n+1)=n! \quad (n>0), \tag{12.55}$$

$$\Gamma(1/2)=\sqrt{\pi}, \quad \Gamma(1)=1, \quad \Gamma(3/2)=\frac{\sqrt{\pi}}{2}. \tag{12.56}$$

12.4.6 Chi-squared distribution

The χ^2-distribution, or the chi-squared distribution, is very useful in statistical inference and the method of least squares. For n independent random variables X_i that are normally distributed with means μ_i and variances σ_i^2, respectively, the sum of these random variables will obey the chi-squared distribution.

Defining the quantity

$$\chi_n^2=\sum_{i=1}^{n}\left(\frac{X_i-\mu_i}{\sigma_i}\right)^2, \tag{12.57}$$

the probability density function for χ^2-distribution is given by

$$p(x)=\frac{1}{2^{n/2}\Gamma(n/2)}x^{\frac{n}{2}-1}e^{-x/2}, \tag{12.58}$$

where $x\geq 0$, and Γ is the gamma function. Here n is called the degree of freedom. The mean of the χ^2-distribution is n, and its variance is $2n$.

12.4.7 Weibull distribution

Weibull's distribution is a distribution widely used in risk analysis and reliability analysis. It has been applied to study many real-world stochastic processes, including the distributions of rainfalls, energy resources, and earthquakes. Weibull's distribution is a three-parameter distribution given by

$$p(x,\lambda,\beta,n)=\begin{cases}\frac{n}{\lambda}\left(\frac{x-\beta}{\lambda}\right)^{n-1}\exp\left[-\left(\frac{x-\beta}{\lambda}\right)^{n}\right], & x\geq\beta,\\ 0, & x<\beta,\end{cases} \tag{12.59}$$

where λ is a scaling parameter, and n is the shape parameter, often referred to as the Weibull modulus. The parameter β is the threshold of the distribution.

This distribution is linked to some other important distributions. It becomes an exponential distribution when $n = 1$, whereas it is a good approximation to a Gaussian distribution when $n > 3.5$.

The CPF is

$$\Phi(x, \lambda, \beta, n) = 1 - \exp\left[-\left(\frac{x-\beta}{\lambda}\right)^n\right]. \tag{12.60}$$

In the particular case $\beta = 0$, the distribution becomes a two-parameter distribution with CPF

$$\Phi(x, \lambda, n) = 1 - \exp\left[-(x/\lambda)^n\right]. \tag{12.61}$$

Example 12.5. The breakdown of a machine in an assembly line obeys a two-parameter Weibull distribution with shape parameter $n = 2.5$. The scale parameter is $\lambda = 60$ months. What is the probability that the machine breaks down within 3 years? What is the probability that it lasts more than 5 years?

Since $\lambda = 60$ and $n = 2.5$, the probability of failure when $x < 36$ (months or 3 years) is

$$\Phi(x < 36) = 1 - \exp\left[-(36/60)^{2.5}\right] = 0.243. \tag{12.62}$$

The probability of any breakdown within 5 years (60 months) is

$$\Phi(x < 60) = 1 - \exp\left[-(60/60)^{2.5}\right] = 0.632, \tag{12.63}$$

and thus the probability that it lasts more than 5 years is

$$P = 1 - 0.632 = 0.368. \tag{12.64}$$

In applications such as the structural reliability analysis, the survival probability is often written as

$$P_s(V) = \exp\left[-\left(\frac{\sigma}{\sigma_0}\right)^n \frac{V}{V_0}\right], \tag{12.65}$$

where V is the volume of the system, and V_0 is the reference volume such as a lab sample. In addition, σ_0 is the critical stress such as the failure stress, and σ is the actual stress of the system.

For example, a critical component such as the axis of a wind turbine is subject to a typical stress σ with failure stress $\sigma_0 = 300$ MPa. It is assumed that $n = 5$ and $V = V_0$ for this system. What is the maximum stress that can be applied to this component so as to ensure it has a survival probability of 99.999%?

The survival probability of 99.999% gives the probability of failure

$$1 - \exp\left[-\left(\frac{\sigma}{300}\right)^5\right] < 0.001\% = 10^{-5}, \tag{12.66}$$

which requires

$$1 - 10^{-5} < \exp\left[-\left(\frac{\sigma}{300}\right)^5\right]. \tag{12.67}$$

This implies that the exponent is very small. Since $\ln(1 + x) \approx x$ when $0 < x \ll 1$, the preceding inequality becomes

$$\left(\frac{\sigma}{300}\right)^5 \leq 10^{-5}, \tag{12.68}$$

which gives

$$\sigma \leq \sqrt[5]{10^{-5} \times 300^5} = 30 \text{ MPa}. \tag{12.69}$$

The component should typically work under a stress of $\sigma \leq 30$ MPa.

12.5. Notes on software

There are many statistical software packages with various capabilities; see the list at https://en.wikipedia.org/wiki/List_of_statistical_software.

Powerful tools includes *R*, *R Studio*, *SPSS*, statistical and machine learning toolbox of *Matlab*®, Gnu Octave, *Python's SciPy*, *Minitab*, *Excel*, *SAS*, *STATA*, *StatGraphics*, *Tableau*, *OriginPro*, and many others such as *WinBUGS*.

Many symbolic computation software tools also have very powerful statistical capabilities, including *Mathematica*, *Wolfram Alpha*, *Maple*, *Geogebra*, *Desmos*, *SageMath*, *Maxima*, *MathCad*, *MathStudio*, and others.

CHAPTER THIRTEEN

Discrete event simulation

Many processes in engineering applications, especially manufacturing engineering and engineering management, can be modeled as discrete events. For example, queueing of parts on an assembly line and queueing in a coffee shop can be modeled by discrete event models. In addition, the service time of a server, such as the check-in desks at an airport or check-out counters in a supermarket, can also be modeled by statistical models. This chapter introduces the fundamentals of discrete event simulation, especially about the queueing process.

13.1. Introduction

The main aim of modeling discrete event processes is to gain insights and then manage such discrete events well. This can minimize the waiting costs and maximize the efficiency of the system under consideration.

13.1.1 Queueing and components

To model a queueing process, we have to analyze its main components.

13.1.1.1 Main components

The main components of a queueing system are:

1. Arrival rate (λ): The arrival rate represents the number of arrivals per unit time in a queue. Here the unit time can be per hour, per minute, per second, or per day, depending on the emphasis of the model.
2. Service rate (μ): The service rate represents how quickly a service is provided, such as processing a request or a service. This is typically represented by the time taken to serve a customer or the number of customers served per unit time.
3. Number of servers (s): The number of servers can be the number of check-in counters of an airline or the number of check-out counters in a supermarket. If each queue is served by one server, then the number of servers can be the same as the number of queues. In some cases, a single long queue or a few queues may be served by multiple servers, which are typically at airport or large public events.

13.1.1.2 Additional components

The three preceding components are the most important components for modeling the queueing process. In reality, additional factors or constraints should be considered.

Engineering Simulation and its Applications
https://doi.org/10.1016/B978-0-44-314084-6.00020-6

For example, constraints can be a finite capacity and a finite population size. Three additional components are:

4. Maximum queueing length (L_{max}): The maximum queueing length can model the maximum capacity of a system, such as a popular restaurant with a limited number of tables. An assembly line usually has a maximum capacity for parts.
5. Queueing rule (R): The queueing rule represents the order of providing a service. The simplest queueing rule is first-come first-served, which is the widely used first-in first-out (FIFO) rule. In different applications, other rules may also be used if appropriate. For example, the last-in first-out (LIFO) can be used for packaging and storage systems, whereas the service in random order (SIRO) may be appropriate for some applications.
6. Population size (N): In most models, it is implicitly assumed that there is a very large population. However, in practice, the population size is finite, and the population size represents the pool of potential customers for a queueing system.

13.1.2 Queue settings

In addition to the key components of a queueing system, there are settings for managing queues. In general, there are four types of queue settings.

For single-phase systems, there are two settings:

1. Single phase and single server: The simplest setting is that only one queue is allowed with a single server. Typical examples are the queues at an ATM or a photocopier. The service is completed in one step or one phase.
2. Single phase and multiservers: In many queueing scenarios, single servers are not sufficient. Thus multiple servers are needed. Queueing in banks and call centers use this system. Each customer in the queue is given a number. The next customer in the queue is called to be served once a server is available.

In many applications such as taking a flight at airport, services can take multiple phases or stages. There are also two different settings:

3. Multiphases and single server: For complicated service activities, they may involve multiple phases. A drive-in restaurant may first have a queue where a customer first orders their meal and then waits for a few minutes to collect their meal. Many job interviews take multiple stages to complete. This setting is called the multiphase single server.
4. Multiphases and multiservers: Multiple-phases and multiple-servers are widely used in practice. For example, to fly from one city to another, customers have to go the airport to check in, go through the security, and then board the plane and take off. Each phase or stage involves some queueing and service with multiple queues and multiple servers.

In some applications, mixed settings may exist because the number of phases can be combined or the number of servers may vary. We will not consider this dynamic scenario here. We will model systems with fixed queueing settings.

13.1.3 Model notations

In modeling queueing systems, standard notation conventions are widely used. Such notations are called Kendall's notations.

There are six parts in the Kendall notation, which can be compactly written as

$$A/B/s/L/P/R, \tag{13.1}$$

where the first part A denotes the arrival model, and B denotes the service time distribution. The third part (s) is the number of servers. L stands for the queueing capacity, whereas P is for the population size. Finally, R is for the queueing rule.

The first part A describes the arrival model in the system. It usually uses M to mean a Markovian process. The key feature of a Markovian process is that it is memoryless and arrivals are independent events. For example, the Poisson arrival model obeys Poisson's distribution, which is Markovian.

The distribution for the service time in part B is typically the exponential distribution, which is also Markovian. Thus many queueing models start with M/M/.

The number of servers (s) in the third part is a positive integer, which can be a single server or multiple servers. For example, the M/M/1 model means that the queue model is for a single server for both arrival and service, with a Poisson (Markovian) arrival and an exponential (Markovian) service time. This simple M/M/1 model does not list other parts, which implicitly assumes that the capacity is infinite and the population size is also infinite. In addition, it also assumes a default FIFO rule. Similarly, the M/M/s model denotes a multiserver system with both arrival and service being Markovian. The assumptions are the same as those for M/M/1. In fact, M/M/1 is a particular case of M/M/s when $s = 1$.

Obviously, more sophisticated models can be used. For example, the model

$$M/M/3/50/700/FIFO \tag{13.2}$$

means that the queueing model has Poisson arrivals, exponential service time, and three servers. This system has a capacity of 50, and the population size is 700. The queueing rule is FIFO. Since FIFO is used so widely and thus considered as a default, we can write this system simply as M/M/3/50/700.

Kendall's notations capture various scenarios. In practice, most simulation models for queueing use either M/M/1 or M/M/s, which will be the main focus in the rest of this chapter.

13.1.4 Model assumptions

Real-world discrete events such as queueing can be very complicated, and their characteristics may evolve with time. However, to build some simple models and to gain good insights, certain assumptions are used in modeling queues.

In many models, the following assumptions are used:

1. *Independence*: Arrivals are independent events, and group arrivals at the same time are not allowed. Thus the arrival of each individual is independent. The arrival of groups should be considered as each individual arrival with a small time difference (say, a few seconds or milliseconds) so as to be consistent with this assumption.
   In addition, the service time for each service is always independent. This means that the slow service of one customer does not affect the service time of the next customer in the queue.
2. *FIFO*: The default queueing rule is FIFO or "first-come first-served", unless specified otherwise.
3. *Stationarity*: The characteristics of the system does not change with time, which means that the whole queuing system is stable with the arrival and service probability distributions remaining unchanged with time.

13.2. Modeling interarrivals

With the above assumptions and standard notations, we are now ready to introduce some key features of queueing models, including interarrival time, service time, and stable queueing models.

For modeling arrivals, the most widely used model is Poisson. The probability density function of the Poisson distribution with time interval t is given by

$$P(k) = \frac{(\lambda t)^k e^{-\lambda t}}{k!}, \quad k = 0, 1, 2, \ldots, \tag{13.3}$$

with mean $\lambda > 0$.

The arrival model for the interarrival times obeys an exponential distribution

$$p(t) = \lambda e^{-\lambda t}, \quad t > 0, \tag{13.4}$$

with mean $1/\lambda$. Here the interarrival time means the time between two arrival events. This relationship can be derived from the Poisson distribution by setting $k = 0$ (no other arrival before the first arrival) and scaling the total probability to unity.

In general, a Poisson process is an arrival process whose interarrival times are independent and identically distributed random variables, and interarrivals t are exponentially distributed: $p(t) = \lambda e^{-\lambda t}$. A Poisson process is memoryless.

In this arrival model, simultaneous multiple arrivals are not allowed. In case of a high arrival rate, the time interval can be subdivided into sufficiently many small intervals, arrivals can always occur in sequence, and thus the above results are still valid.

13.3. Service time model

Though there are different service time models, the most widely used service time model is the exponential distribution

$$P(t)=\begin{cases}\mu e^{-\mu t}, & t\geq 0,\\ 0, & t<0,\end{cases} \tag{13.5}$$

where μ is the average number of customer served per unit time, and thus $\tau = 1/\mu$ is the mean service time.

Based on this model, the service time X has the cumulative probability distribution

$$P(X\leq t)=\int_{-\infty}^{t}\mu e^{-\mu\tau}d\tau=\int_{0}^{t}\mu e^{-\mu\tau}d\tau=-e^{-\mu\tau}\Big|_{0}^{t}=1-e^{-\mu t}. \tag{13.6}$$

Since the total probability sum must be unity, the probability of service time longer than a certain time is

$$P(X\geq t)=1-P(X\leq t)=e^{-\mu t}. \tag{13.7}$$

The service time T is exponentially distributed with a memoryless property. In fact, the exponential distribution is the only memoryless distribution for continuous random variables.

13.4. Queueing models

We can now discuss both single-server and multiple-server models. We will introduce both M/M/1 and M/M/s models.

13.4.1 Single-server model

The single-server system can be modeled by the M/M/1 queue model. Its arrivals obey the Poisson process with arrival rate λ, whereas its service time obeys the exponential distribution characterized by μ. This model is shown in Fig. 13.1.

For this system, if the arrival rate is higher than the service rate (i.e., $\lambda > \mu$), then the system becomes unstable because its queue length will continue to increase and will become unbounded. Therefore the stability requires that $\lambda < \mu$ or that their ratio

$$\rho=\frac{\lambda}{\mu}<1. \tag{13.8}$$

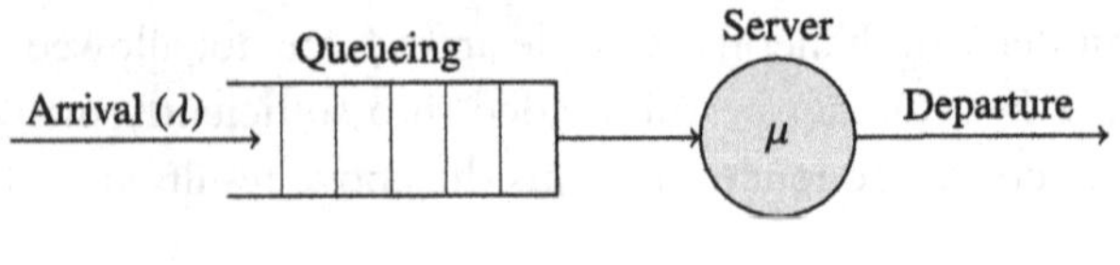

Figure 13.1 Representation of the M/M/1 model.

This ratio ρ is a performance measure for the queueing system, which can be considered as the average server utilization. When $\rho = 1$, the server is 100% busy on average. In addition, ρ can be considered as the averaged number of customers or the probability in service for the server. With this probabilistic interpretation, the probability of no customer at all is thus

$$p_0 = 1 - \rho. \tag{13.9}$$

The objective is to identify the stable, long-time behavior of the queueing system, ignoring short-term time-dependent characteristics. Thus our emphasis is on the steady-state queueing system.

The probability p_n of n customers in the system obeys a geometric distribution,

$$p_n = \rho^n p_0 = \rho^n (1 - \rho). \tag{13.10}$$

To estimate the average or mean number L of customers in the system, we have to calculate the expectation or mean by

$$L = \mathbb{E}[n] = \sum_{n=0}^{\infty} n p_n = \sum_{n=0}^{\infty} n \rho^n p_0 = p_0 \sum_{n=0}^{\infty} n \rho^n. \tag{13.11}$$

From the sum of a geometric series it is straightforward to show that

$$\sum_{n=0}^{\infty} n \rho^n = \frac{\rho}{(1-\rho)^2}. \tag{13.12}$$

Therefore we have

$$L = \mathbb{E}[n] = p_0 \frac{\rho}{(1-\rho)^2} = (1-\rho)\frac{\rho}{(1-\rho)^2} = \frac{\rho}{1-\rho}, \tag{13.13}$$

which is the estimate of the average number of customers in the system. Clearly, L will become infinite as $\rho \to 1$ or $\mu \to \lambda$.

In addition, we know that the number of customers in service is $\rho = \lambda/\mu$, so we have the number N_q of customers in the queue to be served:

$$N_q = L - \rho = \frac{\rho^2}{1-\rho}. \tag{13.14}$$

Furthermore, the service time is $\tau = 1/\mu$, and the average time of a customer in the queueing system is

$$T = \frac{1}{\mu - \lambda}. \tag{13.15}$$

For example, a coffee shop has an arrival rate of about 30 customers per hour, whereas the counter can serve a customer every 1.5 minutes. What is the average queue length for this system?

We know that the arrival rate is $\lambda = 30$ per hour, and the service rate is $\mu = 60/1.5 = 40$ per hour, which gives

$$\rho = \frac{30}{40} = \frac{3}{4}. \tag{13.16}$$

The expected queue length is

$$L = \frac{\rho^2}{1-\rho} = \frac{(3/4)^2}{1-\frac{3}{4}} = \frac{9}{4} = 2.25, \tag{13.17}$$

which should be round up to 3 customers.

The average time for a customer in the system is

$$T = \frac{1}{\mu - \lambda} = \frac{1}{(40-30)} = \frac{1}{10}, \tag{13.18}$$

which is 6 min (or 0.1 hours). For a lucky customer, the probability of no waiting at all is

$$p_0 = 1 - \rho = 1/4. \tag{13.19}$$

For this type of system, there is a well-known Little's law

$$L = \lambda T, \tag{13.20}$$

which links the mean time, the queueing length, and the arrival rate in a single algebraic equation.

13.4.2 Multiserver model

A multiserver queueing system can be modeled by the M/M/s model with $s \geq 1$ servers. Rigorous mathematical analysis requires a full consideration of Markovian models, which are beyond the scope of this chapter. Here we will outline the main results, the and interested readers can refer to more advanced literature.

Let us first define the average utility ratio U_ρ for a queueing system with s servers and n customers. We have

$$U_\rho = \frac{\rho}{s} = \frac{\lambda}{s\mu}, \tag{13.21}$$

which reduces to ρ when $s=1$. Similarly to the earlier discussion, the stability of the system requires that $U_\rho = \rho/s < 1$.

The average number of customers in the system can be estimated by

$$L = \rho + p_0\left[\frac{\rho^{s+1}}{(s-1)!(s-\rho)^2}\right], \tag{13.22}$$

where p_0 is the probability of no customer,

$$p_0 = \frac{1}{\rho^s/[s!(1-U)] + \sum_{k=0}^{s-1}\rho^k/k!}. \tag{13.23}$$

Clearly, the above two formulas reduce to the results for M/M/1 when $s=1$ if we use $0! = 1$.

The average time of a customer spent in the system can be obtained using Little's law, which is valid for both M/M/1 and M/M/s models. So we have

$$T = \frac{L}{\lambda}. \tag{13.24}$$

Let us look at an example. A busy supermarket has an arrival rate of 90 customers per hour. There are 5 check-out counters, and the service time on average is 3 minutes per counter per customer. What is the average number of customers in the queueing system?

From the descriptions we know that $\lambda = 90$ per hour, $\mu = 60/3 = 20$ per hour, and $s = 5$. Thus the utility ratio is

$$U = \frac{\lambda}{s\mu} = \frac{90}{5\times 20} = 9/10 < 1, \quad \rho = \frac{90}{20} = 4.5. \tag{13.25}$$

The probability of no customer in queue is

$$p_0 = \frac{1}{\rho^s/[s!(1-U)] + Q}, \quad Q = \sum_{k=0}^{s-1}\frac{\rho^k}{k!}. \tag{13.26}$$

Substituting the values, we have $Q = 47.89$ and $p_0 \approx 0.0063$. The average number of customers in the queueing system is

$$L = \rho + \frac{p_0\rho^{s+1}}{(s-1)!(s-\rho)^2} \approx 13.2, \tag{13.27}$$

which is about 14 customers. Thus the average time of a customer in queue is

$$T = \frac{L}{\lambda} \approx 0.15 \text{ hours}, \tag{13.28}$$

which is about 9 minutes.

13.5. Applications

The management of queueing processes is very important to many applications, such as management of large events, assembly lines, airlines, and logistics as well as transport systems. In practice, the discrete queueing systems may not be stationary, so that their characteristics will change with time. For example, motorway traffic, the arrival rates in supermarkets, and the number of calls in a call center will all vary with time. Thus the queueing models we have discussed may not provide realistic estimation because these models are simple and only valid for stationary systems. However, some of the average quantities may still provide good insights to the real systems.

The management or optimization of queueing systems is highly needed in practice. Proper management requires to consider many factors, such as physical settings, structures, estimation of key parameters, and rough estimate of arrival rates and service time based on historical data. Efficient queue management should aim to serve a majority (say 95%) within a fixed time limit. This may require the dynamical allocation of staff and servers, and predicting trends.

From the optimization point of view, the minimization of the waiting time in queue is to minimize

$$\text{minimize} \;\; T_w = \frac{\rho^s p_0}{s!(s\mu)} \frac{s^2}{(s-\rho)^2}, \tag{13.29}$$

which is a function s, λ, and μ. Since it is not easy to control the arrival rate λ, the best way for achieving optimality is to vary s and μ. This is usually achieved in practice by increasing s if needed and speeding up the service if possible.

Since the average number of customers in the queueing system is linked to the waiting time, the minimization of the waiting time is equivalent to the minimization of the queueing length, that is,

$$\text{minimize} \;\; L = \rho + p_0 \left[\frac{\rho^{s+1}}{(s-1)!(s-\rho)^2} \right]. \tag{13.30}$$

Which form to choose for optimization will depend on the ease of calculation, though the optimal solutions should be same. However, in practice, the minimization of waiting time T_w seems to be most widely used. Though it is usually not easy to solve such optimization problems, some approximation estimates will be most practical and useful. In fact, the utility measure ratio U can provide a good insight into the system.

Let N be the total number of customers to be served during a total period of T. The arrival rate λ can be approximated by N/T. In addition, the average service time is $\tau = 1/\mu$. Thus we have

$$U = \frac{\lambda}{s\mu} = \frac{N/T}{s\mu} = \frac{N\tau}{sT} < 1. \tag{13.31}$$

After some algebra, we have the so-called Teknomo rule of thumb for estimating the number of servers needed to manage queues,

$$s \geq \left\lceil \frac{N\tau}{T} \right\rceil, \tag{13.32}$$

where $\lceil x \rceil$ is the round-up to the nearest integer.

As a simple example, a supermarket typically have 250 customers per hour. The average check-out time for each counter is 2.5 minutes. How many checkout counters should be available to avoid long queues? Since $N = 250$, $T = 1$ hour $= 3600$ seconds, and $\tau = 2.5 \times 60 = 150$ seconds, we have

$$s = \left\lceil \frac{250 \times 150}{3600} \right\rceil = \left\lceil \frac{125}{12} \right\rceil = 11. \tag{13.33}$$

Thus 11 counters should be open for service.

13.6. Notes on software

There are many different software packages that can simulate discrete events. A comprehensive list of relevant software tools can be found at
https://en.wikipedia.org/wiki/List_of_discrete_event_simulation_software.

Powerful software tools include *Arena*, *FlexSim*, *Enterprise Dynamics*, *Simul8*, *WITNESS*, and many others. For example, discrete event simulation software *WITNESS* is an interactive tool with block-style predefined functions. *SimEvent* tool of *Matlab*® is also powerful. Open-source tools such as *Facsimile*, *DESMO-J*, Python's *Simpy*, and *Simula* are also good tools to carry out discrete event simulation.

CHAPTER FOURTEEN

Simulation by statistical models

In engineering simulation and applications, we have to deal with data, uncertainty, errors, and randomness. This requires statistical methods. This chapter introduces the fundamentals of linear regression, generalized linear regression, model selection, and Monte Carlo simulation.

14.1. Introduction

For a given sample of n independent observations $x_1, x_2, \ldots, x_n$ of a random variable X, such as the pressure variation in an experiment, we can calculate some statistical quantities from these observed values.

The ample mean and sample variance are two most widely used statistic quantities. The sample mean is given by

$$\bar{x} \equiv \frac{1}{n}(x_1 + x_2 + \cdots + x_n) = \frac{1}{n}\sum_{i=1}^{n} x_i, \tag{14.1}$$

which is in fact the arithmetic average of the values x_i. The sample variance is defined as

$$S^2 = \frac{1}{n-1}\sum_{i=1}^{n}(x_i - \bar{x})^2. \tag{14.2}$$

14.2. Regression

For a statistical model with an explanatory or independent variable x and a response or dependent variable y, a data set consists of n data points or pairs:

$$(x_1, y_1), \ (x_2, y_2), \ \ldots, \ (x_i, y_i), \ \ldots, \ (x_n, y_n). \tag{14.3}$$

The aim of regression analysis is to build a model to understand the data. In general, the relationship can be a function

$$y = f(x, a, b, \ldots), \tag{14.4}$$

where the parameters $(a, b, \ldots)$ are model parameters to be determined from the data. The function $f(x, \ldots)$ can be linear or nonlinear. If it is linear, then the regression is called a linear regression. Otherwise, the regression becomes a nonlinear regression problem.

Engineering Simulation and its Applications
https://doi.org/10.1016/B978-0-44-314084-6.00021-8

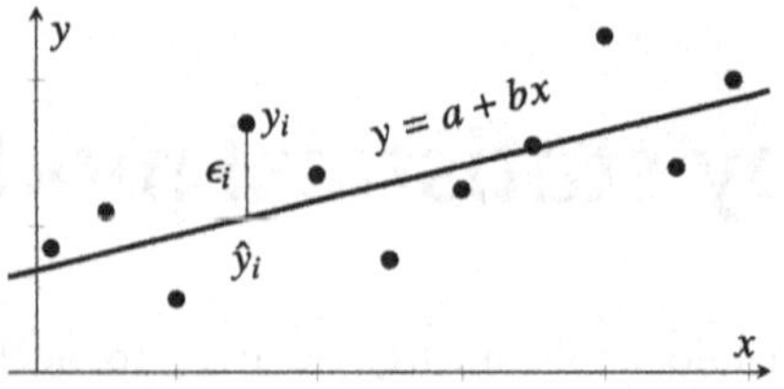

Figure 14.1 Best fit line for a simple linear model.

14.2.1 Liner regression

For a set of n data points (x_i, y_i) $(i = 1, 2, \ldots, n)$, the usual practice is to try to draw a straight line

$$y = a + bx, \tag{14.5}$$

which represents the major trend. This line is often referred to as the best-fit line or the trend line as shown in Fig. 14.1.

In this linear case, there are two parameters, a (intercept) and b (slope). Mathematically speaking, the best-fit line should minimize the overall residual errors or differences between the true value y_i and the model-predicted value $\hat{y}_i = a + bx_i$. The individual residual errors are defined by

$$\epsilon_i = y_i - \hat{y}_i = y_i - (a + bx_i), \tag{14.6}$$

which can be any real numbers (positive, negative, or zero). Thus a simple sum of errors does not represent the overall errors or derivations from the trend line. In regression, the overall error is defined as the residual sum of squares (RSS)

$$\text{RSS} = E_s = \sum_{i=1}^{n} \epsilon_i^2 = \sum_{i-1}^{n} \left[y_i - (a + bx_i)\right]^2. \tag{14.7}$$

From the optimization point of view, the best-fit line will correspond to the parameters a and b so that the RSS is minimized; thus the name the method of least squares (MLS). From the probability theory point of view, the MLS is related to maximize the joint probability or the maximum likelihood.

Since the error E_s is a function of a and b via the model of $f(x) = a + bx$, its minimization occurs at zero gradients, that is, both its partial derivatives should be zero:

$$\frac{\partial E_s}{\partial a} = -\sum_{i=1}^{n} \left[y_i - (a + bx_i)\right] = 0, \tag{14.8}$$

and

$$\frac{\partial E_s}{\partial b} = -\sum_{i=1}^{n} x_i \left[y_i - (a + bx_i) \right] = 0. \tag{14.9}$$

Both conditions can be written as

$$\sum_{i=1}^{n} \left[y_i - (a + bx_i) \right] = 0 \tag{14.10}$$

and

$$\sum_{i=1}^{n} x_i \left[y_i - (a + bx_i) \right] = 0. \tag{14.11}$$

By expanding these equations we have

$$na + b\sum_{i=1}^{n} x_i = \sum_{i=1}^{n} y_i \tag{14.12}$$

and

$$a\sum_{i=1}^{n} x_i + b\sum_{i=1}^{n} x_i^2 = \sum_{i=1}^{n} x_i y_i, \tag{14.13}$$

which is a system of linear equations for a and b. It is straightforward to obtain the solutions:

$$a = \frac{1}{n}[\sum_{i=1}^{n} y_i - b\sum_{i=1}^{n} x_i] = \bar{y} - b\bar{x}, \tag{14.14}$$

$$b = \frac{n\sum_{i=1}^{n} x_i y_i - (\sum_{i=1}^{n} x_i)(\sum_{i=1}^{n} y_i)}{n\sum_{i=1}^{n} x_i^2 - (\sum_{i=1}^{n} x_i)^2}, \tag{14.15}$$

where

$$\bar{x} = \frac{1}{n}\sum_{i=1}^{n} x_i, \quad \bar{y} = \frac{1}{n}\sum_{i=1}^{n} y_i. \tag{14.16}$$

14.2.2 Correlation

Any possible correlation between x_i and y_i data can be described by the correlation coefficient R. For a pair of samples (x_i, y_i), their sample means are $\bar{x}$ and $\bar{y}$, respectively. We can calculate their sample variances S_x^2 and S_y^2 by

$$\text{var}(x) = S_x^2 = \frac{\sum_{i=1}^{n}(x_i - \bar{x})^2}{n-1}, \quad \text{var}(y) = S_y^2 = \frac{\sum_{i=1}^{n}(y_i - \bar{y})^2}{n-1}. \tag{14.17}$$

Table 14.1 Some data points for a linear model.

x	1	2	3	4	5
y	1	1.5	2	2.6	3

The correlation coefficient between x_i and y_i is defined by

$$R = \frac{\mathrm{cov}(x, y)}{S_x S_y}, \tag{14.18}$$

where the covariance is given by

$$\mathrm{cov}(x, y) = \mathbb{E}[(x - \bar{x})(y - \bar{y})] = \frac{\sum_{i=1}^{n} (x_i - \bar{x})(y_i - \bar{y})}{n - 1}. \tag{14.19}$$

It is easy to verify that $S_x^2 = \mathrm{cov}(x, x)$ and $S_y^2 = \mathrm{cov}(y, y)$.

From given n data points (x_i, y_i), R can be calculated directly by

$$R = \frac{n \sum_{i=1}^{n} x_i y_i - \left(\sum_{i=1}^{n} x_i\right)\left(\sum_{i=1}^{n} y_i\right)}{\sqrt{\left[n \sum x_i^2 - (\sum_{i=1}^{n} x_i)^2\right]\left[n \sum_{i=1}^{n} y_i^2 - (\sum_{i=1}^{n} y_i)^2\right]}}.$$

If two variables x and y are independent, then $\mathrm{cov}(x, y) = 0$, and there is no correlation between them, so $R = 0$. The case of R close to 1 means a strong positive correlation, where the increase in x will lead to the increase in y. On the other hand, the case of R close to -1 means a strong negative correlation, where the increase in x will lead to the decrease in y. In addition, R^2 is also called the coefficient of determination, which measures the fraction of variance of y due to the variation of x.

Example 14.1. For the data shown in Table 14.1, we have $n = 5$. To fit a linear model $y = a + bx$, it is straightforward to calculate a and b using (14.14) and (14.15):

$$a = 0.49, \quad b = 0.51, \tag{14.20}$$

and thus the best-fit line is

$$y = a + bx = 0.49 + 0.51x. \tag{14.21}$$

The correlation coefficient R is

$$R = 0.9987, \quad R^2 = 0.9974. \tag{14.22}$$

The best-fit line is shown in Fig. 14.2.

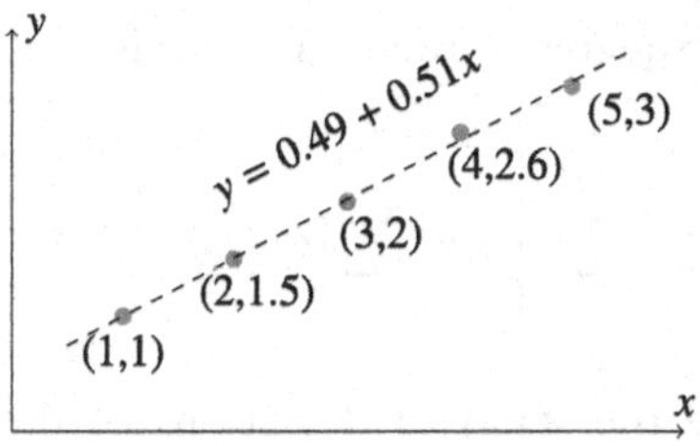

Figure 14.2 The best-fit line by linear regression.

14.3. Generalized linear regression

A straight trend line is only valid for simple linear models. In many cases, it is necessary to use higher-order models that correspond to curves, rather than straight lines. In this case, we essentially use the generalized linear regression, which tries to fit the data to a polynomial of degree p

$$y(x) = \alpha_0 + \alpha_1 x + \alpha_2 x^2 + \cdots + \alpha_p x^p, \tag{14.23}$$

where the coefficients α_i $(i = 0, 1, \ldots, p)$ will be determined from the data. The power functions $x^0 = 1$, x, x^2, $\ldots$, x^p are called basis functions. Since this function $y(x)$ is a linear function in terms of coefficients α_i, this model is called generalized linear regression (GLR).

Obviously, other basis functions can also be used, such as

$$y(x) = a + b\sin(x), \tag{14.24}$$

or

$$y(x) = a\cos(x) + be^x + c, \tag{14.25}$$

because both functions are linear in terms of the coefficients. However, the functions $y(x) = a + \cos(bx)$ and $y(x) = a\exp(bx)$ are nonlinear and thus cannot be fit into the GLR category.

14.3.1 General formulation

Let $f_j(x)$ be the known basis functions, such as x^2 or $\sin(x)$. The GLR model can be written as

$$y(x) = \sum_{j=0}^{p} \alpha_j f_j(x) = \alpha_0 f_0(x) + \alpha_1 f_1(x) + \alpha_2 f_2(x) + \cdots + \alpha_p f_p(x). \tag{14.26}$$

Now the residual sum of squares or the total error is

$$E_s = \sum_{i=1}^{n} \left[y_i - \sum_{j=0}^{p} \alpha_j f_j(x_i) \right]^2 / \sigma_i^2, \tag{14.27}$$

where σ_i $(i = 1, 2, \ldots, n)$ are the standard deviations of the ith data point at (x_i, y_i). Typically, it is assumed that x_i can be accurately measured but y_i can have errors. Thus here σ_i^2 is the variance of y_i.

Since there are only n data points, determining the coefficients uniquely requires

$$n \geq p + 1. \tag{14.28}$$

In case all the standard deviations σ_i are the same constant, the formulas can be simplified by setting $\sigma_i = \sigma$.

Let $\boldsymbol{D} = [D_{ij}]$ be the design matrix given by

$$D_{ij} = f_j(x_i)/\sigma_i. \tag{14.29}$$

The minimization of E_s occurs at

$$\frac{\partial E_s}{\partial \alpha_j} = 0 \quad (j = 0, 1, \ldots, p), \tag{14.30}$$

which gives

$$\sum_{i=1}^{n} \frac{f_k(x_i)}{\sigma_i^2} \left[y_i - \sum_{j=0}^{p} \alpha_j f_j(x_i) \right] = 0, \quad k = 0, \ldots, p. \tag{14.31}$$

Rearranging the terms and interchanging the order of summations, we have

$$\sum_{j=0}^{p} \sum_{i=1}^{n} \frac{\alpha_j f_j(x_i) f_k(x_i)}{\sigma_i^2} = \sum_{i=1}^{n} \frac{y_i f_k(x_i)}{\sigma_i^2}. \tag{14.32}$$

Defining the matrix $\boldsymbol{A}$ and column vector $\boldsymbol{b}$ as

$$A_{kj} = \sum_{i=1}^{n} \frac{f_k(x_i) f_j(x_i)}{\sigma_i^2} \tag{14.33}$$

and

$$b_k = \sum_{i=1}^{n} \frac{y_i f_k(x_i)}{\sigma_i^2} \quad (k = 0, \ldots, p), \tag{14.34}$$

we can rewrite (14.32) as a matrix equation

$$\boldsymbol{A\alpha} = \boldsymbol{b}, \quad \boldsymbol{A} = \boldsymbol{D}^T\boldsymbol{D}, \tag{14.35}$$

where $\boldsymbol{A}$ is a $(p+1) \times (p+1)$ matrix, and $\boldsymbol{b}$ is a column vector. This linear system is also called the normal equation, which can be solved using the standard methods for solving linear systems.

The solution of the coefficients is

$$\boldsymbol{\alpha} = \boldsymbol{A}^{-1}\boldsymbol{b}. \tag{14.36}$$

If all the basis functions are simple power functions $f_i(x) = x^i$ $(i = 0, 1, \ldots, p)$ (or 1, x, $x^2, \ldots, x^p$), then the GLR becomes a polynomial regression. Without loss of generality, we can assume that $\sigma_i = \sigma = 1$. Thus the normal matrix equation (14.35) becomes

$$\begin{pmatrix} \sum_{i=1}^n 1 & \sum_{i=1}^n x_i & \ldots & \sum_{i=1}^n x_i^p \\ \sum_{i=1}^n x_i & \sum_{i=1}^n x_i^2 & \ldots & \sum_{i=1}^n x_i^{p+1} \\ \vdots & & \ddots & \\ \sum_{i=1}^n x_i^p & \sum_{i=1}^n x_i^{p+1} & \ldots & \sum_{i=1}^n x_i^{2p} \end{pmatrix} \begin{pmatrix} \alpha_0 \\ \alpha_1 \\ \vdots \\ \alpha_p \end{pmatrix} = \begin{pmatrix} \sum_{i=1}^n y_i \\ \sum_{i=1}^n x_i y_i \\ \vdots \\ \sum_{i=1}^n x_i^p y_i \end{pmatrix}.$$

The best-fit line is the particular case when $p = 1$ with

$$y = \alpha_0 + \alpha_1 x = a + bx, \tag{14.37}$$

and the matrix equation becomes

$$\begin{pmatrix} n & \sum_{i=1}^n x_i \\ \sum_{i=1}^n x_i & \sum_{i=1}^n x_i^2 \end{pmatrix} \begin{pmatrix} \alpha_0 \\ \alpha_1 \end{pmatrix} = \begin{pmatrix} \sum_{i=1}^n y_i \\ \sum_{i=1}^n x_i y_i \end{pmatrix}. \tag{14.38}$$

Its solution can be obtained by simple inversion. The inverse of the matrix

$$\boldsymbol{A} = \begin{pmatrix} n & \sum_{i=1}^n x_i \\ \sum_{i=1}^n x_i & \sum_{i=1}^n x_i^2 \end{pmatrix} \tag{14.39}$$

is

$$\boldsymbol{A}^{-1} = \frac{1}{\Delta} \begin{pmatrix} \sum_{i=1}^n x_i^2 & -\sum_{i=1}^n x_i \\ -\sum_{i=1}^n x_i & n \end{pmatrix}, \tag{14.40}$$

Table 14.2 Data points.

x	-2.00	-1.00	1.00	2.00	3.00
y	6.05	1.64	−1.23	0.25	3.77

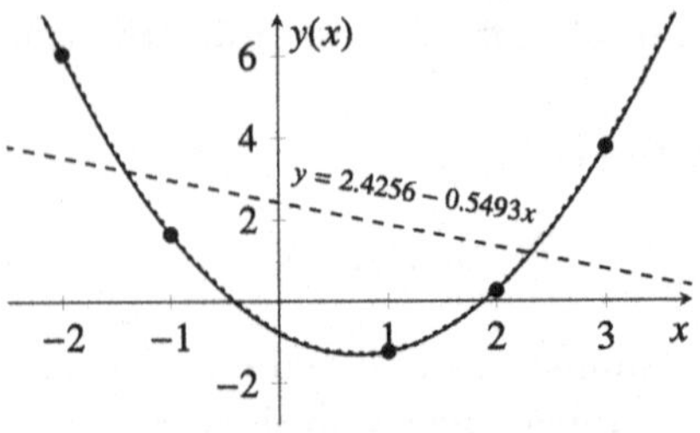

Figure 14.3 Best-fit curves for $p = 1, 2, 3$.

where Δ is the determinant of $\boldsymbol{A}$, that is,

$$\Delta = \det(\boldsymbol{A}) = n\sum_{i=1}^{n} x_i^2 - \left(\sum_{i=1}^{n} x_i\right)^2. \tag{14.41}$$

Thus the solution for the regression coefficients becomes

$$\begin{pmatrix} \alpha_0 \\ \alpha_1 \end{pmatrix} = \frac{1}{\Delta}\begin{pmatrix} \sum_{i=1}^{n} x_i^2 & -\sum_{i=1}^{n} x_i \\ -\sum_{i=1}^{n} x_i & n \end{pmatrix}\begin{pmatrix} \sum_{i=1}^{n} y_i \\ \sum_{i=1}^{n} x_i y_i \end{pmatrix}$$
$$= \frac{1}{\Delta}\begin{pmatrix} (\sum_{i=1}^{n} x_i^2)(\sum_{i=1}^{n} y_i) - (\sum_{i=1}^{n} x_i)(\sum_{i=1}^{n} x_i y_i) \\ n\sum_{i=1}^{n} x_i y_i - (\sum_{i=1}^{n} x_i)(\sum_{i=1}^{n} y_i) \end{pmatrix}, \tag{14.42}$$

which are the same coefficients as those in Eqs. (14.14) and (14.15).

Let us use a simple example to show how the polynomial regression works.

Example 14.2. For the data points given in Table 14.2, we can show these points in Fig. 14.3. It seems that a quadratic model is the best choice. So let us use

$$y(x) = \alpha_0 + \alpha_1 x + \alpha_2 x^2, \tag{14.43}$$

and we have

$$\begin{pmatrix} n & \sum_{i=1}^{n} x_i & \sum_{i=1}^{n} x_i^2 \\ \sum_{i=1}^{n} x_i & \sum_{i=1}^{n} x_i^2 & \sum_{i=1}^{n} x_i^3 \\ \sum_{i=1}^{n} x_i^2 & \sum_{i=1}^{n} x_i^3 & \sum_{i=1}^{n} x_i^4 \end{pmatrix} \begin{pmatrix} \alpha_0 \\ \alpha_1 \\ \alpha_2 \end{pmatrix} = \begin{pmatrix} \sum_{i=1}^{n} y_i \\ \sum_{i=1}^{n} x_i y_i \\ \sum_{i=1}^{n} x_i^2 y_i \end{pmatrix}. \tag{14.44}$$

From the data we know that

$$n = 5, \quad \sum_{i=1}^{n} x_i = 9, \quad \sum_{i=1}^{n} y_i = 10.5. \tag{14.45}$$

The other quantities can be calculated in a similar way. Therefore we have

$$\begin{pmatrix} 5 & 3 & 19 \\ 3 & 19 & 27 \\ 19 & 27 & 115 \end{pmatrix} \begin{pmatrix} \alpha_0 \\ \alpha_0 \\ \alpha_2 \end{pmatrix} = \begin{pmatrix} 10.48 \\ -3.16 \\ 59.54 \end{pmatrix}.$$

By direct inversion we have

$$\begin{pmatrix} \alpha_0 \\ \alpha_1 \\ \alpha_2 \end{pmatrix} = \begin{pmatrix} -0.7886 \\ -1.4447 \\ 0.9872 \end{pmatrix}. \tag{14.46}$$

Finally, the best-fit equation is

$$y(x) = -0.7886 - 1.4447x + 0.9872x^2, \tag{14.47}$$

which is quite close to the formula $y = x^2 - 1.5x - 1$. The data set was generated by using $y = x^2 - 3x/2 - 1$ with 15% noise.

14.3.2 Model selection

In the previous example, after visualizing the data set, we used a quadratic equation or a polynomial of degree $p = 2$. For a large data set, it is not easy to figure out what models we should use to fit the data. In fact, there are two challenging issues in regression, the order p of the polynomial and overfitting.

To use the right regression model for a given data set, it is helpful to have some knowledge of the underlying model. Without that knowledge, we have to look at the data and try to figure out the trend by visualization. For the simple data set shown in Table 14.1, it is easy to see that they have a linear trend. However, for this previous example, the results and data visualization show that we should use a quadratic model with $p = 2$.

Suppose that we have no idea what model to use. One possible approach is to use different models to see which model fits the data best. For the data in Table 14.2, let us try to fit a linear model with $p = 1$. It is easy to obtain

$$y_{p=1} = 2.4256 - 0.5493x, \tag{14.48}$$

which is shown as the dashed line in Fig. 14.3. Obviously, this is not a good model for explaining the data set.

In our example, we have used $p = 2$; we have already obtained expression (14.47), which is a good fit.

Now we can use higher-order polynomials to see if we can improve the goodness of the fit. If we use $p = 3$ as the regression model, then we have

$$y_{p=3} = -0.7847 - 1.4489x + 0.9854x^2 + 0.0010x^3, \tag{14.49}$$

which is shown as the dotted curve in Fig. 14.3.

Again, if we use $p = 4$ to the similar regression, then we have

$$y_{p=4} = -0.7630 - 1.4300x + 0.9646x^2 - 0.0050x^3 + 0.0034x^4. \tag{14.50}$$

Now the question is: Should we try $p = 5$? Since there are only $n = 5$ data points, it is not possible to determine the coefficients unique for $p \geq 5$ because the matrix will be singular due to insufficient information.

Even for the four different models with $p = 1, 2, 3, 4$, which model is the best? Obviously, model $y_{p=2}$ is better than $y_{p=1}$. What about the other two models?

The main question is now: What is the criterion for selecting a good model? This is the main issue for model selection.

One way for selecting a model among many possible models is to look at the errors or residuals. The residual sum of squares (RSS) can be calculated by

$$\text{RSS} = \sum_{i=1}^{5} [y_i - \hat{y}_p(x_i)]^2, \tag{14.51}$$

where $\hat{y}_p(x_i)$ is the predicted value of the model of order p at x_i, and y_i is the observed value.

The RSS values for different orders p are listed in Table 14.3. It seems that the higher orders give the lower fitting errors. This tendency to use higher-order models is called overfitting because it tends to produce more complicated models than the actual underlying true mathematical model.

There are different rules or criteria to do model selection. From the model-fitting point of view, we can look at two features or changes in the best-fit models. On the one

Table 14.3 The residual sums of squares for different regression models.

p	p=1	p=2	p=3	p=4
RSS	27.9245	7.6526×10^{-4}	7.0630×10^{-4}	1.0107×10^{-29}

hand, if we look at the values of RSS, then the errors become significantly lower for $p = 2$ in comparison with $p = 1$. This is a good indication that $p = 2$ could be the right model. However, the RSS values do not reduce significantly further if we use $p = 3$ or $p = 4$ (compared with the change from $p = 1$ to $p = 2$). This may suggest that $p = 3$ and $p = 4$ may not be necessary.

If two models explain the same data equally well, then the simpler model should be chosen. In this case, among $p = 2, 3, 4$, we should choose $p = 2$. This informal criterion is based on the well-known Occam's razor, which states "Entities are not to be multiplied without necessity". This principle is also consistent with Isaac Newton's rule in his *Principia*: "We are to admit no more causes of natural things than such as are both true and sufficient to explain their appearances." Albert Einstein put this simply as "Make everything as simple as possible, but not simpler."

Alternatively, if we look at the coefficients of different models with different orders p, the coefficients at x^2 for all $p = 2, 3, 4$ are typically around 1, whereas the coefficients at x^3 and x^4 are significantly smaller. This also suggests that x^2 should be the right order for the regression model.

In statistics, data mining, and machine learning, there are a few techniques that can be used to avoid overfitting, and such methods often use information criteria, including Akaike information criterion (AIC) and Bayesian information criterion (BIC). Other methods, such as Lasso method and regularization, are also widely used. The interested readers can refer to more specialized literature.

14.4. Sampling and Monte Carlo method

In engineering simulation and applications, there are uncertainty and noise. To evaluate different scenarios, we have to do multiple simulations with different inputs. This requires the Monte Carlo approach. In the design of experiments, weather forecasting, climate simulation, and financial forecasting, the Monte Carol method is widely used.

14.4.1 Monte Carlo method

The essence of Monte Carlo is to generate a large but finite number of random samples to carry out simulation; the main quantities such as rainfalls in weather forecasting or stress variations of a building under wind loading can be estimated by averaging over these random samples.

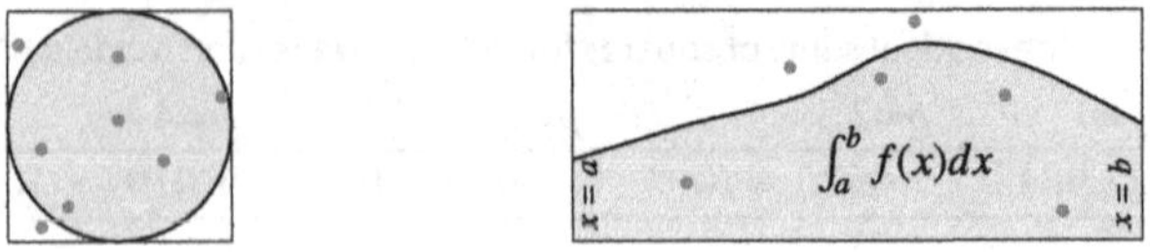

Figure 14.4 Basic idea of Monte Carlo.

For example, to estimate π by Monte Carlo sampling, one of the simplest ways is to use an inscribed unit circle with $r = 1$ inside a square with its side $a = 2r = 2$. Since the area of the unit circle is $A = \pi r^2 = \pi$, and the area of the square is $a^2 = 4$, their ratio is

$$R = \frac{\pi}{4}. \tag{14.52}$$

Suppose that n random points are drawn from uniform distributions so that these n can distribute inside the square, shown on the left of Fig. 14.4. Among the n points, there are k points falling within the unit circle. Thus the area ratio R can be approximated by

$$R = \frac{\pi}{4} \approx \frac{k}{n}, \tag{14.53}$$

which gives

$$\pi \approx \frac{4k}{n}. \tag{14.54}$$

In a simple Monte Carlo simulation, $n = 10000$ random points (x, y) are generated, where both x and y are drawn from a uniform distribution on $[-1, 1]$. Then there are $k = 7869$ points that fall into the unit circle. Thus the estimate of π is

$$\pi = \frac{4k}{n} = \frac{4 \times 7869}{10000} \approx 3.1476. \tag{14.55}$$

For complicated integrals, especially integrals in higher-dimensional spaces, the Monte Carlo method becomes very powerful. The main idea is similar. As shown on the left of Fig. 14.4, the integral

$$I = \int_a^b f(x)dx \tag{14.56}$$

is the shaded area under the curve. The total area of the rectangle is $A = h(b - a)$, where h is the height of the rectangular box. Thus the integral can be estimated by the area ratio

$$q = \frac{I}{A} \approx \frac{k}{n}, \tag{14.57}$$

where n is the number of sampling points, and k is the number of points that fall under the curve. So the Mont Carlo sampling gives

$$I = \int_a^b f(x)dx \approx \frac{k(b-a)h}{n}. \tag{14.58}$$

However, this simple approach is rarely used in practice.

More formally, Monte Carlo integration evaluates the integral with n random samples $x_1, x_2, \ldots, x_n$ drawn in the domain of the integral. Then the integral is estimated by

$$I \approx V_0 \left[\frac{1}{n} \sum_{i=1}^{n} f(x_i) \right] = V_\Omega \bar{f}, \tag{14.59}$$

where V_0 is the volume of the integral domain Ω. For the simple one-dimensional integral, $V_0 = (b-a)$. For multidimensional integrals, $V_0 = \int_\Omega dx$. In addition, $\bar{f}$ is the average over all the sampling points,

$$\bar{f} = \frac{1}{n} \sum_{i=1}^{n} f(x_i). \tag{14.60}$$

When n is sufficiently large, the above integral estimate will approach the true value of the integral.

Sometimes, the integral limits can be large, and thus the volume of the domain may be large. Some mathematical transforms can be used to transform the original integral into a smaller domain, typically [0,1], so that Monte Carlo sampling can be carried out easily. If the domain is in [0,1] for all dimensions, then the integral can be approximated by

$$I \approx \frac{1}{n} \sum_{i=1}^{n} f(x_i). \tag{14.61}$$

Let us use an example to show how the Monte Carlo integration works.

Example 14.3. The exact value of the error function

$$\mathrm{erf}(x) = \frac{2}{\sqrt{\pi}} \int_0^x e^{-u^2} du \tag{14.62}$$

at $x = 1$ is

$$\mathrm{erf}(1) = 0.842700793. \tag{14.63}$$

Let us use the Monte Carlo method to estimate its value.

Suppose we draw $n = 10$ samples

$$u_1 = 0.6020, \quad u_2 = 0.2630, \quad u_3 = 0.6541, \quad u_4 = 0.6892, \quad u_5 = 0.7482,$$
$$u_6 = 0.4505, \quad u_7 = 0.0838, \quad u_8 = 0.2290, \quad u_9 = 0.9133, \quad u_{10} = 0.1524.$$

We now calculate

$$f_1 = \frac{2}{\sqrt{\pi}} e^{-u_1^2} = 0.7854, \quad f_2 = 1.0530, \quad f_3 = 0.7356,$$
$$f_4 = 0.7017, \quad f_5 = 0.6447, \quad f_6 = 0.9211,$$
$$f_7 = 1.1205, \quad f_8 = 1.0707, \quad f_9 = 0.4900, \quad f_{10} = 1.1025.$$

Their mean value is

$$\bar{f} = 0.8625. \tag{14.64}$$

Since $V = 1 - 0 = 1$, we have

$$\text{erf}(1) = V\bar{f} = 0.8625. \tag{14.65}$$

Obviously, if we use $n = 10000$ samples, then we can get more accurate answers.

The Monte Carlo method can be used for other applications, not just for numerical integration. Its applications include optimization, physical and chemical simulation, financial simulation, generation of samples drawn from a probability distribution, weather forecasting, climate change simulation, engineering simulation, uncertainty quantification, risk analysis, computational biology, artificial intelligence, inverse problem and parameter estimation, and many others.

Though pseudorandom numbers are used and most such random numbers are drawn from uniform distributions, however, there is no reason that Monte Carlo methods should all use uniform distributions. In fact, other sampling methods are also widely used, such as the importance sampling and low-discrepancy sequences.

The error in Monte Carlo integration decreases in the form of the order of $O(1/\sqrt{n})$ as n increases. Other methods such as quasi-Monte Carlo can have a better error reduction with the error of $O((\ln n)^d/n)$, where d is the dimension if appropriate methods such as Halton sequences are used.

14.4.2 Quasi-Monte Carlo methods

Quasi-Monte Carlo (QMC) methods work similarly to standard Monte Carlo methods, but low-discrepancy sequences are used in QMC, and the distribution of sample points is more regular or uniform.

There are many different variants of quasi-Monte Carlo methods, such as the higher-order QMC and the multilevel QMC. There are many low-discrepancy sequences, including the Halton sequence, Sobol sequence, Faure sequence, and others. The readers interested in QMC and low-discrepancy sequence generation can refer to more specialized literature.

14.5. Notes on software

There are many statistical software packages for data analysis and a comprehensive list can be found at https://en.wikipedia.org/wiki/List_of_statistical_software.

Examples of such powerful tools are *R*, *R Studio*, *SPSS*, statistical and machine learning toolbox of *Matlab*®, *Gnu Octave*, *Python*'s *SciPy*, *Minitab*, *Excel*, *SAS*, *STATA*, *StatGraphics*, *Tableau*, *OriginPro*, and many others such as *WinBUGS*.

In addition, many symbolic computation software tools also have very powerful statistical capabilities, including *Mathematica*, *Wolfram Alpha*, *Maple*, *Geogebra*, *Desmos*, *SageMath*, *Maxima*, *MathCad*, *MathStudio*, and others.

For regression analysis, there are many tools for carrying out regression, including *polyfit* in Matlab, *lm* and *glm* in R, *Data Analysis* in Excel, and many others.

For Monte Carlo simulation, there are also many tools and packages. For example, Matlab's *simsd* can simulate linear models with uncertainty using Monte Carlo. Python's *NumPy* and *Scikit-Learn* are also widely used for Monte Carlo simulation. In addition, *Mathematica*, *Maple*, and *R* can also do Monte Carlo simulation.

Bibliography

[1] G.B. Arfken, H.J. Weber, F.E. Harris, Mathematical Methods for Physicists: A Comprehensive Guide, 7th ed., Academic Press, Waltham, 2012.

[2] M. Armstrong, Basic Linear Geostatistics, Springer, Berlin, 1998.

[3] K.J. Bathe, Finite Element Procedure in Engineering Analysis, Prentice-Hall, New Jersey, 1982.

[4] J. Banks, J.S. Carson, B.L. Nelson, D.M. Nicol, Discrete-Event System Simulation, Pearson New International edition, 5th edition, Pearson, Harlow, 2013.

[5] J.E. Beasley, Advances in Linear and Integer Programming, Oxford University Press, New York, 1996.

[6] J. Bird, Engineering Mathematics, 7th ed., Routledge, New York, 2014.

[7] J. Bird, Higher Engineering Mathematics, 7th ed., Routledge, New York, 2014.

[8] W.E. Boyce, R.C. DiPrima, Elementary Differential Equations and Boundary Value Problems, 10th edition, John Wiley & Sons, New York, 2012.

[9] S.P. Boyd, L. Vandenberghe, Convex Optimization, Cambridge University Press, Cambridge, 2004.

[10] P. Brandimarte, Handbook in Monte Carlo Simulation: Applications in Financial Engineering, Risk Management, and Economics, John Wiley & Sons, Hoboken, New Jersey, 2014.

[11] H.S. Carslaw, J.C. Jaeger, Conduction of Heat in Solids, second edition, Oxford University Press, Oxford, 1986.

[12] M. Conforti, G. Cornuejols, G. Zambelli, Integer Programming, Springer, Heidelberg, 2016.

[13] R.D. Cook, Finite Element Modeling for Stress Analysis, John Wiley and Sons, New York, 1995.

[14] J. Crank, Mathematics of Diffusion, Clarendon Press, Oxford, 1970.

[15] D.J. Daley, L.D. Servi, Idle and busy periods in stable M/M/k queues, Journal of Applied Probability 35 (4) (1998) 950–962.

[16] G.B. Dantzig, M.N. Thapa, Linear Programming 1: Introduction, Springer-Verlag, New York, 1997.

[17] G. Dantzig, R. Fulkerson, S. Johnson, Solution of a large-scale traveling salesman problem, Journal of the Operations Research Society of America 2 (4) (1954) 393–410.

[18] K. Deb, Optimisation for Engineering Design: Algorithms and Examples, Prentice-Hall, New Delhi, 1995.

[19] J.R. Dormand, P.J. Prince, A family of embedded Runge-Kutta formulae, Journal of Computational and Applied Mathematics 6 (1) (1980) 19–26.

[20] N.R. Draper, H. Smith, Applied Regression Analysis, 3rd edition, John Wiley & Sons, New York, 1998.

[21] S.J. Farlow, Partial Differential Equations for Scientists and Engineers, John Wiley & Sons, New York, 1982.

[22] R. Fletcher, Practical Methods of Optimization, second edition, John Wiley & Sons, Hoboken, NJ, 2000.

[23] C.A.J. Fletcher, C.A. Fletcher, Computational Techniques for Fluid Dynamics, vol. I, Springer-Verlag, Heidelberg, 1997.

[24] C.A. Floudas, Nonlinear and Mixed-Integer Optimization: Fundamentals and Applications, Oxford University Press, Oxford, 1995.

[25] A.C. Fowler, Mathematical Models in the Applied Sciences, Cambridge University Press, Cambridge, 1997.

[26] N. Gershenfeld, The Nature of Mathematical Modeling, Cambridge University Press, Cambridge, 1998.

[27] P.E. Gill, W. Murray, M.H. Wright, Practical Optimization, Emerald Group Publishing, Bingley, 1982.

[28] R. Goodman, Teach Yourself Statistics, Teach Yourself Books, London, 1957.

[29] D. Gross, C.M. Harris, Fundamentals of Queueing Theory, John Wiley & Sons, New York, 1998.

[30] S. Halfin, W. Whitt, Heavy traffic limits for queues with many exponential servers, Operations Research 29 (3) (1981) 567–588.

[31] J. Heizer, B. Render, Operations Management, 11th edition, Pearson, London, 2013.

[32] G.E. Hinton, R. Salakhutdinov, Reducing the dimensionality of data with neural networks, Science 313 (5786) (2006) 504–507.

[33] D.E. Holmes, Big Data: A Very Short Introduction, Oxford University Press, Oxford, 2017.

[34] A. Jeffrey, Advanced Engineering Mathematics, Academic Press, San Diego, 2002.

[35] G. James, Modern Engineering Mathematics, 5th ed., Pearson Education, Essex, 2015.

[36] D.G. Kendall, Stochastic processes occurring in the theory of queues and their analysis by the method of the imbedded Markov chain, The Annals of Mathematical Statistics 24 (3) (1953) 338–354.

[37] T. Koch, T. Ralphs, Y. Shinano, Could we use a million cores to solve an integer program?, Mathematical Methods of Operations Research 76 (1) (2012) 67–93.

[38] G.A. Korn, T.M. Korn, Mathematical Handbook for Scientists and Engineers, McGraw-Hill, New York, 1968.

[39] S. Koziel, X.S. Yang, Computational Optimization, Methods and Algorithms, Studies in Computational Intelligence, vol. 356, Springer, Heidelberg, 2011.

[40] E. Kreyszig, Advanced Engineering Mathematics: International Student Version, 10th ed., John Wiley & Sons, New York, 2011.

[41] C. Lanczos, Linear Differential Operators, Dover Publications, New York, 1997.

[42] A.H. Land, A.G. Doig, An automatic method for solving discrete programming problems, Econometrica 28 (3) (1960) 497–520.

[43] E.L. Lawler, D.E. Wood, Branch-and-bound methods: a survey, Operations Research 14 (4) (1966) 699–719.

[44] J. Ledin, Simulation Engineering: Build Better Embedded System Faster, CRC Press, Boca Raton, 2001.

[45] R.W. Lewis, K. Morgan, H. Thomas, S.K. Seetharamu, The Finite Element Method in Heat Transfer Analysis, John Wiley & Sons, New York, 1996.

[46] J.D.C. Little, A proof of the queueing formula: $L = \lambda W$, Operations Research 9 (3) (1961) 383–387.

[47] Matlab info, http://www.mathworks.com.

[48] J.I. McCool, Using the Weibull Distribution: Reliability, Modeling, and Inference, John Wiley & Sons, Hoboken, New Jersey, 2012.

[49] N. Metropolis, S. Ulam, The Monte Carlo method, Journal of the American Statistical Association 44 (4) (1949) 335–341.

[50] A.R. Mitchell, D.F. Griffiths, Finite Difference Method in Partial Differential Equations, John Wiley & Sons, New York, 1980.

[51] C.B. Moler, Numerical Computing with MATLAB, SIAM, Philadelphia, 2004.

[52] J. Nocedal, S.J. Wright, Numerical Optimization, second edition, Springer, New York, 2006.

[53] M. Okereke, S. Keates, Finite Element Applications: A Practical Guide to the FEM Process, Springer Tracts in Mechanical Engineering, Springer, Berlin, 2018.

[54] A. Papoulis, Probability and Statistics, Englewood, Cliffs, 1990.

[55] C.E. Pearson, Handbook of Applied Mathematics, 2nd ed., Van Nostrand Reinhold, New York, 1983.

[56] R.K. Pearson, Discrete-Time Dynamic Models, Oxford University Press, Oxford, 1999.

[57] J.C. Peterson, Technical Mathematics with Calculus, 3rd ed., Thomson Learning, New York, 2004.

[58] Y. Pochet, L.A. Wolsey, Production Planning by Mixed Integer Programming, Springer, New York, 2009.

[59] W.H. Press, S.A. Teukolsky, W.T. Vetterling, B.P. Flannery, Numerical Recipes in C++: The Art of Scientific Computing, 2nd ed., Cambridge University Press, Cambridge, 2002.

[60] E.G. Puckett, P. Colella, Finite Difference Methods for Computational Fluid Dynamics, Cambridge University Press, Cambridge, 2005.

[61] B. Render, R.M. Stair, M. Hanna, Quantitative Analysis for Management, 9th edition, Prentice Hall, Upper Saddle River, NJ, 2006.

[62] K.F. Riley, M.P. Hobson, S.J. Bence, Mathematical Methods for Physics and Engineering, 3rd ed., Cambridge University Press, Cambridge, 2006.

[63] S. Robinson, The Practice of Model Development and Use, John Wiley & Sons, New York, 2003.

[64] S.M. Ross, Simulation, 4th edition, Academic Press, 2006.

[65] T.L. Saaty, Elements of Queueing Theory, McGraw-Hill, New York, 1961.

[66] T. Sawik, Scheduling in Supply Chains Using Mixed Integer Programming, John Wily & Sons, Hoboken, NJ, 2011.
[67] G.D. Smith, Numerical Solutions of Partial Differential Equations, third edition, Clarendon Press, Oxford, 1985.
[68] J.C. Spall, Introduction to Stochastic Search and Optimization: Estimation, Simulation and Control, John Wiley & Sons, Hoboken, NJ, 2003.
[69] G. Strang, G.J. Fix, An Analysis of the Finite Element Method, Prentice Hall, Englewood Cliffs, NJ, 1973.
[70] K.A. Stroud, D.J. Booth, Engineering Mathematics, 6th ed., Palgrave Macmillan, New York, 2007.
[71] B. Taylor, Introduction to Management Science, 8th edition, Prentice Hall, Upper Saddle River, NJ, 2005.
[72] K. Teknomo, Queueing rule of thumb based on M/M/s queueing theory with application in construction management, Civil Engineering Dimension 14 (3) (2012) 139–146.
[73] V. Thomee, Galerkin Finite Element Methods for Parabolic Problems, Springer-Verlag, Berlin, 1997.
[74] L.N. Trefethen, D. Bau III, Numerical Linear Algebra, Society for Industrial and Applied Mathematics/SIAM, Philadelphia, 1997.
[75] F. Underwood, The particular integrals of a class of linear differential equations with constant coefficients with special reference to a formula by Forsyth, Mathematical Gazette 15 (207) (1930) 99–102.
[76] H.K. Versteeg, W. Malalasekra, An Introduction to Computational Fluid Dynamics: Finite Volume Method, Prentice-Hall, New York, 1995.
[77] E.W. Weisstein, http://mathworld.wolfram.com.
[78] Wikipedia, http://en.wikipedia.com.
[79] A.V. Wouver, P. Soucez, C. Vilas, Simulation of ODE/PDE Models with MATLAB, OCTAVE and SCILAB: Scientific and Engineering Applications, Springer, Heidelberg, 2014.
[80] X.S. Yang, Engineering Optimization: An Introduction with Metaheuristic Applications, John Wiley & Sons, New Jersey, 2010.
[81] X.S. Yang, Mathematical Modelling with Multidisciplinary Applications, John Wiley & Sons, Hoboken, NJ, 2013.
[82] X.S. Yang, Introduction to Computational Mathematics, 2nd edition, World Scientific Publishing, Singapore, 2014.
[83] X.S. Yang, Engineering Mathematics with Examples and Applications, Academic Press, London, 2017.
[84] X.S. Yang, Nature-Inspired Optimization Algorithms, Elsevier, Waltham, 2014.
[85] X.S. Yang, Nature-Inspired Optimization Algorithms, 2nd edition, Academic Press, London, 2020.
[86] X.S. Yang, Introduction to Algorithms for Data Mining and Machine Learning, Academic Press, London, 2019.
[87] M.J. Zaki, W. Meira Jr, Data Mining and Analysis: Fundamental Concepts and Algorithms, Cambridge University Press, Cambridge, 2014.
[88] D.G. Zill, W.S. Wright, 4th ed., Advanced Engineering Mathematics, Jones & Bartlett Learning, Sudbury, MA, 2009.
[89] O.C. Zienkiewicz, R.L. Taylor, The Finite Element Method, vol. I/II, 4th edition, McGraw-Hill, London, 1991.
[90] W.B.J. Zimmerman, Multiphysics Modeling with Finite Element Methods, Series on Stability, Vibrations & Control of Systems, World Scientific Publishing, Singapore, 2006.
[91] D. Zwillinger, CRC Standard Mathematical Tables and Formulae, 32nd ed., CRC Press, Boca Raton, FL, 2012.

Index

Printed in the United States
by Baker & Taylor Publisher Services

Printed in the United States
by Baker & Taylor Publisher Services